For Sau-Ling,

Best,

Jinji   Sept. 21, 98

NARRATING NATIONALISMS

NARRATING NATIONALISMS

Ideology and Form in Asian American Literature

Jinqi Ling

New York   Oxford
Oxford University Press
1998

Oxford University Press

Oxford   New York

Athens   Auckland   Bangkok   Bogota   Bombay
Buenos Aires   Calcutta   Cape Town   Dar es Salaam
Delhi   Florence   Hong Kong   Istanbul   Karachi
Kuala Lumpur   Madras   Madrid   Melbourne
Mexico City   Nairobi   Paris   Singapore
Taipei   Tokyo   Toronto   Warsaw

and associated companies in

Berlin   Ibadan

Jinqi Ling, "Reading for Historical Specificities: Gender Negotiations
in Louis Chu's *Eat a Bowl of Tea*," *MELUS* 20.1 (Spring 1995): 35–51.
Copyright © 1995, The Society for the Study of Multi-Ethnic Literature
of the United States. Reprinted by permission.

Jinqi Ling, "Identity Crisis and Gender Politics: Reappropriating Asian
American Masculinity," in *An Interethnic Companion to
Asian American Literature*, ed. King-Kok Cheung, New York: Cambridge University
Press, 1997. Copyright © 1997, Cambridge University Press.
Reprinted by permission of Cambridge University Press.

Library of Congress Cataloging-in-Publication Data
Ling, Jinqi.
Narrating nationalisms : ideology and form in Asian American
literature / by Jinqi Ling.
p.   cm.
Includes bibliographical references and index.
ISBN 0-19-511116-8
1. American literature—Asian American Authors—History and
criticism.   2. World War. 1939–1945—United States—Influence.
3. Asian Americans—Intellectual life.   4. Asian Americans in
literature.   5. Literary form.   I. Title.
PS153.A84L56   1998
810.9'895'09045—DC21   97-34558

9 8 7 6 5 4 3 2 1

Printed in the United States of America
on acid-free paper

Preface

In *Narrating Nationalisms,* I reread five formative Asian American literary texts written between 1957 and 1980. Through this rereading I attempt to intervene in two interrelated tendencies in current Asian American literary criticism: a privileging of content over form in assessments of "traditional" texts (that is, texts written in the pre-1980 era), an approach that results from the community's emphasis on literature's social or political function during the ethnic canon formation in the mid-1970s and early 1980s; and a prioritizing of "contemporary" over "traditional" writings in the current critical emphasis on the postmodern sublime—a differential treatment that often proceeds on the basis of the incomplete assessment of "traditional" works in prior critical discourse. The continued existence of these tendencies contributes to a perpetuation of the current "crisis" in Asian American cultural criticism, which is frequently manifested in a hypothetically assumed, though rarely admitted, opposition between "traditional" and "contemporary" Asian American literary articulations. In this study I aim to problematize the arbitrary nature of these tendencies and to propose a reconceptualization of the relationship between the past and the present of post–World War II Asian American literary history.

The goal of this critical project is reflected in the title of this book. It is also embodied in the two strains of critical thought that inform my analytical method: cultural studies, as well as postmodern and poststructuralist theories on the one hand, and social history and neo-pragmatic perspectives on the other. By entwining these diverse approaches, I hope to make a serious attempt to negotiate the tension between the older humanist and the uncritical antihumanist impulses in current Asian American literary studies. The most important assumption of my project, however, is that the problematics arising from these conflicting impulses cannot be effectively addressed only through a discourse of theory, or through an exclusive attention to Asian American literary production in the immediate present. Rather, they must be fully grasped and renegotiated at the sites where they were initially produced and hardened into essentialized positions.

In my reading of five Asian American literary works that I identify as the sites of such a critical engagement, I take it as a central task to reentangle the "ideological" with the "formal," terms I use pragmatically throughout this study: the former to refer to a text's power of political persuasion, particularly its implicit evaluative commentary on the social issues faced by Asian Americans in the period; and the latter to indicate the aesthetic characteristics and rhetorical strategies of such texts with an emphasis on their negotiated relationship with their ideological import. By taking seriously the formal properties of these texts' ideological production, I wish not only to offer a corrective to the content-based approach to them that is now common among Asian American critics, but also to contribute to a reconstitution of the material basis for investigating Asian American literary discourse of the post-1980 period as a fully historical process of cultural production and reproduction. In carrying out this task, I engage in extensive dialogue with the positions of various Asian American critics, a dialogue that presupposes that those positions were themselves responsive to the evolving contexts and shifting assumptions of their inquiries. My ultimate goal is to reopen discussions of Asian American literary production of the pre-1980 era as an internally complex and multiply affiliative process, and to rethink interventionary strategies for Asian American cultural studies that recognize their interrelatedness with prior sources of resistance as well as the imperatives posed by new social and ideological formations.

In the opening chapter of this study, I frame Asian American literary discourse from 1957 to 1980 as a fully relational process of cultural negotiation with undecidable but insistently transformative results. I identify two issues in Asian American cultural criticism—the assessment of both realist narrative and Asian American cultural nationalism—as crucial sites for negotiating a reconnection between Asian America's past and its present. The four chapters that follow feature readings of literary discourse in five texts by John Okada, Louis Chu, Frank Chin, and Maxine Hong Kingston. These readings explore four questions: how an individual writer's perception of social conditions forms an important basis for the positions at work in a particular text and informs the author's relationship with the cultural and ideological issues addressed; how the literary texts themselves often become part of the ongoing social circumstances under which emerging concerns are contested and negotiated; how the texts' visions of alternatives to the perceived defects of social reality are enhanced, conditioned, or curtailed by available means of expression; and how these writings prefiguratively contributed to reshaping social and cultural attitudes about race, gender, and class in contemporary Asian American literary works.

More specifically, Chapter 2 focuses on the cultural production of John Okada's 1957 novel *No-No Boy*. My analysis revolves around the relationship between the text's political critique of wartime racism toward Japanese Americans and its novelistic negotiation of such a critique within the context of cold war American nationalism and assimilationist assumptions. I identify rhetorical mechanisms in *No-No Boy* that were fraught with social accents and ideologically open to transformative appropriations by Asian American critics in the 1970s and after.

Chapter 3 treats Louis Chu's 1961 novel *Eat a Bowl of Tea* as implicitly participating in dialogue with community issues such as gender, class, and cultural traditions, and with the early 1960s social discourse about economic and racial injustice in American society. In this chapter I analyze both the historical and aesthetic concerns that inform Chu's realist representation of Chinatown's plight and the fictionality of his fiction within the contexts of the post-McCarthy era and of the prevailing existentialist mystification of the nature of Chinese Americans' social status in the period. Secondarily, I use my analysis to illustrate the politics of reading the novel—for both its original readers and its current audiences—in terms of the political stakes involved in managing the distance between the book's encoding and its subsequent decoding and recoding.

In Chapter 4 I discuss Frank Chin's plays *The Chickencoop Chinaman* (1972) and *The Year of the Dragon* (1974) as examples of how the author employs the dramatic form to privilege demonstrative communication and open engagement with social issues in a period of ethnic activism. I foreground four aspects of Chin's theatrical art: its strategic blurring of boundaries between social and dramatic texts; its manipulation of performance/audience relationships in the author's representation of various forms of Asian America's cultural deformation; its insistence on moral engagement through its ambiguous affiliations to modernist and postmodernist aesthetics; and its dialectical stimulation of Asian American women's rearticulation of gender in their own terms. While my analyses of *No-No Boy, Eat a Bowl of Tea,* and Chin's two plays can be seen as textual explications in their own terms, these discussions are designed to enhance a comparative perspective for my explorations throughout this study of the linkages between writing, reading, and social change reflected in Asian American literary discourse of the 1970s.

In Chapter 5 I analyze Maxine Hong Kingston's 1980 nonfiction *China Men* as the author's implicit response to the consequences of her articulation of ideological differences through her 1976 autobiography *The Woman Warrior*. My assessment of the debate over Kingston's work underscores the tension between her conscious foregrounding of Asian American women's doubly marginalized social status and her unconscious dilution of her critique of racism through a partial reliance on American orientalism in problematizing Chinese patriarchy. From this perspective *China Men* represents Kingston's efforts to renegotiate her unfinished feminist project through a critical engagement with both the male-oriented ideal-

ism that partly informs the ideological controversies over her 1976 position and
the assumptions that underlie her writing of *The Woman Warrior*. My reading of
China Men situates the book in a strategically vital place in postwar Asian American literary history for its conscious effort to reconfigure the existing Asian
American historical imagination and thus to shift community perspectives from
nationalist toward postnational positions.

In my concluding chapter I address three ongoing critical issues that have
marked the community's internal debate since the 1970s: the operation of cultural hegemony as embodied in the reception of Jade Snow Wong's *Fifth Chinese
Daughter*, which I examine in relation to the shifting horizon of expectations and
the changing political contexts of the book's signification; the strategy of ethnic
authenticity adopted by Asian American writers in the period which I see as a
historically necessitated but less-than-ideal cultural choice; and the issue of political responsibility in the critical discourse of the 1980s and 1990s about Asian
American literature, which I (re)read as an ongoing process of negotiation. I conclude by calling on Asian American critics to be more responsive to the complexities of individual Asian American writers' voices, more alert to the dangers of
subsuming or silencing their historical specificity in terms of presentist theoretical agendas, and thus more concerned about the role of their own discourse in
the construction of a progressively pluralistic culture that creatively privileges
multiple centers.

This book has its origins in the dissertation I wrote in the Program in American
Studies at Washington State University. I am deeply indebted to my former
teachers—Sue Armitage, LeRoy Ashby, Alex Hammond, Dick Law, Laureen Mar,
Gail Nomura, Tim Reed, and Steve Sumida—for their intellectual mentoring,
their enabling guidance, and their generous and continuing support. They taught
me to appreciate a historical perspective in reading American culture and encouraged me to enter a field that has profoundly changed my life.

Colleagues at UCLA have been extremely resourceful and generous in providing suggestions for my revision of the manuscript for publication. For their astute
readings and detailed criticisms at different stages of my writing of this book, I
wish to thank Ali Behdad, King-Kok Cheung, James Goodwin, Russell Leong,
Anne Mellor, Vince Pecora, Ken Reinhard, and Jenny Sharpe. My conversation
with Barbara Packer on a specific critical issue proved useful and reassuring. Yuji
Ichioka's correction of aspects of my historical account of the internment of Japanese Americans during World War II saved me from embarrassing errors. My sin-
cere thanks to Paula Gunn Allen, Martha Banta, Joe Bristow, Ken Lincoln, David
Wong Louie, Karen Rowe, Greg Sarris, and Valerie Smith for giving me much
needed and timely encouragement. In its earliest stage of revision, my book project received valuable support form Eric Sundquist, who read a portion of it with

a strong interest and, as department chair, also reduced my teaching load at a crucial moment of my revision of the manuscript for publication. The final version of my book is stronger as a result of the help from all these people. They must decide if I have made correct use of their thoughtful advice; I alone am responsible for the remaining flaws and misinterpretations.

The completion of this book would not have been possible without continuing research grants from both the Academic Senate and the Asian American Studies Center of UCLA since 1992, as well as a Faculty Career Development Award from UCLA during the 1996–1997 academic year. I have been very lucky to work in an institution that provides the most encouraging intellectual environment an Asian American junior faculty member could expect. I wish to thank the four successive chairs in the English Department—Jonathan Post, Rob Watson, Eric Sundquist, and Tom Wortham—for helping to create such an environment. I owe special thanks to Don Nakanishi, Director of the Asian American Studies Center, for his commitment to helping junior colleagues and to providing substantive and multileveled support. Among the students at UCLA whose help in the past few years has led the book to its final form, I would like to thank my research assistants: Nina Ha, Grace Hong, Jim Lee, Darryl Mar, and, in particular, Lynn Itagaki, who also helped with proofing and indexing. My deepest gratitude goes to King-Kok Cheung for being a most understanding and supportive colleague.

I am very grateful to the staff at Oxford University Press who made the publication of this book possible. I especially want to thank Elizabeth Maguire for expressing an early interest in my book project, Susan Chang for being a patient and insightful editor, and Will Moore for careful supervision over the book's production. The anonymous reader assigned to my manuscript by Oxford University Press made thoughtful comments that assisted me in preparing the final draft. An earlier and shorter version of Chapter 3 appeared in "Reading for Historical Specificities: Gender Negotiations in Louis Chu's *Eat a Bowl of Tea*," *MELUS* 20.1 (Spring 1995): 35–51; portions of Chapters 4 and 5 appeared in different forms in "Identity Crisis and Gender Politics: Reappropriating Asian American Masculinity," in *An Interethnic Companion to Asian American Literature,* edited by King-Kok Cheung (New York: Cambridge University Press, 1997, 312–37). I wish to thank the copyright holders for permitting me to use these materials in my book.

I reserve my most profound thanks to my wife, Yi, to whom this book is dedicated.

Los Angeles, California   J. L.
October 1997

Contents

NARRATING NATIONALISMS

I

History, Entanglement, and Negotiated Change

The hegemonic subject cannot have a terrain of constitution different from the structure to which it belongs. . . . [This structure] is inhabited by an original lack, by a radical unde-cidability that needs to be constantly superseded by acts of de-cision. These acts are, precisely, what constitute the *subject,* who can only exist as a will transcending the structure. Be-cause this will has no place of constitution external to the structure but is the result of the failure of the structure to con-stitute itself, it can be formed only through acts of identifica-tion.

        —Ernesto Laclau, "Power and Representation"

To keep alive a sense of alternative ways of life and of struggle requires memory of those who prefigured such life and strug-gle in the past. In this sense, tradition is to be associated not solely with ignorance and intolerance, prejudice and parochi-alism, dogmatism and docility. Rather, tradition is also to be identified with insight and intelligence, rationality and resis-tance, critique and contestation.

        —Cornel West, *The American Evasion of Philosophy*

The 1980s and 1990s have witnessed a tremendous growth in the field of Asian American literary studies. One important aspect of such a growth is reflected in the proliferation of critical approaches to the analysis of literary texts, approaches that range from historical materialism to poststructuralist critiques, from Third World feminisms to gender performance analysis, and from the various persua-sions of cultural studies to postcolonial perspectives. These theoretical and methodological developments have provided readers of Asian American literature

with a formidable body of scholarship, an enhanced critical awareness of witness-
ing a time of unprecedented intellectual ferment, and a deepened understanding
of Asian American literary criticism as an evolving discourse dynamically interacting with Asian American creative energies in the age of global capitalism.

But the implications of this growth for Asian American critics themselves are
not always certain. Here I particularly refer to a significant but ambiguous development that results from increased theoretical and methodological awareness,
that is, Asian American critics' resistance to ethnocentrism through an internal
critique of "Asian American developmental narratives."[1] The antiessentialist
thrust of this critique is clearly informed by postmodern and poststructuralist
problematizations of foundationalist assumptions about Western civilization,
namely, claims for teleological progress, for synthetic vision, or for unitary construction of the subject. Viewed as a whole, such a critical turn has led to profound and largely positive results in Asian American literary studies: it fundamentally revises the existing premise of Asian American critical practice by
emphasizing the indispensability of diasporic and post-identity perspectives; it
inspires creative and critical projects that dynamically draw on and contribute to
such perspectives; and it witnesses the emergence of a whole generation of young
Asian American scholars whose knowledge about literature completely overlaps
their theoretical interest.

But the effort to problematize traditional intellectual categories and to refigure
the human subject also carries with it tendencies that, under conditions of theory
fetishism, often threaten to become the new master code—and indeed a new form
of spatial typology—of our freshly awakened political imaginary. For example,
along with its complication of Asian American interventionary strategies through
refocusing on the local, the contingent, and the interstitial, the critique of developmentalism casts in doubt almost all forms of identity formation, of the pursuit
of objectivity, or of the struggle for social progress. So pervasive is the conviction
that we now occupy a temporality of immediacy and competing differences that
any attempt to think historically, and to be serious about Asian America's past
and its future, is now deemed impossible because such an attempt, as David
Palumbo-Liu points out, is typically seen as a theoretical failure—a failure obviously more damning than other failures—to resist "contamination" by master
narratives (1995, 58).[2] Under such circumstances, what becomes problematized is
not only certain flawed historical projects but also the very notion of history itself,[3] a situation that in turn makes the repeated calls by Asian American critical
practitioners to reconnect the "discursive" with the "material" sound not only ineffective but also perfunctory.

A number of questions emerge from the foregoing observations: Can we effectively deal with the current "crisis" in Asian American cultural studies if we insist
on seeing the community's "tradition"—symbolized by railroads, immigration

exclusion, or internment—as not possessing some deep and extended structural basis that connects to our present, or if we see ourselves as living in entirely discrete social and cultural spaces that generate sensibilities totally different from those produced by traditions?[4] Can we still meaningfully conceive any social or cultural process that truly "moves forward, that renews itself, that is self-critical and purposive" if our critiques of "developmentalism" involve a rejection not only of mechanical progression but also of historical approaches generally?[5] Is the narrative in "traditional" Asian American literary writings inherently developmental, oppressive, and totalizing, or is it mainly constructed to be seen as such through the philosophical and anthropological lens of poststructuralism,[6] which, in their theoretical expression of skepticism about systematic attempts to understand the world, tend to offer in return another general theory? If current developments in Asian American literary production and criticism are not a simple negation of earlier Asian American literary practices, what historical roles did the latter perform in facilitating—rather than simply stifling—the emergence of more recent concerns in Asian American literature or in transforming the political horizons presupposed by Asian American literary and critical articulations in the late 1980s and after?

In this chapter I attempt to address these questions from a theoretical-pragmatic perspective by means of a three-pronged argument. The basic component of my critical effort is that the Asian American literary articulations of the pre- and post-1980 periods should be conceptualized not as mutually exclusive entities but as participating in a nonlinear process of cultural dissent with indeterminate but insistently transformative results. First I describe specific mechanisms of cultural contestation and negotiation in the pre-1980 period as discursively paving the way for contemporary Asian American creative and critical concerns. I then focus on two issues in current Asian American literary criticism—realist narrative and cultural nationalism—which I identify as crucial sites for negotiating a reconceptualization of the relationship between the "traditional" and the "contemporary" in Asian American literary history. I substantiate the critical perspectives developed in this chapter through specific textual analyses in subsequent chapters. For immediate purposes here, I begin my discussion with a critical dialogue with Lisa Lowe's conceptualization of "cultural difference" in her influential 1991 essay "Heterogeneity, Hybridity, Multiplicity," a conceptualization that, in my view, is illustrative of the dichotomous views of history in current Asian American critical thinking.

Toward a Production of Cultural Difference

The term "Asian American developmental narrative" has become in recent years almost a synonym for the literary view proposed in the 1974 anthology *Aiiieeeee!*,

edited by Frank Chin, Jeffery Chan, Lawson Inada, and Shawn Wong, and the re-
iteration and extension of that position by the same editors in 1991 in *The Big Aiiieeeee!* Both anthologies emphasize contributions to the development of an Asian
American literary tradition by two groups of authors—Chinese American and
Japanese American (with Filipino American writers included in the earlier anthology)—on the basis of an "Asian American cultural integrity" characterized by
American birth, exclusive use of English, and participation in an "Asian American heroic tradition" distinguished by courage, wisdom, and pioneering male
ethos (Chin et al. 1974, xvi). Identifying qualities in Asian American works emphasizing racial and class oppression by figures such as Carlos Bulosan, John
Okada, Toshio Mori, and Louis Chu, the editors view Asian American authors
who use different representational strategies with deep suspicion (Chan et al.
1991, 8). The editors' problematic distinction between "the real" and "the fake"
in Asian American literary expression implicitly reflects their continued preoccupation with survival and ethnic solidarity as a political necessity for Asian Americans in contemporary America, and they accordingly canonize Asian American
writings that, in their view, are exemplary of their envisioned Asian American
ideal and prophetic of its future development. The editors' emphasis on the desir-
ability of defining an Asian American literary tradition as a self-contained and
self-referential continuum obviously collides with the various Asian American literary voices they exclude, while it invites both challenges to and rearticulations of
their definition of being "Asian American."

Lowe's 1991 essay was, within this context, a timely intervention in the oppositional economy initiated by *Aiiieeeee!* and reaffirmed by *The Big Aiiieeeee!* In it,
Lowe identifies a false dyadic opposition between nationalism (a term she sometimes uses interchangeably with "nativism") and assimilation in the editors' notion of Asian American identity, an identity maintained, according to Lowe,
through a "vertical transmission" of "exclusively hierarchical" cultural values,
with an "oedipal resolution" in favor of a male-oriented monologism that essen-
tializes Asian American culture and suppresses its gender, class, and national differences (1991, 27, 26, 35). As an alternative, Lowe describes a multileveled and
multidirectional "nomadic" model that features Asian American culture as a
"fluctuating composition of differences, intersections, and incommensurabilities"
within "the general social terrain of culture [that] is open, plural, and dynamic"
(39, 27, 29). The vision that Lowe articulates of Asian American identity as an internally heterogeneous and externally associative entity that resists conceptual fixation or closure is at once complex and historical. It not only illustrates the arbitrary nature of ethnic identity as an ideological construct whose unity depends on
the exclusion of differences, but also provides new conceptual tools for a nonessentialized investigation of Asian American experience as a contradictory process of
multiple affiliations and outcomes.[7]

Although Lowe's articulation constitutes a necessary move beyond the positions taken by the editors of *Aiiieeeee!* and *The Big Aiiieeeee!*, her conceptualization of Asian American cultural differences appears to fall short of full development. For example, she does not make crucial distinctions between Asian Americans' heterogeneous "origins" and the "fundamental condition" of their articulation of heterogeneous differences (1991, 31–32), or between the various social-demographic changes in the Asian American community since 1965 and the delayed expansion of their political space commensurate with those changes. As a result, Lowe's argument pays only limited attention to specific forms of social power that can hegemonically condense the conditions she describes into circumstances inaccessible to Asian Americans' attempts at equal expression or equal exchange, and similarly limited attention to the significant differences between the theoretical potential of her vision of cultural hybridity and the existentially experienced reality of Asian Americans' living with multiple social identities.

This uneven development in Lowe's conceptualization of cultural difference, I would suggest, prevents her from making two further distinctions regarding "traditional" Asian American cultural projects: that between specific Asian American writers' contingent claims of essence and their intentional "desire to essentialize" (1991, 34), and that between their variously motivated essentialist moves across diverse concerns and their actual participation in a unified project of cultural nationalism (I discuss Asian American cultural nationalism later in this chapter). The inadequately debated elements in Lowe's otherwise reflexive move lead her in the end to privilege untrammeled "nomadic" play across cultural or national boundaries as abstract as Descartes's grid. Elsewhere, Lowe explains her notion of "nomadism" as follows:

> The space of nomad thought is smooth, not gritted like ruled or regulated spaces. From the smoothness of nomad space, one can travel to any other point, through a variety of routes, by a variety of means; its mode of operation is the *nomos,* extending forward in an open space, rather than the *logos* entrenching in a closed, discrete space. . . . [T]he nomadic suggestively designates a practice which traverses . . . settled distinctions, which shifts and displaces them, and ultimately resituates them as different *loci.* (1993, 46–47)

This generalized postmodern concept of the nomadic, which forms the basis of her call for a paradigm shift for Asian American studies, is posited against what she sees as nationalist stagnation and oppression in earlier literary representations of the ethnic group's cultural struggles.[8]

Because the past is now viewed as a nondiscursive bygone which can be easily grasped and analyzed, what becomes significant and worthwhile is only the present, which is constructed as infinitely complex, associative, and subversive. What follows then is Lowe's foregrounding of a logic that is at once antidevelopmental and devoid of her intended historical materialism via claims of "strategic essentialism"; that is, as she reformulates Gramsci's concept of subaltern struggles vis-à-vis a historical bloc, "the significant practices of the subaltern groups may not be understood as hegemonic until they are viewed with historical hindsight" (1991, 29).[9] From this perspective, provisional unity or hegemony is simply impossible to grasp or conceive in a tangible, purposive, and pragmatic sense; it is always undesirable because foregrounding such tendencies implies a tacit acceptance of the teleology of the historical process in question. Under such circumstances, difference can only derive from and lead to difference, and Asian Americans' heterogeneous "origins" are necessarily the same as "the fundamental condition" of their equal access to such differences in a material sense. Such a view of cultural difference presupposes a given "coordination of distinct, yet allied positions, practices, and moments" (Lowe 1991, 29) in a largely synchronic situation, and it omits what Gayatri Spivak calls "the crucial middle term" of an oppositional cultural politics (1988, 286), that is, an account of the production of ideology as an emancipatory process of identifying and unpacking historically produced conditions of *fundamental power imbalance.*

I want to complement Lowe's critical effort from another direction: whereas Lowe provocatively imagines the complex operation of Asian American cultural differences as a fluid, differential, and multidirectional process on a plural and open cultural terrain, I attempt in this book to describe the material production of difference under historically more condensed situations from 1957 through 1980, with an emphasis on the specific ways in which difference is oppositionally articulated into ideological positions in particular Asian American writings. As will become evident over the course of this study, the historical vision that emerges from my analysis ultimately converges with Lowe's, but through a different route and under a different set of assumptions about the relationship among "ideology," "culture," and "difference." More immediately, my position in the present chapter consciously negotiates the tensions between the critical models offered by the editors of *Aiiieeeee!* and *The Big Aiiieeeee!* on the one hand and by Lowe's 1991 theoretical intervention on the other. For example, I disagree with the belief implicit in *The Big Aiiieeeee!* that Asian American writers must participate in a male-oriented heroic struggle against cultural domination along a singular, predictable path. But I also question the countersuggestion that the literary operations engaged by early Asian American literary works (particularly those celebrated by *Aiiieeeee!* and *The Big Aiiieeeee!*) simply live out the results prescribed for them—a view that disregards the works' own discursive productions. I argue, on the contrary, that the political visions of the five Asian American literary texts examined in this book are both less predictable and more effective than presupposed by subsequent theorizing. In reference to the assumptions in *The Big Aiiieeeee!,* I emphasize that Asian American writing's textually signified desires for social change are never free from historically constituted contextual constraints on their articulation, a situation that inevitably renders their meaning contradictory, tentative, and contingent, and prevents easy fulfillment of their strategically conceived counterhegemonic goals. But I also argue that the subversiveness of texts such as Theresa Hak Kyung Cha's *Dictée* is often a theoretical construct, and that overemphasis on the "materiality" of such subversiveness not only increases the distance between theory and practice but also works falsely to justify ahistorical tendencies toward avant-garde celebrations of difference. As for the widespread theoretical skepticism about "developmental narratives," I acknowledge its critical value but find it counterproductive to elevate the relativism of such conditionally useful Western self-critiques to the status of a rigorous meta-theory for Asian American critical issues. In particular, I feel that such Nietzschean perspectivism does not arise from the actual historical condition of Asian Americans' displacement, and that its uncritical application can have the effect of preventing the socially disfranchised[10]—those with little hope of fulfilling dreams of human dignity or individual coherence—from talking meaningfully about their social betterment.

Negotiating Transformations

In what follows, I sketch the critical assumptions that inform my view of Asian American literary discourse from 1957 to 1980 as a contested and multiply negotiated process of transformation. My position differs from two commonly held views in prior treatments of Asian American literary discourse of the period. The first designates the production of this literature in the epochal moment of the early 1970s as both its only point of canon engagement and its exclusive ownership of the political vision it articulates (e.g., Kim 1982, 173–213; Li 1992, 324–29). I do not deny that these years were a crucial stage of a formation process, a stage that is characterized by Asian American literature's self-espousal as an alternative presence in American culture and by its conscious demystification of its hegemonically defined relations to majority society and culture. But this stage was constitutive of an Asian American agency that had been long in the making—an agency made up of subject formations attempted with different degrees of success or failure by various earlier Asian American writers. Furthermore, this moment anticipated a subsequent uncovering of this agency's buried history and its more effective articulation to new conditions. At the same time, the era's appropriation of empowering elements from various pre-1970s Asian American literary works—both by the editors of *Aiiieeeee!* and by women writers such as Maxine Hong Kingston—depended on retrospectively granted meanings relevant to their immediate cultural or political needs. These discursively produced sensibilities in turn generated new polemics for Asian American literary discourse and gave new incentives to the writers who negotiated its revision, rearticulation, and reconfiguration.

A second commonly held view equates the articulation of individual Asian American writers at given historical moments in the period with the actual presence of fully realized Asian American agency.[11] Such an equation characteristically leads either to ahistorical expectations of thorough treatments of a full range of important social issues (e.g., race, gender, class, sexuality, postcoloniality, imperialism) in each individual work or to reductive assessments of writings unable to live up to these expectations. Conversely, texts that appear to address these issues relatively successfully are often praised as if they were the products of their own histories—products that are not only self-generative but also unrelated to other social meaning–making resources or processes that play important, though often indirect, roles in their production. At the heart of this equation lies a failure to see that Asian American literary voices of the 1957–1980 period were often constructed out of contexts of differential power and unequal access to cultural apparatuses or resources. Within this context, the cultural mechanisms that actively excluded Asian American literary expression also defined discourses available to writers who attempted to articulate their differences. Consequently, individual acts of articulation in Asian American literary works of the period did not always manifest themselves as explicit political struggles.[12] In addition, the construction of agency in one text may reflect struggles in others or may unintentionally facilitate the emergence of forms of agency in unexpected sociocultural loci (Grossberg 1992, 114). In this sense, either promotion or demotion of Asian American texts on the basis of such an equation masks the differential effects of social power on individual Asian American works' formal and ideological orientations, effects that often reveal the traces and indicate the flow of agency. As we shall see in the chapters that follow, tracing the construction of a necessarily incomplete and multifarious Asian American agency enables us to sort out how specific historical visions of social transformation intersect with particular rhetorical decisions and changing historical circumstances in the texts examined.

In using the terms "Asian American literature" and "Asian American literary discourse," I am aware of totalizing implications, especially when the majority of the texts examined in this study are by Chinese American writers. It seems no less problematic, however, to talk about "Chinese American literature" or about "Japanese American literature" in the period, as if each were not part of an overlapping and interrelated set of literary articulations, or as if each delineated a coherent and reducible group of writings. For lack of more precise terminology, I choose "Asian American literature" and "Asian American literary discourse" with an explicit purpose of destabilizing the terms and unpacking the various meanings and sensibilities that they dually suggest and suppress. I am also aware that in focusing on Asian American works such as *No-No Boy, Eat a Bowl of Tea,* and *The Chickencoop Chinaman,* I may create the impression of reifying them because they were first given "classic" status in 1974 by the editors of *Aiiieeeee!,* who prioritized particular Chinese American and Japanese American literary works in terms of the political and aesthetic agendas of the era. Yet assessments of the meaning of canonization must take into account not only the act of selection itself but also its conditions and long-term effects. More specifically, we should investigate what specific needs the initial canonization of these texts fulfilled and at what expense, as well as the extent to which the insistence on these texts' fulfilling those needs, both by the editors of *Aiiieeeee!* and by their critics, created over time circumstances for these texts' salutary neglect, if not "decanonization" (by this term I mean that these texts have continued to receive inadequate critical analysis as cultural or aesthetic productions since the mid-1970s).

The readings in this study analyze how specific Asian American literary writings of the period were influenced by, responded to, and attempted to effect changes in discourse about Asian Americans both as a collective group and as hybrid positionalities interacting with one another and with a society marked by hierarchically arranged racial, gender, and class differences. I explore how such interactions are mediated through the ideological stances and formal choices of specific Asian American texts in terms of "negotiations," a term I use purposefully to refer to the intricate and often ambiguous textual and intertextual relationships in these works. Not only has the term "negotiation" gained a certain currency among practitioners of cultural studies who draw upon postmodern, New Historicist, and pragmatist theories,[13] but also it bears particular relevance to the nature of the cultural interactions reflected in the Asian American literary works under examination. Specifically, I use "negotiation" to describe cultural mechanisms both consciously employed by Asian American writers and unconsciously impinging on their creative practices in the period. On the one hand, such mechanisms involve contestatory strategies that inform the positioning of Asian American authors in relation to cultural conventions and to the diverse voices within their own communities; on the other hand, they also involve larger historical and cultural processes that operate independently of purposive human interventions and are fraught with undecidable consequences.

Not coincidentally, both Frank Chin and Maxine Hong Kingston, two influential writers who led the radical Asian American cultural resurgence of the 1970s, prefer a metaphorical use of the word "war" instead of the term "negotiation" for their literary articulations of difference. This usage reflects the embattled contexts out of which their positions emerged and were felt to be necessary, while it bespeaks the writers' realization that they faced fundamental power imbalances based on race, gender, class, and other historical experiences, and that the circumstances were appropriate for initiating a confrontational bargaining process

with the cultural establishment. The usage also points toward tensions between a
newly awakened ethnic, gender, or class consciousness on the part of these Asian
American writers and the obvious lack of social and cultural space for their self-
representation. The possibilities and the problems of using "war" as a strategy for
articulating differences can be seen in the heated debates in the Asian American
community since the 1970s over issues of identity, gender, and the relationship
between literature and community interests. Whether we like such conflicts or
not, they have persisted as part of post-1960s Asian American literary discourse
and are continuously shaping our responses to the issues they raise, particularly in
view of the continued existence of social inequalities faced both collectively and
individually by various Asian Americans. If we recognize that such conflict and
fragmentation within the community is but an inevitable part of a protracted
process of democratization, we can also see the battles in these "wars" not just as
reactive, negative events but as dynamic, though not necessarily effective, efforts
by individual Asian American writers to address power imbalance in particular
contexts. The term "negotiation" becomes immediately relevant in this regard for
its resonance with the well-known military metaphor formulated by Gramsci,
who distinguishes "war of maneuver" from what he calls "war of position." By
"war of maneuver," Gramsci refers to the historical stage where everything is condensed into one front in one "strategic" moment of struggle for the purpose of
opening a single victorious "breach" in the "enemy's defenses"; by "war of position," he refers to a continuous struggle across different fronts at various levels
where there is rarely any discrete, clear breakthrough in a protracted yet progressive historical transition toward a "decisive" reorganization of existing power relations (1971, 232–34, 238–39).[14]

Michael Omi and Howard Winant were among the first American critics to apply Gramsci's war metaphor to the analysis of race as "the fundamental axis of social organization in the United States." In their important 1986 study *Racial Formation in the United States,* they observe that under conditions prevalent in the
United States, "war of maneuver" is applicable mainly to nineteenth-century race
relations, when racial minorities—blacks, Native Americans, and Asians—were
effectively banned from the American political system through repeated white-
led race riots and military assaults. This situation denied racial minorities the
minimal necessary social and conceptual flexibility for contesting the hegemonic
racial state. "War of position," by contrast, signals for these authors the ability of
racial minorities to wage political struggles, to mount oppositional ideological
projects, and to "make sustained strategic incursions into the political process" as
they gradually achieved political gains after World War II. Along with the
changed historical contexts and the transformed political climate in the era, Omi
and Winant suggest, "war of maneuver" is giving way to "war of position" in
racial minorities' political and social struggles in the contemporary United States

(1986, 73–75). Their application of Gramsci's war metaphor vividly describes the historical transition of American racial contestation effected through different modes of political initiatives within different hegemonic formations, and it correctly emphasizes the need for "a deepening and [an] articulation of a variety of antagonisms" in recognition of "the expansion of the Keynesian State [in postwar America] in which the interests of the different sectors were no longer defined along clear-cut class lines" (see Laclau and Mouffe 1985, 74–75).

Nevertheless, in respectively associating the two kinds of metaphoric wars with discrete historical periods—in ways that reflect the general belief that Gramsci himself favors only "war of position"—the authors inadvertently simplify both the social realities and the nature of the political choices faced by Asian Americans in the postwar era.[15] For example, they pay little attention to the fact that until the late 1960s, Asian America's social and economic subordination remained largely invisible to the majority society; that, even into the 1970s, Asian American political voices were still on the fringe of the protest movements that occupied the attention of mainstream institutions; and, for these reasons, that the political gains of American racial minorities in the period were not only limited but also quite uneven. A better grasp of Asian Americans' experience with race in the period therefore requires a more naunced appropriation of Gramsci's war metaphor, not as a closed paradigm, but as a self-reflexive analogy open to rearrangement of its themes and reorientation of its cultural politics. In view of Asian Americans' social status during the decades since 1945, I would suggest that both types of war referred to by Gramsci existed simultaneously in Asian American literary discourse in the 1970s; indeed, the massive power imbalance facing their small, fragmented communities required innovative combinations of strategic and tactical interventions both within and across the available spaces of cultural struggle. Under such circumstances, launching a radical literary "war of maneuver" may not be a suicidal gesture; rather, it can be understood as a strategic move that mobilizes collective will, opens up space in the cultural establishment, and reveals the "overall relation of the forces in conflict," in anticipation of a tactically protracted "war of positions" (Gramsci 1971, 234). Yet the more tactical "war of position" must be conceived along with radical political alternatives in order to be affiliative in a progressive sense, and to avoid the possibility of reducing its "exceptional qualities of patience and inventiveness" to a mere dependence on solutions implemented only through preestablished institutional practices (Gramsci 1971, 239; see also Laclau and Mouffe 1985, 74–75).

Historically, Asian American literary discourse of the 1970s developed through what might be termed a war of words, a process that featured individual articulations of contestatory positions conditioned by the discursive formations of race, gender, class, and other social experiences at given historical moments. For example, in the early 1970s, when the editors of *Aiiieeeee!* used race and manhood as central categories in their effort to promote a collective Asian American identity, they were launching a strategic assault aimed at creating a breach in Asian Americans' exclusion from American public discourse. They explicitly attacked the majority culture's habitual reduction of Asian Americans to a feminized, alien and monolithic racial other, a group with neither relevance nor significance to American society. Such claims, however inaccurate and counterproductive for contemporary readers, had the practical effect of exposing what Alan Wald calls the "mode and consequences" of Asian Americans' incorporation in the social fabric of the United States in the pre-1965 era—violent social subjugation, economic exploitation, and cultural trivialization and distortion, mainly on the basis of their racial difference (1987, 23, 28). Along this line, E. San Juan, Jr., argues that racial categorization in American society plays a central role in "the preservation and reproduction of the U.S. social order," as well as in the "exclusion and inclusion that continues to inform and reinforce all other social antagonisms" in American society (1992, 5). The position that the editors of *Aiiieeeee!* took in arguing for ethnic solidarity on reactive and unidimensional grounds clearly reflects both the limitations of the ideological horizons available to them and their provisional need for a one-directional method of contestation, which was required by "the limits asserted in a flat denial" (Lang 1992, 301). The subsequent challenges to their position, particularly by Asian American women, and the hardening of the original counterstance constitutes a transitional stage in which much energy was spent on internal debate within the emergent Asian American literary discourse. From today's perspective, the evolution of such a discourse might have moved more forcefully to engage the dominant culture once it refused fixation of its reference to the reigning racial and gender ideology, recognized its internal complexities and differences, and avoided counterstances that froze into essentialist dogma. But in light of the mutually dependent relationship between the two types of metaphoric wars enacted in the era, the strategic breach opened by *Aiiieeeee!* can be understood primarily in terms of the productivity of its confrontation with the cultural establishment,[16] its transitional revelation of additional possibilities for engagement, and its function as a precondition for the adoption of more reflexive and tactical positions both within and across the initially articulated differences. For only during struggle launched from such a provisional unity, as Amilcar Cabral argues in a different context, can the complexity of cultural problems be raised in all its dimensions, and only through struggle capable of opening up space in the dominant culture can the options for successive adaptations of strategies and tactics be fully exposed (1973/1994, 63).

Other arguments by the editors of *Aiiieeeee!* testify to how self-conscious Asian American writers of the 1970s became about the unequal balance of power under which they and their texts carried out confrontational bargaining. The editors' well-known position on the colonial character of the English language is illustrative:

The assumption that an ethnic minority writer thinks in, believes he writes
in, or has ambitions toward writing beautiful, correct, and well-punctuated
English sentences is an expression of white supremacy. The universality of
the belief that correct English is the only language of American truth has
made language an instrument of cultural imperialism. Minority experience
does not yield itself to accurate or complete expression in the white man's
language. (Chin et al. 1974, xxxvii)

The argument here reflects deep tensions between an emergent Asian American
literary voice and an unyielding cultural establishment. On the one hand, the editors see the era's refusal to recognize Asian American literary voices as the result of
institutional codification of Euro-American cultural archetypes and the naturalization of their attendant linguistic conventions. In the editors' view, exclusion of
Asian American literary articulations on the basis of unfamiliar linguistic usage is
another manifestation of the institutional power that had continually denied
Asian Americans access to America's social discourse. The editors' claim to ownership of their own language thus points toward a crucial context of their contestation to cultural domination; that is, the unequal conditions underlying their attempt to exercise power were partly constituted by and maintained through
ideological uses of language by the cultural establishment.

On the other hand, the editors' strongly worded challenge to the adequacy of
"white man's language" for expressing "minority experience" is not without its
problems. For one thing, there is an implicit assumption in this argument that
"white America" was not only a cultural monolith with a discourse devoid of internal complexities and differences but also a fixed social entity incapable of evolution
or change.[17] Clearly, the rhetoric of total rejection of the "white man's language"
best describes the editors' moral outrage, but it does not address the more serious
historical issue of how an emergent Asian American literary discourse was itself inextricably entangled with mainstream language and cultural traditions. The historical dimension of *Aiiieeeee!*'s assertion of linguistic differentiation therefore suggests that its claim on an "Asian American language" was not a matter of actual
practice. On the contrary, the existence of such a discourse can be said to depend on
"finding new forms or adaptations of forms" from prior cultural and linguistic conventions, and its meaning can be understood "only in relation to a full sense of the
dominant" (Williams 1977, 126, 123). The concept of negotiation offers a means of
dealing with this complex relationship. The emergent Asian American linguistic
tradition had no new or "pure" language available to it; rather, it had to fashion its
rhetoric out of the archive of cultural conventions and historical circumstances, including both non-Western and Western traditions, while taking bargaining positions that would reshape and enlarge that archive, make space for more diversified
cultural and linguistic symbols, and enlist new audiences.

Such a negotiated process necessarily involves political contestations, rhetorical innovations, articulation of extreme positions, acceptance of undecidable consequences, and modification of prior stances. It also involves recognizing the dangers posed by assimilation to the self-interest of an emergent culture, which might be defined as accommodation to the interests of the dominant culture without risking the potentially negative outcomes of confrontation/bargaining. But the voicing of positions will not be constructive if minority discourse, as Mae Henderson suggests, involves only a consciousness of speaking about external conditions from the position of the oppressed at an empirical level; the engagement in such a process must also involve simultaneous recognition of the fact that discourse also speaks *to* the other from the vantage point and site of complex historical interconnections (1989, 19). For only when Asian American writers actively engage with the discourses of others can their self-inscriptions of the hitherto invisible become pragmatically effective in a social and historical sense. Such active engagement, I suggest, makes possible articulation of ideological differences in a way that such articulation can simultaneously be recognized by the cultural establishment and create pressure for a process of negotiated change. In tactical terms, the voicing of such differences must be forceful enough to create both commitment in the emergent community of dissent and inducements to accommodation from the established cultural construct without either collapsing the engagement of communication between the "center" and the "peripheries" or sacrificing the less powerful party's interests.

As I mentioned previously, one key limit that gave shape to the cultural and ideological symbols in which an emergent Asian American literature could articulate its position was the incompatibility between the ethnic community's demands for recognition of the validity of its literary voice and the cultural establishment's demands for aesthetic conformity. As a result, Asian American writers' articulated positions are often marked by a discrepancy between what a certain narrative strategy promises and what the text actually delivers, between the writer's intentions and the external constraints on the opinions expressed, and between the text's aesthetic form and its ideological content. In most cases, Asian American literary discourse at once confirms and disrupts established value and belief systems because it simultaneously adopts broadly shared linguistic and cultural conventions and articulates noncanonical and marginalized cultural sensibilities. For Asian American writers, the tactical problem in the era involved negotiating the disruptive element in their works, which was likely to close off communication, while recognizing that reliance on existing cultural and linguistic codes threatened to make their literary voices indistinguishable from those in the mainstream. Indeed, the impulse to look for common ground with the cultural mainstream ignores the crucial fact that the confrontation-negotiation process by which Asian American literary voices seek self-definition, change, and redress becomes pragmatically meaningless if one of its outcomes—"heterogeneity"—is assumed at the outset by the aggrieved parties.

Although the race-centered, manhood-centered positions and the rejection of "white language" by the editors of *Aiiieeeee!* can be seen as productive strategic moves taken to open a breach in the cultural establishment for Asian American literary voices, the turn of events was determined not by the editors' stated goals but by the indeterminate social and cultural conditions stimulated by their exertion of ideological differences. Ironically, their disruption of the dominant culture gave rise to multiple possibilities at sites they never imagined—disruptions of the critical projects they set in motion, critiques of their own positions within the community they purported to represent, or the emergence of new forms of cultural intervention in works by other Asian American writers. From today's vantage point it can be argued that the extreme positions taken by the editors proved most effective when they were self-consciously constructed to prevent communicative closure and interpreted provisionally to acknowledge the complexity of Asian American experiences and differences. Nevertheless, even if a writer is totally conscious of the political stakes and cultural risk of deploying a strategically essentialist move, he or she can hardly determine the point at which a "strategic use of essentialism" ceases to be provisional and becomes permanent (see Fuss 1989, 32).[18] In other words, the effects of the "strategic use of essentialism" in Asian American literary discourse can be best understood only in hindsight.

By way of comparison, many antiessentialist critiques, because of their alertness to the dangers of claiming essence, pose their own problems for the writer, for they tend to suggest scenarios that characteristically ignore the determining social factors in favor of idealist solutions. Lawrence Grossberg has noted the impasse between the idea of totally conscious negotiations implicit in the concept of "strategic use of essentialism" and the tendency to suspend action in many antiessentialist positions. He suggestively links the need to understand agency at "sites of struggle" with the need to trace its movement on "planes of struggle" (1992, 121), thus opening up avenues for rearticulating strategies of resistance from a global perspective. Only by recognizing the imperatives of making counterhegemonic moves against particular forms of oppression, and the undecidable effects of such moves on both temporal and spatial terrains, can critical discourse evaluate the consequence of essentialist and antiessentialist positions in ways that are not only theoretically sound but also practically meaningful. In taking such a position, however, I do not aim to prescribe a single global perspective that could successfully map out all the various tensions that Asian American writers and critics juggled in efforts to effect change in the 1957–1980 period. Rather, I intend to show how the mobilizing vision of social transformation has historically inhered in the myriad articulations of difference in Asian American literary writings of the period, and that the means of expression and negotiation available to individual writers necessarily limited their articulations of such a vision, as it does my own reconstructions of them.

In deciding which texts to examine, I have been concerned with historical periods and the contexts of these texts' production. I have also kept in mind the horizon of expectations of the different and changing readership of these texts, especially in terms of a text's tendency either to confirm or to challenge popular cultural perceptions or value systems. It is never easy to distinguish ideologically transformative texts from ideologically reinforcing ones, for judgments of a text's meaning are formed not only out of its immediate reading environment but also out of its retrospective use by subsequent interpretive communities. In this sense there are no explicitly "oppositional" or inherently "conservative" texts but only texts that function in such ways in specific contexts. As critics we need to look into the use to which such texts have been put under specific circumstances and to explain why they generate the responses they do. My interpretations are of course ideologically and culturally associated with the critical approaches with which I align myself; they can be regarded as acts of participating in the ongoing negotiation I find at work in Asian American literary discourse itself. My readings aim at transformative understanding of textual signs—through consciously activating submerged meanings and critically incorporating interventionary values—in order to produce new sensibilities and to move postwar Asian American critical discourse toward a fully historical perspective on Asian America's past, present, and future. Identifying specific forms of negotiation, describing the modes in which they operate in specific works, and disclosing "options and alternatives for transformative praxis" (West 1990, 31) will, I hope, encourage further recognition not only of the complexities of Asian American literary production from the 1950s through the 1970s but also of how these writings have contributed to reshaping subsequent social and cultural positions in American society about race, gender, class, and other historical experiences. With these mechanisms of negotiation in mind, I now turn to the historical roles of Asian American realist narrative and Asian American cultural nationalism, two critical issues that often receive simplistic treatments in postmodern Asian American cultural criticism. Through such an analysis, I hope to illustrate how understanding Asian American literary discourse of the pre- and post-1980 periods as a negotiated process is inseparable from a transformative rearticulation of these issues as ongoing textual practices and social-symbolic acts.

Resituating Realist Narrative

Contemporary debates over the limitations of realism as a residual modernist problematic have engaged the attention of Asian American critics because of the

obvious explanatory model they offer for critiquing a male-oriented cultural nationalism within the ethnic community. One provocative argument that emerges
from such a context emphasizes the complicity of the notion of realist imitation
with the logic of Asian American identity politics, a complicity that is seen as affirming the linear assumptions about bourgeois nationalist closure and as sup-
pressing Asian American particularities and differences. The critical value of this
argument is beyond doubt: it underscores the structural dependence of an essentialist Asian American identity claim on developmental narrative as a necessary
mode of the ethnic subject's individual formation, and it usefully complicates traditional debates over realism, which treat the issue of political representation only
as a tangential concern. Within this analytical framework, for example, Shelley
Wong observes that "the choice of realist forms that centered on the development
of autonomous selfhood made possible the literary representation and achievement of an Asian American subjectivity (a subjectivity that had been conspicu-
ously absent in mainstream depictions or objectifications of Asians) that could
serve as a prelude to the Asian American subject's achievement of political representation." Such a use of realism, Wong further observes, invariably led to a formal and thematic reproduction of the developmental narrative of American *Bildung* under the hegemonic conditions of the 1970s, when the ethnicity paradigm
of immigration dominated discussions of race in the United States (1995, 130,
128).[19] As a counterstrategy Lisa Lowe suggests, with regard to the significance
of *Dictée,* that this work successfully

> resists the core values of aesthetic realism—correspondence, mimesis, and
> equivalence—and approaches these notions as contradictions. Rather than
> constructing a narrative of unities and symmetries, with consistencies of
> character, sequence, and plot, it emphasizes instead an aesthetic of frag-
> mented recitation and episodic non-identity—dramatizes, in effect, an aes-
> thetic of infidelity. Repetition itself is taken to its parodic extreme, and dis-
> engaged as the privileged mode of imitation and realism. (1995b, 37)

Despite the relevance of these observations, however, their critical force depends mainly on a negative understanding of realism as an aesthetic principle that
only privileges positivist reflections of immediate reality and homogenizes complexities and differences. They give no consideration, for example, to the multiple
forms and heritages of realism as an internally complex and contradictory representational strategy historically, or to the sophisticated reworking of realism
since the 1920s by Theodor Adorno, Walter Benjamin, Mikhail Bakhtin, Gérard
Genette, or Hayden White.[20] Instead, they identify an obsolete form of realist
claim and then argue almost effortlessly about specific Asian American literary
works' generic and epistemological breakthroughs and about others' aesthetic and
ideological defects.[21] Such a distinction between the "realist" and the "nonreal-

ist"—with the former used as a metaphoric substitution for ideological totalization and the latter as a synonym for heterogeneous recognition of difference—
problematically confounds the nature of realist representation in literature. For
example, it constructs Asian American social experience as totally passive and easily representable; it assigns undue power to the subjective will to duplicate the
world in contexts of differential social relations; and it emphasizes only how Asian
American realist representation can be co-opted or victimized into mimicking the
dominant while ignoring how such representation simultaneously subverts linear
hegemonic arrangement. In overestimating the adequacy of the ethnicity-based
immigration paradigm as a viable analytical framework within which to judge
literary realism, the negative assessment of realism thus affirms an extreme appropriation of the poststructuralist critique of representation, while neglecting the
fact that this critique, in its best moments, aims only to problematize Hobbesian
assumptions about political representation rather than dismiss representation altogether (e.g., Bennett 1987; Spivak 1988; Laclau 1993).[22]

There is no denying that traditional Asian American literary studies privileges
a sociological reading of literature, and, as a caution against the dangers of such a
tendency, reminders of the limitations of collapsing the figurative into the material are always pertinent and justifiable. It should also be noted, however, that
there is a difference between literature's mimetic claims and the actual result of its
representation, and between realist literature's alleged mimetic essence and such
an essence attributed to a realist work through predisposed schematic reading.
Ted Gong's 1980 sociological characterization of Louis Chu's realist novel *Eat a
Bowl of Tea* is illustrative.[23] In his analysis Gong suggests that the novel delin-
eates "a pattern of cultural development from Chinese to Chinese American"
through its representation of the father-son relationship as "the most critical juncture in the erosion of a traditional Chinese value system and the emergence of a
Chinese American character." Gong then asserts that "change from Chinese to
Chinese American begins here" (73, 74–75). Because Gong's characterization affirms the perceived defects of a realist imitation of the dominant ethnicity paradigm in the 1970s, it has become a major reference point for the poststructuralist
argument about the existence in traditional Asian American literary representations of a master narrative of "masculinist generational symbolism" (Lowe 1991,
34). Yet Gong's nonliterary reading of *Eat a Bowl of Tea* constitutes precisely an
instance of epistemic violence on Chu's work through its decontextualization of
the novel on the one hand and its imposition of an anthropological view of Chinese Americans' acculturation as a process of linear cultural transmission on the
other. By substituting Gong's misreading of Chu's work for the novel's own limitations, however, readers who rely on Gong's view of its realism typically dismiss
the novel in ways that not only repeat this critique's epistemic violence but also
preserve, in the process of such a repetition, the pedagogical authority of Gong's

method. The result, paradoxically, is that these readers frequently reinscribe, through more sophisticated hermeneutic abstractions, Gong's sociological omission of the race, class, and gender determinants of the novel's realist portrayal, precisely in the name of rejecting Gong's simplistic approach.

As this example suggests, a literary work's realist detail often implies "mimetic essence" not because such "essence" is an inherent feature of the work in question but mainly because readers tend to construct such an essence from ideological continuums that recognize only sequential plot and causal connections. I also wish to suggest that if we presuppose realism to be an aesthetic form exclusively concerned with a pre-given signified, the content of a realist work must accordingly be seen as both paraphrasable and susceptible to reductive generalizations. My own position is that a realist narrative cannot be fully grasped or explained only by relying on ideological analysis within a sociological framework. Rather, it must be understood in relation to its primary site of production and usage, that is, its affiliations with the literary and with the aesthetic. Furthermore, because of the subjective nature of any textual representation, a realist narrative unavoidably rewrites the material world temporally, linguistically, and ideologically, offers no easy access to its origins, and interpellates the text within social and cultural forces that do not yield easily to interpretive reconstructions. Thus, realist narratives do not necessarily produce "mimetic" results or intellectually less demanding meaning for readers, nor do they have to be seen for this reason as natural accomplices of bourgeois nationalist totalization.

Nonetheless, my argument about the difficulty of seamless realist representations does not lead to another extreme view held by some contemporary practitioners of narratology, namely, that there is no such thing as "realist" literature. Rather, I underscore the need of investigating the contextual specificity of realist deployment not as a naive form of representation but as a unique form of social engagement under given historical conditions.[24] In a discussion of realism within the context of Euro-American Marxist literary practices in the 1920s and 1930s, San Juan rearticulates the political need for maintaining a reflexive materialist theory of reflection in contemporary American cultural studies. The principles of realism he has reformulated, though exclusively concerned with the problematics of the "realism debates," seem useful for clarifying some of the confusions surrounding the current realism "controversy" in Asian American literary criticism. These principles can be briefly summarized as follows: (1) a creative use of realism is crucial to producing politically effective art that foregrounds its signifying processes in relation to their contradictory social referents; (2) realism emphasizes a view of art's "broad intelligibility" and the graspability of the social tendencies mediated through such signifying processes; (3) realism engages in serious but ironic construction of consistency and coherence against the mystifying forces of culture that conceal the actual insufficiency of the social situation; and (4) realism is dynamically motivated by urges to expose social contradictions and to transform contemporary conditions (1995, 58–60).

Under these principles, realism always produces mimetic surplus, a feature that prevents realist productions from becoming "self-sufficient" works of art. At the same time, the apparent lack of aesthetic playfulness in these works frustrates poststructuralist attempts to "conquer" texts in totalizing terms. Abdul JanMohamed and David Lloyd regard such a lack of aesthetic playfulness in writings by American minority writers as one textual emblem of racial minorities' social deformation, as well as an "expression and sublimation" of the indignities historically suffered by them (1990, 5–6). From this perspective, realist narrative must be seen both as a conventional literary form historically available to Asian American writers in much of the pre-1980s period and as a necessary ideological tool, however chosen, for their social and political struggles. Owing in part to externally inflicted contradictions and to the mediational character of all representational discourse, realist portrayal of "reality" in Asian American literature of the era is always incomplete and asymmetrical, and consequently writers who attempt to represent social reality "objectively" or project "organic wholes" simultaneously reveal the inherent problematics of their own efforts. As such efforts, realist texts such as *Eat a Bowl of Tea* or *No-No Boy* are no more transparent in meaning than postmodern narratives such as *Dictée* or *Dogeaters,* and their interpretation demands that readers adjust their ideological assumptions and become receptive to alternative meanings attainable only through unconventional glosses of their discourses.

Confirming that the *absolute* distinction between the realist and the nonrealist (which, in the context of my discussion, involves a false differentiation between the nonliterary and the literary) is arbitrary in practice, these modes of representation often coexist in hybrid forms in both pre- and post-1970s Asian American writings. For example, how else do we account for the "utopian" moments of hope or the role of "magical" solution in predominantly realist works such as *No-No Boy* and *Eat a Bowl of Tea,* or for the stark "realist" portrayals in more self-referential texts such as *Dogeaters* and *Dictée?* Or for Maxine Hong Kingston's juxtaposition of documentary accounts of Chinese immigration history in the United States against surrealist descriptions of the cultural genesis of Chinese America in *China Men?* The combination of these different narrative strategies in works characterized either as mainly realist or predominantly nonrealist suggests that the interdependence/interpenetration of the two modes was not only an available aesthetic phenomenon but also a necessary cultural strategy in Asian American writings of the 1957–1980 period. Such a dialectical relationship finds a cogent elaboration in T. V. Reed's discussion of the significance of sociologically coded photographic documentary works in relation to postmodernist modes of representation:

Where in much postmodernist work fragmentation, stylistic heterogeneity and anti-estheticism are themselves *aestheticized* . . . [these works] keep the question of the real, and particularly the real plight of the marginalized, on their political agenda. Their didactic interventions are truly anti-aesthetic in that they recall the political stake in claims to represent the real, and they point to the political contexts of reception. Politically effective texts today need the rhetorical power generated by sophisticated textual play through and against the complex symbolic-material webs of domination. And they also need an analytic, explicitly political dimension to shape the text's reception through direct contestation with the incorporative power of the postmodern, late capitalist order. (1988, 174)[25]

Recognizing both the difference and the continuity between realist and nonrealist works helps reveal not only the ideological and rhetorical complexities of representation in much pre-1980s Asian American writing but also its ongoing relevance as active cultural agent to contemporary cultural formations in Asian American history. Realism is potentially both open and closed, its meaning and significance contingent on both its contextual usage and its wider cultural and ideological determinations. Ignoring or caricaturing the historical roles of Asian American realist narrative deprives us not only of an important critical resource but also of a part of history in which art's serious commitment to its social and political function was considered either essential or at times even decisive. By calling attention to the historicity as well as the complexity of realism, however, I am not advocating a revival of the mid-twentieth-century modes of realism that are no longer answerable to the need for contemporary Asian American literary representation. What I am suggesting is that realism is a historically constituted aesthetic phenomenon; that its negative and incomplete assessment in current Asian American cultural criticism is entwined with a linear perception of pre-1965 Asian American history, a perception that often results in a hierarchical distancing of Asian America's past from its present; and that its ongoing relevance lies in both its careful historicization and its conscious rearticulation into new forms of social and political commitments.

Cultural Nationalism in Context

"Asian American cultural nationalism" is a term closely associated with the 1974 articulation of an "Asian American cultural integrity" by the editors of *Aiiieeeee!* The severe limitations of the editors' pronouncements have led some critics to draw parallels between the effects of their claims and those of postcolonial bourgeois constructions of the nation, effects often seen as totally complicit with the dominant ideology and practice that the editors attempted to expose. To the extent that such a comparison complicates our understanding of the relationship between "margins" and "the center" and alerts us to the dangers of an essentialist use of identity politics, a postcolonial critique of early Asian American cultural self-definitions has been and will remain an indispensable ideological intervention. I would caution, however, that collapsing the subaltern cultural nationalist contestation in *Aiiieeeee!* with a colonial representation of the nation risks fetishizing the dominant form of nationalist essence through an inverted fixation on binaries. In particular, it risks obscuring some of the irreducible differences between the given postcolonial theory's assumptions about nationalism and "the gritty, ground-level texture"—to use Frank Lentricchia's phrase—of *Aiiieeeee!*'s 1974 articulation of the nation.[26] In posing the issue this way, I wish to register a slight demur about the now popular use of the Foucauldian concept of discourse reversal in critiquing essentialist tendencies in Asian American cultural nationalist struggles (Foucault 1976/1980, 100–102). Although a thorough discussion of Foucault's philosophical position about this concept is not possible within the scope of my inquiry here, it is important to recognize that it derives from his influential formulation of "discursive formations" (1972, 8, 13), a formulation that has been very useful to literary and cultural criticism for its emphasis on the embeddedness of practice with power and culture as multiply implicated processes, as well as for its effective refutation of reductive approaches to history and to subject formation. But such a theory also partially depends, as critics have pointed out, on a conceptualization of discursive "regularities" or regularity in dispersion (by which Foucault does not dismiss incompatible or differential elements in formation processes but suggests their predictable modes of operation), as well as on a belief in the inescapable complicity between power and knowledge within the Western system of cultural production.[27] Despite its best insights, I would therefore argue, Foucault's concept of discourse reversal does not—and does not aim to—give an adequate account of the results of hegemonic encounters between Asian American and Western nationalist projects in cross-cultural and cross-linguistic situations. In other words, Asian American nationalist claims, because they do not occur *entirely* within the context described by Foucault, cannot be a complete reversal or a seamless duplication of the bourgeois nation. Rather, such claims must be analyzed as both a site of ideological mimicry of the dominant and a place of the "différend" (Lyotard's term), that is, as Gayatri Spivak writes, of "the inaccessibility of, or untranslatability from, one mode of discourse in the dispute to another" (1988, 300–301).

In his thought-provoking analysis of the rise of Bengali nationalist ideologies and politics in late nineteenth-century India, Partha Chatterjee calls attention to the internal complexities of the anticolonial nationalist project, particularly its ambiguous relationships with colonial domination. Chatterjee argues that such a nationalist project does not develop according to the modular forms of Western nationalism prescribed for Third World elites by Benedict Anderson; rather, it engages in a creative construction of the nation based on assumptions and practices quite different from those defined by the Western bourgeois nation. Specifically, Chatterjee sees Bengali anticolonial nationalism as being waged in two domains: the material (economy, science, technology, legal institutions) and the spiritual (language, education, religion, community). In the former, anticolonial nationalism imitates the approved models offered by the West because of the absence of other options; in the latter, it locates its subjectivity and declares its sovereignty from Western cultural dominance. Such a contradictory approach to nation building, Chatterjee further suggests, is not motivated by an unambiguously rationalist and self-conscious attempt at identity formation on the part of the colonized; rather, it is a gesture toward a simultaneous adaptation to and disruption of the discursive power of colonial oppression with "instrumental," though highly problematic, implications and consequences (1993, 5–13, 19). Although exclusively concerned with situations in India in a particular historical period, Chatterjee's consideration of a little discussed dimension of Third World nationalisms is illuminating for my examination of Asian American cultural nationalism in several ways. It suggests, first, that the articulation of counterhegemonic nationalist concerns depends on access to recognizable and accessible enunciative modalities and repertoires of knowledge which derive from differential and unequal histories; second, that the imitative aspects of such articulation tend to be severely restricted by the dominant practices and the ruling assumptions of the nation, while the hostile aspects of it tend to exaggerate spiritual independence or achievement; and finally, that such articulation necessarily produces conflicting themes and contradictory results.

When the editors of *Aiiieeeee!* angrily affirmed their Americanness through a discourse of citizenship, for example, they mobilized a dominant cultural trope and a universalist claim on liberty and progress. From a presentist perspective, such a move may appear to be not only politically naive but also radically exclusionary. But when it is resituated in the discursive context from which the editors' early 1970s position emerged, its ideological thrust becomes quite specific: we see that it constituted, for the first time since the mid-nineteenth century, a public claim on rights that Asian Americans were entitled to but denied historically. As such, it signified to most Asian American critics of the period a dissension against, rather than a co-optation by, the hegemonic discourse of citizenship because it symbolically transgressed the established terms of the mainstream sociology of ethnicity, revealing their "partial representation/recognition" of America's national objects while alienating the fetishized rhetoric of Americanization (see Bhabha 1994, 86, 88). The editors' extreme assertion of their American identity—and their simultaneous questioning of such identity's ideo-

logical coherence—thus functioned as a staunch polemic against liberal notions
of assimilation and integration that dominated the public discourse on race relations in American society in the early 1970s. Such a polemic is symptomatically manifested in the editors' deep suspicion in the era of a steady influx of
largely middle-class Asian immigrants who, in the editors' eyes, ignored pressing social issues in American society, avoided transgressive politics, and impul-
sively embraced the American dream.[28] Nevertheless, claiming to be "American" under the circumstances could not lead to a reconstitution of the cultural
nationalist subaltern as an unproblematic citizen-subject, or to his or her easy
absorption into a normative narrative of upward mobility. Rather, the very idea
of "the citizen's rights" splits the figure of the racial/sexual subject into public
and private parts of the self (Chakrabarty 1994, 352), a splitting that, I would
suggest, both deepens and intensifies the tension Chatterjee has described between a simultaneously material and spiritual subaltern claim on the nation.
This situation points toward a crucial dilemma in making an Asian American
cultural nationalist claim: its necessary failure completely to realize itself socially and materially according to the paradigms offered by the Western notion
of the Enlightenment, and its simultaneous tendency to obscure the institutional constraints on the effects of its assertion of subaltern nationalist presence
through appropriating the language of the dominant. Such inconsistency of the
Asian American nationalist subject necessarily involves a continued postpone-
ment of its realization of a desire for social amelioration and a constant internal
reenactment of its socially and historically experienced contradictions. Thus, it
often results in what Homi Bhabha calls a "vacillation of ideology," in which the
nationalist discourse "slides from one enunciatory position to another" (1990a,
298).[29]

We sense the contradictory impulses of the editors' positions when they emphasize their American birth even as their government continually refused to redress the unjust treatment of U.S.-born Japanese Americans during World War
II,[30] and when they insist on the primacy of English as the only language spoken
and understood by Asian Americans even as publishers repeatedly rejected the
initial submissions of the manuscript of *Aiiieeeee!* partly on the ground of its language (Chin and Chan 1972, 78–79). Notice as well that when Frank Chin assumed his self-styled oppositional position as the "Chinatown cowboy" in this period (Chin 1972a), he also felt the need to evoke a combative and resourceful
"Kwan Kung"—Chinese god of war and literature (McDonald 1981, xxvii–
xxviii)—for cross-cultural reinforcement. Chin's wavering between these two cultural figures of resistance is particularly revealing with regard to the rhetorical
and incomplete nature of the nationalist positions he represents. At the same
time, it affirms Chatterjee's observation that we tend to take the *claims* of nationalism to be a political movement much too literally and much too seriously

(1993, 5), without considering, I would suggest, the possibility that such claims can perform ironic and ideologically destabilizing functions.

The double-voiced construction of Chin's nationalist stance is similarly reflected in the editors' simultaneous but contradictory endorsement of American nativism and the separatist Asian cultural revival movement influenced by Third World struggles and black nationalism. The coexistence of these contradictory nationalist tendencies in the editors' positions in *Aiiieeeee!* suggests both a failure of the American system in the period to come to terms with its racial minorities on the basis of the founding principles of the nation and the editors' keen awareness of the difficulty of becoming an "American" subject in those terms even when they imitate the voice of the dominant. This inherent irony in Asian American cultural nationalism shows that the phenomenon is both more and less than what its critics have often made it seem. On the one hand, the structural ambiguity of the editors' position defies any convenient categorizations of it. On the other, its dual concerns, which suggest deep divisions in the editors' feelings, prevent the position they take from achieving the ideological coherence necessary for stimulating their desired collective insurgency in the Asian American community. In addition, the contradictory nature of the editors' nationalist position reflects a discrepancy between what the editors claimed to do and what the discursive context of their interpellated subject position allowed them to perform, a discrepancy that leads, in turn, to "a continuing questioning" of Asian Americans' social contingency in relation to the majority society, as well as reproducing in them the perpetual psychic ambivalence of "the strangeness of the familiar" (Bhabha 1990b, 70, 72).

What provided the editors' disparate nationalist arguments with a provisional unity was their unconscious or unintentional recognition of the interrelatedness of race, gender, and class: they problematically use the trope of "feminization" of Asian American men as a position from which to attack racism rather than as a point of entry into sustained investigation of the historical process of racial gendering of Asians in America, hence condensing the complexities of these issues into a manageable surface of contestation. Such unity was structurally deficient because it prioritized a (straight) male gender as a sufficient ground for ethnic solidarity. It was also historically contingent because it attempted to turn the temporary lack of articulated ethnic, gender, cultural, and sexual heterogeneity within the Asian American community into a unidimensional mobilization of race-based resistance. (I therefore do not see the suppression of these diverse interests in the community as *entirely* the result of Asian American cultural nationalism; rather, a thorough investigation of such suppression must involve a consideration of its role in relation to institutional power in the period in question.) Such a strategy in turn obliterated the multiply inflected voices within the community through a structural reproduction of the socially sanctioned either/or bifurcation

of Asian American identity, a bifurcation also reflected in Chin's competing oppositional models of nationalism. Because of the discrepancy between the editors'
rhetorical idealization of masculinist symbols and the material diversity of individual Asian Americans' lived experiences, the images they promoted did not
elicit the responses they expected from the community. But such images did generate as side effects an oppositional consciousness exposed to the shifting social
dynamics of the 1970s, allowing not only crossing and recrossing of the symbolic
boundaries of the editors' nationalist constructs but also appropriation and reap-
propriation of their political import. Because of Asian American cultural nationalism's "continued interaction with different emancipatory social movements"
(Pease 1994, 3), it could not attain a full development as a unitary political project, nor did it successfully create an alternative to its oppressor's ideological apparatus within the given social relations. Yet the Asian American nationalist project's structural liminality repeatedly released the incommensurate values it
subsumed within its imagined spaces and stimulated the suppressed subjects of
social and canonical regulation to demand belated recognition.

It must be emphasized that the structural split in Asian American cultural nationalism did not automatically lead to a self-conscious postnational position
because its discursive ambivalence remained conditioned by the continuing narrative authority imposed by American nationalism. (I propose a reading strategy for
disrupting such narrative authority in my analysis of Kingston's *China Men* in
Chapter 5).[31] This situation points to an unresolved contradiction in current
academic, postcolonial critiques of the nation: while such critiques are quite successful in conceptually dismantling various nationalist projects, they tend to show
little interest in examining the material practice of the United States as itself a
powerful imperial nation (Amy Kaplan 1993, 15, 17). Such critiques are especially
negligent, in my view, of investigating the domestic manifestations and consequences of America's often racially based global exertion of power from the 1950s
through the 1970s, and the specific ways in which Asian Americans' early efforts at
self-determination went contentiously—and contradictorily—through the hegemonic operations of America's nation-state. In calling attention to the structural
complexity and ideological ambivalence of Asian American cultural nationalism, I
therefore emphasize existing postcolonial studies' inadequate theorization of the
national question,[32] as well as the need for Asian American critics to attend to the
actual constituencies of cultural nationalism from both within and outside its
boundaries, to disarticulate elements in cultural nationalism that suppress differences and reproduce American exceptionalism, and to rearticulate cultural nationalism's interventionary potential toward transformative directions or possibilities.

The evolution of Asian American literature since the publication of *Aiiieeeee!* in
1974 suggests that the unfolding of an Asian American cultural plurality could
only have been a halting, contested process that partly depended on recognizing

the internal contradictions of Asian American realist and nationalist narratives of the pre-1980s era as a precondition for its subsequent hybridization. Many features of recent Asian American literature—including a diasporic or an international perspective—were already embedded in suppressed or distorted forms in Asian American writers' responses to the hegemonic processes of the 1950s, 1960s, and 1970s, and the positions of subsequent Asian American writers should accordingly be seen in implicit dialogue with these earlier articulations (although it is obvious that the political and economic contexts of contemporary Asian diaspora are qualitatively different from those of the previous era). *Aiiieeeee!*'s use of *Eat a Bowl of Tea* and other works to promote a nationalist position, viewed within this context, does not disqualify these texts as active cultural agents that contribute to emancipatory social conditions. On the contrary, the ambiguous purposes for which these texts were used call for rigorous aesthetic and ideological responses to them as sites for investigating the social discourses and political intentions surrounding their production and ongoing reception. Walter Benjamin refers to such a dialectical relationship between historical continuity and discontinuity as "the always-new in the contexts of the ever the same."[33] The newness of recent Asian American literary articulations lies not in their inherent power of being contemporary nor in their actual severance from previous sources of resistance, but in their fuller expression, under more enabling (or seemingly more enabling) social conditions, of the possibilities of liberation problematically or incompletely envisioned by earlier Asian American realist and/or nationalist literary voices. In this sense, Asian Americans cannot move easily beyond the limitations of their past simply on the basis of new social formations. For historical transitions are always ambiguous, protracted, and unpredictable, constantly throwing up obstacles to development and frequently demanding recontextualization of current problematics in light of the past and reexamination of the past in relation to its residual forms in the present. But recognizing the entangled, nonlinear, and multidimensional nature of historical development, as I have emphasized throughout this chapter, should not lead to a diminished sense of history or to giving up thinking progressively altogether. For history, despite its sheer discursiveness, does possess what Satya Mohanty calls "minimal rationalities" (1992, 138), and historical conditions, as Raymond Williams also agrees, "could be and were made better" (1989, 283).

In reconstituting the relational networks and the formation processes of Asian American literary discourse from 1957 to 1980, I therefore take as my central task in this study to reassess five formative Asian American texts of the period. I do not regard these texts as engaging in a grand narrative of identity formation according to some shared logic of resistance, or as inherently agonistic to current critical sensibilities about heterogeneous cultural differences. Rather, I see them as interrelated products of different levels and moments of social formation, with each constituting a creative response to the social and cultural conditions it entered. At the same time, I also view these diverse and contradictory literary attempts as implicitly participating in an ongoing yet nonteleological process of disarticulating social and cultural conventions, and as collectively shaping, through their revision of existing cultural codes and their production of new literary significations, an unstable yet insistently transformative vision about Asian America's future. In this process, these texts' ideological tendencies and formal characteristics, as well as the specific forms of their social imagination, were shaped not by any single determinant but rather by the complex interplay between authorial design, available social space, and accessible cultural resources—on a social-material terrain that was only partially open, conditionally heterogeneous, and dynamically fluid yet frequently inhospitable to the voices of the emergent.

Such a recognition points to the related question of how to read the "failures" of some of these works when they were first published. To readers who assume a criterion in favor of an ideally instant agency, such "failures" are often taken as a sign of these works' ideological inadequacy. As I argued earlier in this chapter, however, resistance is never an inherent feature in a cultural product, the social effects of which depend mainly on its accessibility to institutional apparatus and on its social and cultural usage. The "failures" of these works, from this perspective, indicate their incompatibility with and inaccessibility to established modes of literary response in their time rather than their inability to voice desires of transformation with available aesthetic and ideological means of expression. With their disruptive cultural influence contained by the presiding values, some of these texts went out of print; but the social conditions that produced them did not disappear. On the contrary, these conditions were expanded both temporally and spatially as a result of the ideological exertion and then the marginalization of these texts. Such unresolved social and cultural tensions then formed, to use Daniel O'Hara's words, "a part of the new situation, the new dilemma or condition," which later Asian American writers would confront in their new historical present. Indeed, these Asian American texts became cultural sites for "conscious preservation" of the history of Asian American writers (1992, 49). The accumulative effects of these diverse articulations in turn helped multiply the grounds for renewed Asian American cultural dissent that built on and then moved beyond earlier articulations.

2

Writing the Novel, Narrating Discontents

Race and Cultural Politics in John Okada's *No-No Boy*

Narrative always says less than it knows, but it often makes
known more than it says.
— Gérard Genette, *Narrative Discourse*

The lieutenant believed him this time. "Hell's bells," he ex-
claimed. "If they'd done that to me, I wouldn't be sitting in
the belly of a broken-down B-24 going back to Guam from a
reconnaissance mission to Japan." "I got reasons," said the
Japanese-American soldier soberly.
— John Okada, *No-No Boy*

The changing reception of John Okada's 1957 novel *No-No Boy* raises important
questions about the nature of its production in the Eisenhower era, of its surviv-
ability into the 1970s as a cultural agent of resistance, and of its ongoing relevance to contemporary Asian American cultural criticism. The cultural politics of
No-No Boy therefore provides an initial case study of how the theorized process of
negotiation which I discussed in Chapter 1 is enacted by an Asian American literary text. As Okada's contemporary Japanese American readers would have known
without opening the book, his title refers to a controversial phenomenon that derived from the already problematic internment of Japanese Americans by the U.S.
government during World War II. The decision to relocate Japanese Americans
was made on February 19, 1942, under Executive Order 9066, approximately two
months after Japan's attack on Pearl Harbor. The stated rationale for the decision
was "military necessity," namely, to safeguard the national security of the United
States against possible Japanese sabotage. Unstated was American policy makers'
conviction that all persons of Japanese ancestry residing in the United States were
actually engaged in subversive activities on behalf of the Japanese militaristic
government. Under the terms of the executive order, over 120,000 Japanese
Americans were uprooted from their homes throughout the West Coast and con-

fined initially to assembly centers and later to more permanent internment camps in desolate interior lands.

At the beginning of 1943, the War Department decided to recruit the interned nisei (American-born, second-generation Japanese Americans) into an all-Japanese American combat unit for the U.S. military. As a security clearance measure, the War Department conducted a voluntary registration among the interned nisei males by way of a questionnaire (known as the "Statement of United States Citizenship of Japanese Ancestry"), which all nisei males over the age of seventeen were required to answer. Key to the questionnaire were questions 27 and 28, which read: "No. 27. Are you willing to serve in the armed forces of the United States on combat duty wherever ordered? No. 28. Will you swear unqualified allegiance to the United States of America and faithfully defend the United States from any or all attack by foreign or domestic forces, and forswear any form of allegiance or obedience to the Japanese emperor, to any foreign government, power, or organization?" (Weglyn 1976, 136).[1] The security clearance was carried out by the War Relocation Authority (WRA), which had collaborated with the War Department in devising the questionnaire but decided to use it also for administrative purposes—to sort out and segregate the "troublemakers" from the camps, which had been experiencing sporadic resistance since the latter half of 1942. Under such circumstances, the registration not only became compulsory but also was extended to all adult internees—male and female nisei seventeen years old and over, and all issei (first-generation Japanese immigrants).

Ichiro Yamada, the "no-no boy" of Okada's title, is among the interned nisei who answer the two questions negatively and are jailed for "disloyalty."[2] Okada's novel appears to tell a story of the return of the prodigal, one who comes to recognize his "error" and to reembrace the promise of America. But within this seemingly innocent treatment of Ichiro's return, Okada has created a protagonist who fails to regain his selfhood and whose ongoing predicament epitomizes the consequences of the racism that fueled the wartime internment of Japanese Americans and continued to condition their lives and identities in the postwar years. Partly because of the sensitive nature of the novel's subject matter and partly because of the ambiguous meaning of its double voicing, No-No Boy received little attention when it first came out in 1957. Indeed, on the eve of its rediscovery in the mid-1970s, the book's first edition of 1,500 copies had not yet been sold out (Chin et al. 1974, xxxvi).

Okada's Rhetorical Decision

A brief history of the reception of No-No Boy since the 1970s opens the way to discussing the discourses available to Okada for negotiating an intervention in the mid-1950s. Until the late 1980s, the predominant view of the novel had focused on its apparent call for ethnic recuperation and moral reconciliation, with an emphasis on Ichiro's ability to overcome his self-hatred and to complete his quest for a sense of "wholeness" through a difficult but ultimately successful process of redemption (Chin et al. 1974, xlii; McDonald 1979, 25; Kim 1982, 147–56; Lim 1986, 63). Such a view was based on the critical community's traditional emphasis on "defining Asian American realities through literature" (Kim 1990a), an emphasis affirmed, during the ethnic formation in the mid-1970s and the early 1980s, through a paradigmatic reading of one of Ichiro's interior monologues in which he allegorically identifies himself with the hero of a Japanese folk tale, Momotaro, a boy born from a split peach who avenges the wrongs done to his aging parents and restores the wholeness of his family through bravery and the help of his friends (15–16).

Since the early 1990s, this interpretation has been challenged by critics informed by emerging concerns of contemporary critical developments. These critics find an exclusive emphasis on the novel's temporal succession as a way of affirming the ideological continuum of extratextual concerns to be inadequate, and attempt to reexamine the text in ways that bring out its suppressed meanings and unrecognized ideological dimensions (e.g., Sato 1992; Jinqi Ling 1995a; Lowe 1995a, 59–60). Of these more recent positions, Gayle K. Fujita Sato's problematization of the traditional emphasis on the novel's theme of recuperation through the Momotaro story is especially provocative. Sato identifies, through close engagement with both the novel and the folk tale to which it is related, some significant contradictions between Okada's portrayal of Ichiro's identity quest and the experience of Momotaro. Seeing these contradictions manifest in two basic textual registers—the novel's repetitive and halting syntax, and the irresolution of Ichiro's inner struggle—Sato argues that the novel's lack of linear development ironically strengthens the power and the logic of assimilation while it disrupts the redemptive process that critics traditionally prescribe for Ichiro. Sato accordingly suggests that Okada fails to deconstruct the racial dichotomy in postwar America and allows Ichiro's identity crisis to be ultimately resolved "through a binary opposition valuing '(white) American' over 'Japanese'" (1992, 256).

My analysis of *No-No Boy* recognizes the insights of both the traditional and the more recent readings of the novel. But I find, in the examples just cited, that critics tend to affirm uncritically the contingently constructed centrality of the Momotaro tale, and consequently either overestimate the success of Ichiro's search for identity by focusing only on the parallels between his experience and Momotaro's, or misunderstand Okada's attempt to create an ambiguous protagonist by pointing out aspects of Ichiro's life that contradict the Momotaro story. Such an overemphasis on the interpretive authority of the Momotaro tale depends, I would suggest, on a partial but continued suspension of critical consciousness about analyzing *No-No Boy* as a work of fiction.[3] In particular, I would argue, this approach obscures some of the fundamental questions about the book's status in post–World War II Asian American literary history, that is, its specific forms of engagement with the social and aesthetic discourses of the cold war era; its actual conditions of emergence, disappearance, and belated recognition; and its connections with Asian American literary writings over which its articulation takes precedence. I treat the Momotaro tale seriously but as only one component of Okada's larger rhetorical scheme for the production and reception of *No-No Boy,* a component whose formal and ideological significance can be effectively accounted for only in relation to the tensions and contradictions of the novel's historically wrought structure of feeling.

Specifically, my view of Okada's work foregrounds the ambiguous nature of Ichiro's search and the uncertainty of his return. But this characteristic of Ichiro's quest is determined mainly by the limited range of dissent permitted in the social and aesthetic discourses in which Okada conceived his fictional project, as well as by the contradictory state that such discourses create in Ichiro's consciousness. This situation prevents Ichiro from either thinking about or reacting against his plight totally outside the available social options, while making it difficult for his struggle to become simply recuperative. At the same time, I also suggest, Okada does not for this reason turn Ichiro's existential liminality into ideological fatalism. Rather, he negotiates the indeterminacy of Ichiro's dilemma through a deployment of several interrelated positionalities: an implicit critique of either/or assumptions about cultural identity in the portrayal of Ichiro's troubled experience with both assimilation and Japanese nationalism; a use of the mother-son conflict as a crucial site of revelation of the historical tragedy inflicted on Japanese American life during the war; an illustration of both the promise and the difficulty of resolving Ichiro's identity crisis through a metaphorical use of the folk hero Momotaro; and an attempt to differentiate and enlist multiple audiences for the novel's political vision by subversively rehearsing the broadly shared humanism of the era through the love affair between Ichiro and Emi, a nisei woman abandoned by her husband. The groping, unsteady Ichiro who emerges from such a narrative process remains highly conflicted: he does not develop sequentially according to the novel's plot, nor does he entirely dissolve into the social roles designated for him by the dominant discourse. The primary significance of the publication of *No-No Boy* in 1957, from this perspective, lies neither in the work's thematic affirmation of Ichiro's survival through positive connections with individuals in his community, nor in his rejection of Japanese nationalism in favor of the hegemony of white America, but rather in Okada's inserting the outcast Ichiro into the space opened up by the novel itself. Ichiro's muffled voice resonates with the ethnic dissent of the 1950s and implicitly challenges the social power that suppressed the construction of the Japanese American subject. In this sense, the novel constitutes an act of participating in the cultural dialogue of its time and of demanding attention from the mainstream to Japanese America's ongoing social and moral dilemma.

The available biographical records indicate that Okada started writing *No-No Boy* in the early 1950s while working as a librarian first in Seattle and then in Detroit. Despite the fact that the library job required him to work "overtime" and to put up with "disrupted vacation plans," he kept his writing a "disciplined" avocation and managed to complete the entire manuscript sometime around 1955. Okada's constant struggle to find "more time to write" while he was starting a family and moving across the country for jobs (Chin 1979a, 259–60) suggests both a sense of urgency on the part of the writer and the cultural tensions that surrounded the production of *No-No Boy*. Okada wrote and published the novel in an era of conflicting social tendencies in America. On the one hand, the 1950s ushered in a decade of mass consumerism, popular cultural styles, suburban domesticity, and technology fetishism.[4] On the other, it witnessed a profound sense of alienation among American intellectuals, who resisted corporate values, lamented the dissolving individual, and explored alternatives by appealing to resources of the self. Throughout most of this period, however, the individual struggle against external imposition of social and cultural norms took place within the more general tendency to divorce questions of the personal from those of the political, a result of postwar liberalism's distrust of the legacy of the naive left politics of the 1930s on the one hand and of its inability to effectively counter America's cold war domestic politics on the other (e.g., Leer 1991; Molesworth 1988; Schaub 1991, 163–84).

In this era many writers embraced existential philosophy as a major form of intellectual dissent because it effectively dramatized the individual's moral anguish of living in an increasingly "other-directed" world (Reisman 1950/1961, 8). But the existentialist emphasis on the truthfulness of the inner experience only reinforced the writers' tendency toward "self-absorption over social involvement" (Leer 1991, 487), a tendency further strengthened by the privileging of textual signs over social contexts in New Criticism, the dominant aesthetic tenet for American literary studies in the period. Paradoxically, it was precisely within the cultural space produced by such a convergence of the personalized politics in existential philosophy with the dehistoricized aesthetics in New Criticism that progressive writers of the decade such as Ralph Ellison, J. D. Salinger, Tennessee Williams, Bernard Malamud, and Norman Mailer, among others, distinguished their political voices. This situation underscores, conversely, the essential mood of a society that self-consciously avoided direct examination of grievances about its own political, economic, or racial injustice, especially those suffered by racial minorities such as Japanese Americans during and after the war. The general public inattention to the political consequences of the wartime treatment of Japanese

Americans was ironically contrasted with a growing interest in the literary market in "Japanese" culture. This culture was deemed praiseworthy for its supposedly patient, docile, and law-abiding tradition, despite the rationales for incarcerating thousands of Japanese Americans in wartime internment camps, and despite the distinctions made during the war between the "evil" Japanese and the "good" Chinese in the American popular imagination.[5] The specific contexts of this new interest were America's need to refute communist bloc charges of racial discrimination and class oppression in the United States, Japan's postwar alliance with America in the global contest with communism, and civil rights agitation on the home front by African Americans. In this political climate, a few American publishers began to develop a market for Japanese American writers willing to function as cultural mediators and to tell stories of successful assimilation.

This ideologically conditioned literary market presented both obstacles to and opportunities for Okada's attempt to explore the tragic nature of race hatred in American society. On the one hand, the initial poor reception of *No-No Boy* suggests that Asian American writers (who, in the context I refer to, were Chinese, Japanese, Korean, and Filipino Americans) were effectively excluded from participating in the 1950s social discourse on race and ethnicity, which was dominated by African Americans' social drive to end racial segregation and typified by such angry literary voices as Ralph Ellison's in *Invisible Man* (1952), Richard Wright's in *The Outsider* (1953), and James Baldwin's *Go Tell It on the Mountain* (1953). By contrast, most Asian American writers who were published appeared to confirm the era's reigning discourse on Americanization and to avoid denunciations of racial injustice. Reflecting the cultural identity of alien but "safe" minority assigned to Asian Americans was the rigid distinction drawn by the literary establishment of the era between "intrinsic" and "extrinsic" values in literature, a distinction that reproduced Asian America's social marginalization in the realm of aesthetics by denying Asian American literature not only its literariness but also its rich human potential. Reduced to making sociological documentation of immigrants' struggles and their children's accommodation and assimilation, Asian American writers found that autobiography was almost the only commercially publishable form available to them. For example, the most important Japanese American literary work published in the 1950s prior to *No-No Boy,* Monica Sone's autobiography *Nisei Daughter* (1953), became an instant commercial success for its mainstream publisher, presumably because it satisfied what the age demanded of the Japanese American literary voice: representations of the differences between being "Japanese" and being "American," explanations of the exotic but nonthreatening otherness of Japanese American life to mainstream readers, and accounts of successful transition into the mainstream. What was ignored in Sone's book was its nuanced critique of racial discrimination against Japanese Americans through the female protagonist's contradictory narrative voice and her constant puzzlement about the outcome of her inner struggle (e.g., Kim 1982, 74–81; Sumida 1992; Sau-ling Wong 1993, 93–112). The disruptive fictional elements of Sone's book were not recognized because the hierarchical generic assumptions of the era selectively occluded the meaning of her work, just as these assumptions excluded examination of nonconformist perspectives in Jade Snow Wong's *Fifth Chinese Daughter* (1945/1950), the most important Chinese American autobiography of the cold war years.[6]

The question that faced Okada, one may speculate, was how to convey the severity of the World War II rupture in Japanese American life within the limited cultural space allowed for Asian American literary expression. Reflecting Okada's awareness of this tension is both the sense of urgency with which he wrote *No-No Boy* and his rhetorical decision to write a novel. Okada himself had been an internee, albeit one who chose to serve in the U.S. Air Force during World War II (Chan et al. 1991, 478–79). His status as a veteran gave him an implicit license to deal with the no-no boy issue; the era's conditional receptivity to Asian American literary writings opened a space for the attempt. But an autobiographical—hence documentary—account of Japanese Americans' wartime sufferings would have been shocking for postwar readers and vulnerable to ideological censorship within that space. By writing a novel with a fictional hero, Okada adopts a strategy that enables him to speak the ideologically unspeakable while keeping his narrative position usefully ambiguous.

The Racial Dimension of Ichiro's Split Self

The novel begins in 1945 with Ichiro's return from prison to his own community in Seattle. Yet from the outset he is caught between two opposing forces that repeatedly foreground the irresolvable nature of his dilemma. On the one hand, nisei who accept the assumptions of the internment greet Ichiro's return with hatred and hostility, a position made clear by Ichiro's encounter with Eto and Bull, two insolent war veterans who humiliate him publicly, and with Taro, his teenage brother, who out of contempt joins in a violent physical attack against him. On the other hand, Ichiro's mother affirms his no-no decision through fervent expression of Japanese nationalism, self-righteous assertions of motherly authority, and a total denial of his own view of his wartime experience. These extreme attitudes in the Japanese American community indicate that the "home" Ichiro returns to is no less fragmented than his divided self, a situation that intensifies rather than alleviates the originary crisis in his identity. The liminality of Ichiro's return is structurally manifested in the novel's clogged and circular narrative movement beneath its given plot sequence, a feature that, as I noted earlier, is identified by Sato as a symptom of the novel's ideological complicity with the assumptions of the loyalty oath. But I would suggest that this textual feature is determined mainly by the novel's intertextual engagement with the tension between the overwhelming pressure for Japanese Americans to prove their "loyalty" in the immediately postwar period and Ichiro's inability to do so because of his refusal to accept the terms of the draft while interned as an "enemy alien." The syntactic stasis that entraps Ichiro is, in this sense, neither a passive reflection of Okada's transparent intentionality nor, on the other extreme, a sign of the author's conscious refutation of what postmodern theory would term "developmentalism" (see Lowe 1995a, 59–60). Rather, it is simply a rhetorical strategy that Okada uses to enhance the effects of his depiction of Ichiro's moral plight by eliciting empathy from readers who understand the negativity of America's racial politics yet do not underestimate the nature of its hegemonic operations in the post-McCarthy era.

The ironic potential of Okada's structural demonstration of the social impasse faced by no-no boys can be illustrated by his depiction, later in the novel, of Bull's realization of the emptiness of the assimilationist bargain he and other nisei youths have naively accepted when he grieves over the death of another no-no boy, Freddie, who, in trying to defy Bull's insolence, is accidentally killed in a car crash (250). It can also be shown in Okada's portrayal of Ma's gradual translation of her refusal to accept her alien status in America into fanatical Japanese nationalism coupled with an extreme form of self-inflicted social ostracism. In the positions taken by the hostile nisei and the suicidal Ma, Okada dramatizes the fatal weaknesses of two available strategies for dealing with racism—either a naive assimilationism or separatist Japanese nationalism—in the wartime treatment of Japanese Americans. Both work to strengthen the unjust power these various characters face, and reaffirm rather than dismantle the presumed opposition between "Japanese" and "American" identities. Between Ichiro's rejection by the three nisei youths and his conflict with his mother, an alternative space is opened for complicating Ichiro's ideological position as well as for multiplying the novel's narrative vision.

One such instance can be recognized in the "sundry reasons" Ichiro offers for refusing to be drafted while a prisoner in the relocation camp (34). The grounds for his refusal are similar to those of other no-no boys standing before the judge: the U.S. government's differing treatments of Japanese, German, and Italian nationals living in America; young nisei's unwillingness to fight against their brothers from Japan because of parental prohibitions;[7] suspicion of the U.S. Army's profiteering motives in carrying out the relocation; and anger at the government for depriving Japanese Americans of their possessions and for infringing on their rights as American citizens. One no-no boy particularly contends, "If you think we're the same kind of rotten Japanese that dropped the bombs on Pearl Harbor, and it's plain that you do or I wouldn't be here having to explain to you why it is that I won't go and protect son-of-bitches like you" (32). Implicit in Ichiro's position is both a rebelliousness which the complying nisei fail to voice and an insistence on equal rights within the existing political system, an insistence that is missing from Ma's separatist protest. Ichiro's confrontation with the legal authorities in court, however, and his questioning of both the constitutionality of the internment decision and the logic of the draft order are in many ways positions forced by law. These external pressures reproduce the contradictions in Ichiro's consciousness and prevent him from translating the political demand for racial equality implicit in his act of protest into fully conscious or consistent postwar resistance. Consequently, after he is released from prison in 1946 bearing the stamp of "traitor," his understandable desire for a new life becomes highly susceptible to the ideological force fields that surround him: his search will be increasingly characterized by a wavering between Japanese nationalist and American assimilationist attitudes from which he distances himself and yet with which he becomes inextricably entangled.

Ichiro's difficult relationship with these external impositions, however, is not experienced symmetrically. As a dominant social discourse in the cold war period, assimilationism is public, coercive, and shame instilling, while Japanese nationalism, as a political antithesis both constructed and condemned by the force of assimilation, threatens to become real even in the last sanctuary of Ichiro's emotional retreat—his Japanese American home. As Ichiro is forced to pass through these various forms and levels of social power, his reaction is necessarily both unbalanced and incoherent. This is reflected early in the novel in his shutting himself in his bedroom so that he can avoid further humiliation from meeting acquaintances. "Lying there, he wished the roof would fall in and bury forever the anguish which permeated his every pore. He lay there fighting with his burden" (11–12). Ichiro's burden is his history as a no-no boy, one rendered illegitimate by the official definition of the only acceptable past for young Japanese American men: a record of serving in the U.S. military. Lacking such a past makes Ichiro feel that his strong and perfect body is "only an empty shell" and that his postwar existence in American society is but a lingering death. His deep sense of shame leads to intense self-hatred (60), which is reflected in his desire to trade his life with that of the wounded veteran Kenji, an amputee whose missing leg is, to Ichiro, both a red badge of courage and proof of belonging:

> I'll change with you, Kenji. . . . Give me the stump which gives you the right to hold your head high. Give me the eleven inches which are beginning to hurt again and bring ever closer the fear of approaching death, and give me with it the fullness of yourself which is also yours because you were man enough to wish the thing which destroyed your leg and, perhaps, you with it but, at the same time, made it so that you can put your one good foot in the dirt of America and know that the wet coolness of it is yours beyond a single doubt. (64)

Ichiro's envy of the dying Kenji—as well as of Kenji's mutilated physical condition—illustrates not only the crushing weight of assimilationist pressures during and after the war but also the depth of the crisis facing Japanese Americans of the era. Kenji's terminal physical wound will eventually deprive him of his life, while Ichiro's festering psychological wound robs him of the ground for moral recovery. The price for either complying or failing to comply with the pressures exerted by the dominant discourse of Americanization which the text insists upon is high indeed.

Okada obviously recognizes that one consequence of the conditions suffered by Japanese Americans during this period—the disintegration of their communities, their political powerlessness, and their unconscious internalization of assimilationist assumptions about their identity—is an inability to fashion alternative arguments in any but the dominant discourse, a discourse in which they tend to turn upon one another. Ichiro's relations with his parents illustrate this point. Throughout the novel, Ichiro is seldom able to vent the pent-up fury resulting from his repeated frustrations except against his parents, who are themselves largely passive victims of racial oppression. Ichiro's father is characterized by his utter inability to protest and his unconditional detachment from any conflict at home. He ceases to question either his own social status or his wife's domestic tyranny, believing that the forces that have made him what he is are irresistible. Pa's passive acceptance of Ichiro's bitter outpourings elicits only additional contempt from the son, who regards him as "a goddamned, fat, grinning, spineless nobody" (12). In Ichiro's eyes, the old man's leniency toward him indicates nothing but moral and psychological weakness, a perspective compounded by Ma's aggressively assuming the role of his moral guide who oversees his education and his extracurricular interests. But her inability to express either her pride or her grievances in terms relevant to Ichiro's experience renders her utterly ineffectual as a moral adviser. Ma believes that Ichiro's refusal to fight in the war results from the "growth of a seed planted by the mother tree and that she was the mother who had put this thing in her son and that everything that had been done and said was exactly as it should have been and that that was what made him her son because no other would have made her feel the pride that was in her breast" (11). Ma's insistence on seeing Ichiro's choice as an unequivocal sign of his complete identification with Japanese culture contrasts starkly with Ichiro's condemnation by other nisei youths on precisely the same ground. As Ma's fanatic nationalist pride increasingly turns her into a specimen of the "alien" Japanese and hence into an ironic signifier of Americanization, Ichiro's self-hatred grows into hatred of his mother, whom he begins to see as the force that prevents him from becoming "American" and thus as the source of his sufferings. Despite the various reasons he offers for saying no to the judge, Ichiro comes to put all blame on his mother: "It is she who opened my mouth and made my lips move to sound the words which got me two years in prison and an emptiness that is more empty and frightening than the caverns of hell" (12). "The mistakes you [his mother] made were numerous enough and big enough," thinks Ichiro, "so that they, in turn, made inevitable my mistake" (186).

Stephen Sumida calls attention to the connection of Ichiro's blaming of his mother with the perspective of a young nisei sociologist who tours the camps on behalf of the relocation authority and scolds the issei for failing to understand their American-born sons and daughters (1986, 66–67). Viewed within its critical context, this connection is illuminating not only for its invocation of the historical subtext of the generational conflict in Japanese American families but also for its implicit designation of Ichiro's conflict with his mother as "official" in origin. Historically, the conflict between issei and nisei had been largely shaped by a phenomenon of dual citizenship, which repeatedly called into question the nisei's American identity because Japanese law designates the offspring of a Japanese father, regardless of place of birth, as a natural Japanese citizen, while American law recognizes anyone born on American soil, regardless of the parents' ethnicity or nationality, as a U.S. citizen (Sucheng Chan 1991, 112–15). This phenomenon continued from the late nineteenth century through World War II despite a 1924 Japanese act that specified limited conditions under which nisei were exempt from their Japanese citizenship on the basis of paternal descent (Ichioka 1988, 196–210). No issei could become a U.S. citizen until the passage of the 1952 Mc-Carran-Walter Act, however.[8] As nisei came of age in the 1930s and 1940s, their identity remained a source of their social and emotional suffering because of the continued existence of conflicting legal stipulations about their national citizenship, their discriminatory treatment in American society because of their race, and their ambiguous relationship to their parents' birthplace. Despite the fact that conflict between issei and nisei had been a constant ingredient in prewar Japanese American family life, this conflict was, as Sumida points out, rarely one of cultural or ideological confrontation (1986, 64–68).

But under the stress of the internment of 1942 and the draft order of 1943, this familiar conflict in Japanese American family life was exacerbated and transformed into a destructive political struggle, one that Japanese Americans interned on the United States mainland were particularly forced to face. With Ichiro positioned against his mother, the novel shows how wartime American racial politics both invaded and structurally distorted the most basic form of Japanese American social life, and how such politicized generational conflict became, in turn, a justifying ideology for the false dichotomy in Japanese American identity enacted in the internment camps. The dichotomy takes on additional forms as other grievances are enacted in the novel. For example, Eto, Bull, and Taro are victimized by the bargain offered them by the dominant culture: to be accepted as "American" they must accept assimilation and its "obligations." When they are nevertheless regarded as "Japs" following their army service in World War II, they take revenge by turning on Ichiro rather than face the real causes of their negative experience. In a similar way, Emi's husband, Ralph, blames his brother Mike (an American-born World War I veteran disillusioned by the treatment of Japanese Americans during the war) for choosing to go to Japan rather than blame those who force Mike to make that choice. From this perspective, Ichiro's antagonism toward Ma is neither a logical step in his quest for acceptance as an "American" nor an effective refusal of the false racial dichotomy applied to Japanese Americans during the war. Rather, it should more properly be seen as a rhetorical construct through which Okada critiques the warping effects of cultural racism on traditional family bonds crucial to the Japanese American community. Okada recognizes as effects of racism both the ideological confusion in his community and the misdirected grievances against those who are innocent of creating their particular situations.[9] Furthermore, he dramatizes how assimilationist pressures are able to create arbitrary divisions both in the individual psyche and in the material foundation of the Japanese American family. In effect, Okada's construct demonstrates how, using the techniques of the "realistic" novel, an Asian American writer in this period could represent the parent-child relationship in ways that expose the sociopolitical economy embedded in these arbitrary divisions.

Okada's ironic critique of the false dichotomy between Japanese "nativism" and American "assimilation" in terms of generational conflict clearly offers a more complex view of Asian American literary discourse in this era than recent critical paradigms in Asian American cultural studies would grant. Okada reminds us that the opposition between nativism and assimilation is not an Asian American textual invention, nor is it Asian American writers' preferred way of staking out their positions. Rather, this false opposition is constructed by the dominant sociology of American nativism, a construction that actively and hegemonically defines the terms of racial minorities' efforts to understand the nature of their displacement in American society. In addition, Okada's portrayals of the fate of Eto, Bull, and Kenji suggest that Asian American writers are not only fully aware of the arbitrary nature of such an externally imposed frame of reference but also capable of transforming its false assumptions into an effective counterstrategy within the cultural space available to their enunciation. To gloss the irony that often accompanies Asian American writers' critical redeployment—and their deliberate foregrounding of the racial underpinnings—of the nativism/assimilation binarism solely in terms of a culturalist rendering of generational conflict is therefore to sidestep the vital social and political determinants embedded in its construction, circulation, maintenance, and evaluation.[10]

Reinventing a Trope of Transgression

As a crucial site of revelation of the effects of wartime social injustice on Japanese American life, Okada's rhetorical construction of the tortured mother-son relationship foreshadows Ichiro's occasional awakenings to the consciousness that the root cause of Ma's madness is the racism of the country to which she has immigrated. For example, Ichiro ponders: "Sometimes I think my mother is to blame. Sometimes I think it's bigger than her, more than her refusal to understand that I'm not like her" (152). He asks:

> Did it matter so much that events had ruined the plans which she cherished and turned the once very possible dreams into a madness which was madness only in view of the changed status of the Japanese in America? Was it she who was wrong and crazy not to have found in herself the capability to accept a country which repeatedly refused to accept her or her sons unquestioningly? (104)

Ichiro's insights into the conditions entrapping his mother powerfully evoke the memories reported earlier through the Momotaro story. He recalls that "there was a time" when "it was all right to be Japanese" and when his mother "used to smile a mother's smile" and tell him stories "about gallant and fierce warriors who protected their lords with blades of shining steel and about the old woman who found a peach in the stream and took it home, and, when her husband split it in half, a husky little boy tumbled out to fill their hearts with boundless joy." Admitting that "I was that boy in the peach and you were the old woman," Ichiro contemplates the division of self that plagues him after the internment:

> And the reason I do not understand it is because I do not understand you who were the half of me that is no more and because I do not understand what it was about that half that made me destroy the half of me which was American and the half which might have become the whole of me if I had said yes I will go and fight in your army because that is what I believe and want and cherish and love. (16–17)

Ichiro's evocation of an ideal mother-son relationship and a complete Japanese American identity crushed by wartime internment and the draft order is a highly deliberated authorial ploy: through the connection of Momotaro and Ichiro, Okada filters the social issue of racism suffered by Japanese Americans through the lens of Japanese culture, a strategy that provides a basis for comparative commentary on Ichiro's predicament and suggests a coherent way of healing the disrupted Japanese American life in terms that are not only understandable but also empowering to the community. Implicit in this ploy is Okada's attempt to raise the community's ethnic consciousness and thus its potential for resistance. Yet the era that Ichiro evokes through the phrase "there was a time" suggests a nostalgic vision of prewar history. Even the relative stability of Japanese American community life and the brief flourishing of Japanese American literary creativity in the period are at the best signs of community endurance despite the harsh economic and political conditions they faced, conditions marked by the immediate and long-term effects of such anti-Asian legislation as the 1907 Gentlemen's Agreement, the 1913 Alien Land Law in California and a similar 1921 land law in Washington (a state where the Yamadas lived), and the 1924 National Origins Act. Okada's resurrection of the tale of Momotaro's struggle as a nostalgic, community-oriented analogy to Ichiro's cross-cultural identity crisis in postwar America therefore also reveals the strategy's inherent difficulty: Should a desire for cultural cohesion as a defense mechanism against racial oppression on a psychological level lead to efforts to restore a community whose social structures were both temporally and spatially bounded by overwhelming state power? Or can this strategy sustain the ideological force and the rhetorical appeal of the cultural particularity of the Japanese American community if its members do not unanimously endorse such a cultural construction of their origins and if the readers outside the community fail to recognize or empathize with its analogy? With Ma's anti-American stance hardening and her communication with her son and her husband broken down,[11] the novel's underlying discourse, which is organized through the Momotaro story and composed of a series of painfully drawn-out interior monologues, calls for the invention of a more flexible rhetorical figure that can simultaneously resist narrative closure and convey to wider audiences the collective crisis of Japanese Americans epitomized by Ichiro's identity struggle.

To do so, Okada needed both to preserve the ethnic vision he had evoked for the community through the Momotaro tale and to expand the interpretive possibility of the self-contradictory Ichiro so as to suggest to the postwar audience a common understanding of the no-no boy issue. Okada's strategy for achieving this end seems no less deliberated: he offers a provisional resolution of Ichiro's emotional suffering through his love affair with the compassionate and patriotic Emi, a relationship simultaneously invested with the values of and ideologically appropriable by multiple communities of readers. Emi's initial involvement with Ichiro occurs on the eve of Kenji's death, when Ichiro is consumed by self-hatred; her last significant contact takes place when she dances with him in a symbolic celebration of life after Ma's suicide. The intervening events show that Ichiro's muddled healing process is significantly shaped by his close relationship with Emi, especially by her ambivalent attitude toward the no-no boy issue. The existing scholarship on *No-No Boy* pays little attention to the meaning of Emi's ambivalence. This lack of interest may spring from the fact that Emi, like Ma, is essentially a one-dimensional character, a portrayal that occasionally gives rise to questioning Okada's narrative control or even charges that his representation of women favors both "white" and male standards (e.g., McDonald 1979, 22–23). But within the novel's rhetorical context, Emi does not have to be viewed as an embodiment of the subaltern per se; rather, she needs to be seen as mediating, and indeed facilitating, the emergence of a collective subalternity embedded in Okada's construction of Ichiro and his social relations. Emi's mediational function can be better understood in light of her connections with two important characters in Ichiro's life—Ma and Kenji—who directly influence the course of his identity quest. Specifically, Emi relates to Ma through physical contrast and to Kenji through emotional affiliation. In the novel, Ma is portrayed throughout as a physically deformed woman, "flat-chested, shapeless," whose figure "was the awkward, skinny body of a thirteen-year old which had dried and toughened through the many years following but which developed no further" (10–11). Emi, by contrast, is a woman with heavy breasts, rich, black hair falling on her shoulders, and strong and shapely legs (83). Both Sato and Sumida suggest that Mrs. Yamada's physical traits metaphorically reflect the dehumanizing effects of her immigrant experience and of the self-destructive consequence of her rigid response to it (Sato 1992, 246; Sumida 1989b, 224). Symbolically, Ma's stunted physical growth finds its alternative expression in Emi's sensuous body, while Emi's compassion toward Ichiro partially compensates for what Ma has failed to provide him. Viewed from this perspective, Emi can be seen as functioning in the novel as both a negation of and a symbolic substitution for what Ma represents.

More significantly, Emi is introduced to Ichiro by the dying Kenji, with whom she shares not only a critical view of racism in American society but also a sense of moral obligation to help free Ichiro from his self-hatred and regain his moral strength.[12] But a closer examination shows that Emi inherits only part of Kenji's legacy. Like Kenji, she questions the racism suffered by Japanese Americans: "It's because we're American and because we're Japanese and sometimes the two don't mix. It's all right to be German and American or Italian and American or Russian and American but, as things turned out, it wasn't all right to be Japanese and American. You had to be one or the other" (91). But unlike Kenji, who believes that racism will persist in America (134–36), Emi is optimistic about the future prospects for racial relations. For example, while disagreeing with the internment policy, she urges Ichiro to admit his own "mistake" and to do something to atone for his past (95). Similarly, though suffering from a broken marriage indirectly caused by the internment, she advises Ichiro not only to forgive but also to thank the relocation authority, which she considers to have been generous in its response to Ichiro's disobedience (96). "This is a big country with a big heart. There's room here for all kinds of people" (95), Emi tells Ichiro:

> Make believe you're singing "The Star-Spangled Banner" [as if at school assemblies] and see the color guard march out on the stage and say the pledge

of allegiance with all the other boys and girls. You'll get that feeling flooding into your chest and making you want to shout with glory. It might even make you feel like crying. That's how you've got to feel, so big that the bigness seems to want to bust out, and then you'll understand why it is that your mistake was no bigger than the mistake your country made. (96)

By combining in Emi a symbolic substitution for Ma with an optimistic continuation of Kenji, Okada ventures a rhetorical strategy redolent with contextual overtones, a strategy that usefully illuminates what Stuart Hall calls the "connotative" use of an ideological sign in cultural discourse. Hall distinguishes two levels of meaning in a communicative message: "the denotative"—fixed, stable, strictly referential—and "the connotative," or relatively unbounded, fluid, and changeable. According to Hall, the latter level of meaning can become ideologically associative because of its contact with meanings not fixed in natural perceptions or discourses, and consequently its decoding may depend on the use of nonconventional codes (1980/1993, 96–98). As a "connotative"—and ideologically mobile—sign, Emi enlivens Ichiro's "denotative" textual situation through her relationship with him, and together they constitute a new figure of desire which in turn calls for the reader's adoption of nonconventional values for decodings. Yet Okada's partial appropriation of Kenji's cynical attitude toward racism in his construction of an ideologically moderate Emi determines that her alliance with the deeply troubled Ichiro cannot be a seamless match. As a consequence, despite Emi's understanding of the nature of Ichiro's intense inner conflicts, the advice she offers him is at best a softened version of the very discourse that tends to create and to entrap Ichiro in those conflicts. Emi's contradictory vision of error and forgiveness, confounded by Ichiro's tentative but growing love for her, is the ground on which he recognizes his "mistake" and, intermittently, desires to "forget the past" (112). Illustrative of the terms in which Ichiro conceptualizes his "mistake" in resisting the draft is his reflection on his wartime experience while riding on a bus toward the end of the novel: "I have been guilty of a serious error. I have paid for my crime as prescribed by law. I have been forgiven and it is only right for me to feel this way or else I would not be riding unnoticed and unmolested." Feeling "a little wiser" and "a bit more settled in heart and mind" as a result of his reflections, he murmurs: "After the rain, the sunshine" (232). Rather than continuously agonizing over his sufferings as a no-no boy, Ichiro has come to admit his "crime," accept his punishment as just, and thus unconsciously subject himself to yet another form of the dominant ideology—"forgiveness" earned by self-chastisement. He is repentant for his "serious error," grateful for the "generosity" shown him, and expectant of ultimate acceptance by the society that will continue to see him in split terms and to reject him on the basis of a narrow definition of a "real American."

A dramatic manifestation of Ichiro's desire to turn over a new leaf as a result of Emi's influence is his decision to remove himself physically from the Japanese American community in Seattle in order to "keep away from the Japs," "to get away from Pa and Ma," and "to start clean" (112). Yet once out of Seattle, Ichiro finds that society does not readily forgive, nor does he easily forget. The insulting treatment given to him and Kenji by the uniformed cop in Midvale, the young waiter's purposeful display of a discharge pin at the Burnside Cafe in Portland, his difficulty in answering a question about his past experience when filling out a job application at a hotel, and, back in Seattle, Mr. Morrison's remark about the incurability of "[his] kind of illness" (220), all bring back to Ichiro the painful memory of his imprisonment and make him see the impossibility of escaping from the past. Ultimately, Ichiro's change in attitude is a superficial shift in mood; beneath the surface he remains troubled by external judgments, and his new vision of life renders him no more free than his previous psychological imprisonment.

Okada's treatment of Emi's influence on Ichiro is both problematic and revealing: on the one hand, it underscores the ongoing difficulty of conceiving Japanese American subjectivity within the dominant ideology; on the other, it points toward the author's commitment to the healing power of love, a love that is embodied in his portrayal of Emi as a benevolent woman of profound moral compassion (McDonald 1979, 23). Yet the contradictory nature of Emi's character—her emotional involvement with Ichiro and mental detachment from his bitterness, her unconventional attitude toward sexual love and political pragmatism, and her sense of America's "weakness" and belief in its "strength"—suggests deliberate irony at work in both textual and contextual senses. More than a simple representation of giving and returning love to a world permeated with hate, Okada's rendering of Emi's contradictory attitudes and her relationship with Ichiro problematizes both the textual solution of Ichiro's plight and the assumption that postwar racial divisions in America can be healed by strategies of forgetting and benevolence. Such problematization is reinforced through Kenji's observation of the society's treatment of the internees who have returned home at the end of the internment: "name-calling, busted windows, dirty words painted on houses. People haven't changed a helluva lot" (163). In a related context, Okada reminds the reader, by recalling two instances of discrimination against African Americans—the racial dilemma of a light-skinned black male who suffers discrimination from both whites and people of color (135–36) and a black elder who is denied a seat in the church to which he belongs (230–31)—that racism in the United States continues to structure the space of Ichiro's personal struggle. When, through Kenji's discourse, Okada offers Ichiro the cynical advice that he leave his own community for good (164), the reader recognizes the irony: flight or escape offers only an illusion of liberation.

The relationship between Ichiro and Emi can therefore be read in at least two ways. On one level, the relationship seems to imply the author's hope for the re-generation of the no-no boy and for his recovery from his psychic wound through the agency of love. Such a fusion would be consistent with Okada's emphasis, as some critics suggest, on the importance of familial harmony and Christian for-bearance in a society marked by ideological contradictions and racial inequalities and hatred (Inada 1976, vi; Sato 1992, 246–53; McDonald 1979, 23–24). On an-other level, the Ichiro-Emi relationship can be seen as a textual juncture where the needs of the author, the expectations of the audience, and the era's require-ments of the novel's production are negotiated—with the possibility for protest compromised. Even if, by authorial design, Emi constitutes Okada's attempted intertextual solution to the textual impasse of Ichiro's return, she inevitably bears the imprint of the particular cultural milieu in which Okada was writing. In ad-dition, the fact that some of Emi's remarks sound like parodies of the mainstream culture's portrayals of the United States as a happy melting pot raises an alterna-tive possibility: that Okada was aware of the limitations of Emi's discourse and was suggesting that Ichiro had not found, in his relationship with her, an ade-quate solution to his moral and cultural dilemma. Thus, the "hopeful" ending for Ichiro in No-No Boy may not represent an effort by Okada, a veteran of the U.S. Army in World War II, to assuage mainstream concerns about the resistance im-plicit in the no-no boy's position; rather, it may signal his awareness of the limita-tions of Emi's discourse, and his resourcefulness in dealing with audience expecta-tions by offering a resolution that proves to be no solution at all.

The Social Logic of Cultural Displacement

In his discussion of the relationship between the codes of the dominant genteel culture and those of emergent alternative cultures in nineteenth-century Ameri-can dime novels, Michael Denning identifies two forms of ideological appropria-tion in these works—"ventriloquism" and "impersonation." The first involves throwing one's own voice into characters of another class, the second assuming the voice of another in one's own form (1987, 83). The struggle experienced by Okada in managing the resolution of No-No Boy and his literary discourse in positioning himself relative to his readers can be aptly described in these terms. Conscious of the ideological tensions that both surrounded and directly affected his writing of the novel, Okada practiced both "ventriloquism" and "impersonation": he pro-jected the voice of one segment of his implied audience—the interned Japanese Americans—through the character of Ichiro in order to suggest a message of protest; and he projected an "official" voice—that of the apologist for the United States and its race policies during the war—through the character of Emi in order to create a resolution acceptable to the majority of his potential postwar readership. In negotiating the contradictory demands placed on the novel—readerly demands for emotional resolution and familiar values, writerly demands for exposing moral and cultural contradiction, and presumably publishers' demands for conformity to such dominant cultural ideologies as assimilation—Okada was performing a difficult balancing act in managing the relationship between Ichiro and Emi.[13] As a result, the novel's ending reflects the conflicting concerns of the author, the reader, and the cultural establishment.

It is worth noting in this connection that, throughout the novel, Okada rarely lets Ichiro directly voice his disagreement with racism in American society. Instead, the strongest critique of America's wartime treatment of Japanese Americans is made by two characters of non-Asian backgrounds: by the tall blond lieutenant flying a B-24 on a reconnaissance mission between Guam and Japan, who angrily complains about the U.S. government's unjust treatment of its own citizens (ix–xi), and by Birdie, a young African American man working at the Christian Rehabilitation Center in Seattle, who physically confronts those who insult Gary, another no-no boy working at the center (225–26). Okada's transferential use of a white army officer and an outspoken black worker to condemn the unfair treatment of Japanese Americans both during and after the war is contrasted with his deliberate rendering of Ichiro's search for identity, as some critics have recognized, as a process of redemption through compassion and love on one level of the novel's narrative. Such a contradictory approach to the issue of race, while indicating Okada's skillful insinuation of the subversiveness of his work into the given cultural hegemony, more strongly reflects the unresolved tension between his art and his social experience, as well as his self-conscious suspension of his ability to make an ultimate judgment about the nature of his protagonist's dilemma. However Okada himself saw the social impact of his novel, one can argue that the tendency to gloss over the contradictions and historical consequences of racism with images of healing love is actually part and parcel of the overall cultural climate of his time and reflects how particular historical conditions that enabled Okada to expose racial injustice in American society simultaneously limited his response to such injustice—a result, in part, of his reliance on evoking (presumed) human universals.

With *No-No Boy,* Okada offered a work filled with the angry, self-contradictory voices of the victims of racism, resonant with other voices struggling to find languages of human warmth and moral reconciliation, and deeply ambiguous about its central character's "recovery," which remains entangled, as does the divided Emi, in a discourse that reflects the dominant culture's ideology. Although Ichiro has not found an adequate alternative discourse by the novel's end, his voice does not totally dissolve into the dominant one. The fundamental inconsistency of his position, which is grounded in rejection of both wholesale assimilation and fanatic Japanese nationalism coupled with continued dependence on these categories, keeps Ichiro inconclusively "chas[ing] the faint and elusive insinuation of promise" in "the darkness of the alley of the community that was a tiny bit of America" (251). At the same time, such inconsistency prevents Ichiro's struggle from totally merging into either assimilationist impulses or his mother's nationalist isolation, maintains his painful resistance to power, and keeps his own voice contradictory and problematic even while it profoundly dramatizes both the need for a Japanese American discourse and the difficulties of finding a place to stand in order to invent one. The novel's poor sales suggest that the ambiguous Ichiro created by Okada failed to provide a comfortable ideological stance or clear narrative guidance for the majority of readers of his novel, who, as we have seen, were accustomed to autobiographical representations of Asian American life that did not explicitly challenge assimilationist positions. Yet Ichiro's ongoing confusion about his predicament also marks the political potentials of Okada's novel in the 1950s: it kept alive a marginal sensibility replete with the author's moral anguish about racial oppression against Japanese Americans during World War II and with his yearning for social change which had not yet found its agents. Furthermore, with his fictional packaging of Ichiro's moral dilemma in *No-No Boy*, which implicitly critiques the social power responsible for producing it, Okada subversively transformed the conventional realistic novel by making it unfamiliar and problematic. The effects of Okada's critical transformation were similarly ambivalent. By choosing to write a novel that resists prevailing aesthetic tastes and preferences, Okada not only challenged the assumptions of "canonical audiences" who experienced his work under "canonical conditions" (Barbara Herrnstein Smith 1988, 35, 40) but also rendered unintelligible the fictional value of his work for readers predisposed to see it according to existing generic expectations. Small wonder that critics mercilessly found fault with the linguistic and syntactical innovations in *No-No Boy* upon its publication and then left it in oblivion (Chin et al. 1974, xxxv).

The literary establishment's rejection of *No-No Boy* was followed by a period of silence about representations of the internment in Japanese American novels, presumably because the rejection discouraged further marketing of politically sensitive Japanese American literary works by large commercial presses. During the first two decades following the publication of *No-No Boy*, for example, the only other Japanese American novel that came off the press of Charles E. Tuttle, the publisher of *No-No Boy*, was *Hawaii: The End of the Rainbow* (1964) by Kazuo Miyamoto, a Hawaiian-born Japanese American. This novel was followed in 1975 by Supa Press's *All I Asking for Is My Body* by Milton Murayama, another Hawaiian-born writer.[14] To different degrees, both novels deal with the ramifications of the internment in Hawaii, yet neither raises the issue as controversially as Okada does in *No-No Boy*, partly because neither mass evacuation nor a coercive draft comparable to that on the West Coast took place in Hawaii during World War

II.[15] It was not until the second half of the 1970s that the issue of the internment was brought up again openly as a constitutional issue through the redress movement led by the Japanese American Citizens League (JACL), whose efforts led eventually to the passing of the Civil Liberties Act of 1988, which issued an official apology to Japanese Americans who had been interned and provided funds for surviving internees in reparation for their losses during the war.

It is important to stress here that the literary establishment's initial rejection of *No-No Boy* was accompanied by the Japanese American community's shunning of Okada's novel, which surprised its publisher, who had hoped that the community "would be enthusiastic about it" (Chin et al. 1974, xxxix). One reason for the negative community response to Okada's book, most commentators agree, clearly lies in Japanese Americans' internalization of mainstream assumptions about their social status and in their consequent passivity toward the no-no boy issue; both prevented the community from making the moral response demanded by the publication of *No-No Boy*. Another reason for the community's lack of interest in the novel was the dominance, both in the majority society and within the ethnic community, of the new stereotype of nisei as "loyal" Americans as a result of the wide publicity given to the heroic wartime exploits of nisei soldiers (see Ichioka 1998, 45). In view of the societal and communal pressures surrounding the writing and publishing of the novel, it is no coincidence that Okada himself refrained from mentioning the title of his book in an autobiographical essay written right before its release (Chin 1979a, 260). Okada's silence may reflect the inner conflict resulting from his awareness of the controversial subject he chose to address, his realization of the difficulty of his own moral choices, and his assessment that the effects of the internment experience and of postwar pressures to conform and belong were still taking a toll on his community a decade and a half after the end of the war. A cultural process with favorable outcomes for dissenting Japanese American literary voices in the post–World War II era would not be set in motion until the more charged social period of the late 1960s and early 1970s. Retrospectively, the appearance of a work such as *No-No Boy* prior to that time can be seen as a sign that the social transformation that Asian American writers would negotiate was still embryonic.

In rejecting *No-No Boy*, the literary establishment succeeded in obliterating the political message of Okada's novel. But such obliteration did not erase what the book had already articulated, nor did it eliminate Japanese America's unresolved social crisis epitomized in Ichiro's failed identity quest. On the contrary, the text's emergence and disappearance exposed the social power embedded in the process of the novel's production and reception. Indeed, the exclusion of *No-No Boy* from 1950s public discourse indicates the difficulty of materializing either the presumed ideological wholeness or the idealized heterogeneous opposition in Okada's work. For such retrospectively imagined possibilities remained, at the time of the novel's production, well beyond the ideological horizon of Okada's artistic creation and the hegemonic range of Japanese Americans' social existence. But the institutional alienation of *No-No Boy* produced unexpected results: it let Okada's seemingly inconsequential articulation of discontents dissolve into the political unconscious of Japanese America's unrealized desire for social justice; and it allowed Okada's "failed" literary project to function as both a deferred ideological catalyst and part of a renewed social condition for rearticulating Japanese Americans' ongoing social dilemma; it thus became an unstable, prefigurative cultural agent which later generations of Asian American readers could recognize and build upon.

Despite the various textual and intertextual linkages made in this case study of the role of *No-No Boy* in postwar Asian American literary history, my intent is not to label Okada a visionary. He was, however, an important contributor to an evolving, collective Asian American literary archive. As we have seen, he wrote through the active mediation of a type of racially inflected cultural deformation which simultaneously marks his negotiating strategy in the novel as a process of bricolage. It is precisely in the novel's manifestation of both the necessity and the incompleteness of such a process that we recognize its signifying power on a range of diverse but similarly produced Asian American works in the era of its publication: Carlos Bulosan's *America Is in the Heart* (1943); Bienvenido Santos's "Scent of Apples" (1948), Toshio Mori's *Yokohama, California* (1949), Hisaye Yamamoto's "The Legend of Miss Sasagawara" (1950), and Louis Chu's *Eat a Bowl of Tea* (1961). Such a recognition depends on reading the politics and aesthetics of Okada's text in ways both specific to its historically produced local knowledge and open to larger sociocultural forces that determine its macrological significance. Given the lack of such readings upon its publication, as we shall see, the externalization of the internal polemics in Okada's work was not felt until almost two decades after the novel's initial production, when *No-No Boy* began to be recognized as a vivid Japanese American narrative intervention in traditional American literary treatments of race relations and assimilationist pressures.

3

Realist Intervention and the Return of the Repressed

Reading Class, Gender, and Culture in Louis Chu's *Eat a Bowl of Tea*

If the removal of difference is the origin of representation, it follows that the origin will always be present in the product.
—Wolfgang Iser, "Representation: A Performative Act"

The problems of meaning and representation that beset the "Third World" are very different from the slippage of meaning and of the "real" which currently confronts *academic* discourses of Europe and America. To say this is not to claim the possibility of arriving at some essential indigenous truth by a more tortuous route, but to insist that the epistemological problem is *itself* a historical one. Both meaning and the need for locating meaning are conjunctural; and it is useful to maintain a distinction between the realized difficulty of knowing and the preasserted or a priori difficulty of knowing.
—Kumkum Sangari, "The Politics of the Possible"

Continuing the exploration of race and generational conflicts begun in my discussion of *No-No Boy,* this chapter extends its analysis to questions of decoding class and gender relationships and cross-cultural signs in Louis Chu's 1961 novel *Eat a Bowl of Tea.*[1] Before examining these questions, a full contextualization of the novel's production as a realist narrative seems in order because the assessment of this generic aspect of Chu's work has both informed and mediated the Asian American literary community's critical and imaginative reproduction of its discourse since the novel's rediscovery in the mid-1970s. One assumption that needs to be problematized at the outset of such analysis is the category "Chinatown literature," a conceptual framework in which most critical study of Chu's novel has been conducted. The editors of *Aiiieeeee!,* for example, situate *Eat a Bowl of Tea* squarely in an indigenous, English-speaking Chinese American literary tradition, in contrast to two other traditional literary treatments of Chinatown maintained through mainstream culture: Euro-American writers' anthropological reportage of Chinatown and its inhabitants, and China-born émigré intellectuals' politically detached cultural "translation" of the community from upper-class perspectives (Chin et al. 1974, vii–xvi). Because of the editors' insistence on English as the only language used by an indigenous Chinese American literary practice, they locate the value of Chu's novel primarily in relation to the linguistically congenial part of the tradition they promote—a tradition represented by writers such as Sui Sin Far, Diana Chang, Frank Chin, Jeffery Chan, and Shawn Wong—and neglect the novel's possible relationship with resources not based in the English language. One such resource can be identified in a progressive Chinatown literary movement from the 1930s through the 1940s, a movement that, according to Marlon Hom, drew its inspiration from both the left-wing Chinese literature during the Sino-Japanese War (1937–1945) and American left literature of roughly the same period that espoused "social realism" as the most politically effective means of literary representation. One purpose of the movement, according to Hom, was to expose the social plight of Chinatown and to foster, by codifying its own non-English linguistic and cultural idioms, a Chinese American working-class political consciousness (1982, 76–77, 94–95). The reluctance of the editors of *Aiiieeeee!* to acknowledge connections between Chu's novel and this movement thus leads them to see the production of *Eat a Bowl of Tea* as a purely "cultural" phenomenon, one both coherent and continuous with their narrowly defined Chinese American literary tradition. Rather than treating Chu's novel as an instantiation of the latter cultural vision, I see it instead as an example of how Chu negotiates a narrative perspective on Chinatown that both registers and engages the tensions among local knowledge, diasporic concern,[2] political awareness, and cross-cultural ventriloquism. Such a perspective, as I will show in my analysis of Chu's text later in this chapter, not only renders abstract the era's hegemonic definitions of Chinese American life but also asserts, on the level of ideological and aesthetic concreteness, the historicity of the novel's alternative view of "truth."

Subversive Realism

The social and cultural conditions under which Chu wrote and published his novel were similar to those that witnessed the production of Okada's *No-No Boy,* although attention to racial injustice was markedly increasing in American society in the late 1950s as a result of African Americans' mounting drive to end institutionalized segregation in the American South, a struggle that drew wide support from the white middle class, particularly from cities in the Northeast. Ethnic awareness among African Americans grew in parallel with progressive intellectuals' efforts to expose poverty in American society. In two essays published in 1959 and 1960, Michael Harrington reported that 50 million Americans were still living below the "standards which we have been taught to regard as the decent minimums for food, housing, clothing, and health." He asserted that whites made up the majority of the poor, while some minorities—blacks, Puerto Ricans, Mexican Americans, and Native Americans—made up the rest (1959, 19–22; 1960, 120–21). Significantly, Asian Americans were left out of both the civil rights movement of the era and the picture of Harrington's demystification of America as an "affluent society." Not only were Asian Americans invisible, they were also silent about their political and economic marginality, as well as their racially subordinated social status. Such silence was reinforced by the increasing perception of them as a "model minority," a stereotype constructed in the late 1950s by sociologists attempting to explain the low levels of juvenile delinquency among Japanese Americans (Omatsu 1994, 63).

Chinese Americans had particular reasons for being silent on the eve of the publication of Chu's novel. Since the communist victory in mainland China in 1949 (a victory that forced the American-backed Nationalists to retreat to Taiwan), the Chinese living in America had been politically divided because of the United States' different policies toward the Chinese living on either side of the Taiwan Strait. During the early phase of McCarthyism, for example, the pro-Nationalist Chinese Consolidated Benevolent Association of New York and the Six Companies of San Francisco organized large-scale anticommunist campaigns in Chinatowns throughout the United States in order to demonstrate their loyalty to the United States (although such campaigns were not infrequently used within the community to resolve territorial, clan, or personal differences). In 1954, the year of the Supreme Court's decision on *Brown v. Board of Education,* the All-American Overseas Chinese Anti-Communist League was formed in New York (Takaki 1989, 414–16). In 1955 the American consul in Hong Kong warned that Chinese communist spies were using false papers to secure American passports and enter the United States, a warning that sent waves of alarm and renewed oppression through Chinese communities and led in 1957 to the institution of a "Confession Program," whereby Chinese violators of immigration laws were called upon to confess to their true identities in return for immunity from prosecution and deportation (Chen 1980, 214–15). Toward the end of the 1950s, Congress passed the McCarran Internal Security Act, authorizing the internment of communists during a national emergency.

One consequence of continued pressure for conformity to cold war anticommunist ideology and of prolonged suspicion of the Chinese in the United States was a total elimination of the aforementioned progressive Chinatown literature movement. During the "Red Scare" of the 1950s, Hom observes, many left-wing Chinese American literary groups disappeared and numerous Chinatown literary publications were destroyed for fear of government prosecution (1982, 76–77). The dissolution of this Chinatown literary movement, aimed at the non–English-speaking sector of the ethnic community, notably contrasted with the simultaneous flourishing on the American literary market of Chinese American literary works not only written in English but also published by major commercial presses: Jade Snow Wong's *Fifth Chinese Daughter* (Harper & Row, 1945; reprinted 1950), Hazel Lin's *The Physicians* (John Day, 1951), Eileen Chang's *The Rice Sprout Song* (Scribners, 1955), Diana Chang's *Frontiers of Love* (Random House, 1956), and Chin Yang Lee's *Flower Drum Song* (Farrar, Straus & Cudhay, 1957). Although these works offer complex representations of Chinese American life in the period from diverse perspectives, they are largely portrayals from upper-class points of view and consequently shed little light on the "existence of a non-Christian bachelor population that represented the vast majority of Chinese Americans for nearly a century" (Jeffery Chan 1979, 3).

With its unflattering yet sympathetic depiction of New York Chinatown bachelor society, a depiction not only rendered in English but also presented from a cultural insider's perspective, Chu's 1961 work constitutes a significant Chinese American novelistic attempt to represent the ethnic community—both for its indigenous population (who speak both Cantonese and English) and for its possible readers in mainstream culture—as predominantly working class.[3] And, as such, Chu's effort indirectly revives the critical energy of "social realism" once practiced by the vanished progressive Chinatown literary movement, although the artistic and historical visions of Chu's novel were shaped not by the left politics of the previous decades but by the particularities of his own experience as a diasporic writer.[4] Born in China in 1915, Chu immigrated to the United States with his parents in 1924, the year the National Origins Law banned all subsequent immigration from Asia. He went through the American educational system, receiving a bachelor's degree in English and sociology from Upsala College in New Jersey, and then a master's degree in sociology from New York University. For a while, he found employment in New York City's Department of Welfare before he enlisted in the army and was dispatched to China for a year in 1945. After the war he became director of a social center and later served as executive secretary for the Soo Yuen Benevolent Association in New York's Chinatown, where he also hosted a radio program called "Chinese Festival" (Chan et al. 1991, 506). As this biographical sketch makes apparent, Chu did not belong to the New York Chinatown lower class he portrays in his fiction, nor did he have any connections with the radical social activism of the late 1950s and early 1960s. But having lived through some of the harshest years in Chinese immigration history in the contemporary United States, he was a witness to all the social and economic dislocations experienced by his own ethnic community. For example, when Chu was writing *Eat a Bowl of Tea*, nineteenth-century antimiscegenation laws forbidding marriages between Asians and white Americans were still in effect in many parts of the United States. Such laws, and a sequence of exclusionary immigration policies,[5] had made Chinatowns in America into primarily "bachelor societies," a condition, though slowly changing in the immediate postwar era, indexed by the fact that Chu and the protagonist of his novel, Ben Loy, must go back to China to find wives in the late 1940s. As a university-trained sociologist working for government welfare agencies, Chu could not have failed to notice bureaucratic indifference toward Chinatown's continued marginal existence both before and during the cold war. And certainly as a member of New York's Chinatown community in the 1950s and 1960s, he could not have been unaffected by the consequences of the relentless anticommunist campaigns, the widespread distrust of people of Chinese origin or descent, and the deep political rifts among the Chinese living in America,[6] although he himself was presumably "secure" owing to his education, work position, and service in the U.S. military during World War II.

These factors not only combined to inform Chu's choice of the narrative mode for his novel but also determined the range of his social critique through the chosen generic form: he depicts the poverty, isolation, and despair of New York's Chinatown bachelors with starkly realistic detail yet does not make his representation either an explicit moral outcry against racism or a didactic protest against the social and economic marginalization of the Chinese in the United States. Critics informed by poststructuralist perspectives characteristically dismiss this aspect of the novel as either aesthetically uninteresting or politically disengaged. But in my view, it precisely points toward the complexity, as well as the subversiveness, of the novel's production in an era of uneven cultural development in American society. To put it differently, the obvious lack of ready-made sensibilities to which Chu's narrative approach may appeal in today's reading environment suggests that the novel needs to be read through a different interpretive procedure, one that takes seriously the contextual implication of the novel's form and the formal embodiment of the novel's content, without prejudging its significance according to reductive formulas of naive representation.

A list of some of the influential American novels published around the time of *Eat a Bowl of Tea*'s appearance may be illustrative: John Barth's *The End of the Road* (1958) and *The Sot-Weed Factor* (1960), Saul Bellow's *Henderson the Rain King* (1959), John Updike's *Rabbit, Run* (1960), and Joseph Heller's *Catch-22* (1961). Although these works powerfully confronted the cultural mystification of the individual's alienation and dislocation in contemporary American society, their existential manipulations of oppositional mythic symbols did little to assuage the widespread blurring of the factual condition of American cultural and political life in the period, a tendency that effectively obscured both Chinatown's

historically produced problems and its ongoing social plight. Chu's choice of a realist mode of representation and his resort to a "sociological imagination"[7] became, in this sense, a self-conscious aesthetic and ideological intervention in the
formalism of turn-of-the-decade American literary modernism: it exposes,
through its radical representability, Chinatown's disjunctive present concealed by
the teleologically constructed permeability between text and context; it injects a
sense of crisis not only into the realm of social morality but also into the structure
of social relations; and it thus constitutes a valiant attempt to lead American writing out of the failing "empire of signs" (Barthes's phrase), to which many dissenting American writers of the period were attracted but in which their critical projects tended to dissolve because they failed to reestablish "institutionally"
scrambled signs and their referents.[8] My reading of the subversive function of
Chu's realist approach in his novel should not be mistaken for an impulsive endorsement either of a putatively oppositional cultural alterity or of a transparent
originary truth to be obtained only through becoming "the native informant." On
the contrary, I emphasize "the lived contradictions of place and event" (Probyn
1990, 182) in a temporality that remained unquestioned by the predominant literary assumptions in the period. I also underscore Chu's conscious "repudiation of
any motivated relation to the criteria of majority culture" (Harper 1994, 17), as
well as his implicit efforts to dialogize the unperturbed American cultural discourse so as to reveal the radical figuration of difference submerged in its hegemonic operation.

The unofficial form of knowledge exposed by Chu's realist challenge to the aes-
theticism of his time not only renders the dominant cultural assumptions indeterminate but also allows the realist economy of his novel to function contingently
in an ideologically destabilized intratextual situation. Several critics have noted
Chu's depiction of certain melodramatic characters or situations in the novel, elements they call "comic" or "tragicomic" (Chua 1982, 40, 44–45; Hsiao 1992,
152). Viewed in isolation from the contexts of the novel's production, however,
this feature leads either to an affirmation of the universality of classic European
tropological traditions or to an underestimation of Chu's capacity for discursive
engagement. I see this comic dimension of the novel's realist portrayal as performing a function similar to that of what one might call "carnivalesque realism."[9] In
its most general sense, carnival is a parodic critique of dominant ideologies
through symbolic displacements or inversions that privilege imagery associated
with vulgarity, foolishness, error, or self-contradiction. In Mikhail Bakhtin's
thoughtworld, the value of such imagery lies not only in its ability to provoke
ironic critique but also in its being part of larger systems of transgressive cultural
signs (1984, 11). Such transgressive signs, I would suggest, can be identified in
abundant forms in Chu's novel: in sites such as the New York Chinatown slum,
the filthy barber shop, Wah Gay's dimly lit gambling house, the troubled mar-

riage between Ben Loy and Mei Oi, and Ben Loy's sexual impotence; and in behaviors such as whoring, cursing, gossiping, exchanging obscene jokes, and self-deluded actions. Because these tragicomic details are able to reveal the absurdity of taken-for-granted reality and to heighten "the deforming effects of power" (Stam 1988, 131), they produce textual and intertextual contradictions: on the one hand, they explicitly affirm the novel's realistic portrayal of settings, character traits, or commonplace actions designed to persuade readers into accepting its depiction as plausible; on the other, they prevent such portrayal from becoming either a passive mimetic production of the "real" or a fixated surface phenomenon. In addition, their ability to perform rhetorical—that is, comedic—rather than explicitly political or referential functions allows Chu to keep a distance from his radical exposure of Chinatown reality through adopting a nonintrusive but ironic narrative voice. At the same time, they insinuate, through the socially and morally inverted characters and events in the novel, an authorial desire for recoding New York Chinatown's social relations at a time of its transition from bachelor society to a family-oriented community. Such a mode of realism frustrates hermeneutic attempts to establish easy and permanent correspondence between the novel's signifier and the signified, while it also problematizes the view held by some Chinatown inhabitants of the time that traditional practice can be kept intact in the face of social change. In a word, the interventionary value of *Eat a Bowl of Tea* can be appreciated only when we situate the novel fully within the discursive context of its production. By the same token, only through such situatedness can Chu's realism be recognized as capable of subverting, by its deliberate deployment of textual linearity, the teleological mystification of Chinese Americans' social life in cold war American culture.

Because Chu's strategy confronts readers with disturbing images of New York's Chinatown while effectively withholding from them these images' referents, he shows a world at odds with the commonly assumed social reality of Chinese Americans, yet at the same time blurs points of entry into discovering the causes of the textual disparities to which he insistently draws his readers' attention. In effect, the content and form of *Eat a Bowl of Tea* shift the burden of the novel's decoding largely onto its audiences: the interpretation of the novel depends both on its readers' possession of conceptual and linguistic categories for constituting the novel's characters and events and on their ability to locate and make sense of the book's "ideological seams"—its imperfectly joined ideological meanings (Radway 1986, 108–9). The novel's poor reception upon its publication, from this perspective, may reflect both the constraints that the novel imposes on its own interpretation and the lack of a horizon of expectations that would encourage critical reconstruction of contingent correspondence between the novel's encoding and decoding. Indeed, the general public inattention to Chinatown's economic conditions in the late 1950s and the early 1960s suggests that the textually exposed social cleavages in *Eat a Bowl of Tea* were not recognized as part of the existing social order by its readers. During the Asian American social movement of the late 1960s and early 1970s, some textual disjunctions of Chu's novel did become socially meaningful and allowed the book to serve as an active cultural agent for Asian American writers' self-empowerment. One commonly recognized value of the novel in the period is its illustration of how issues of race and class can be used to legitimize Asian Americans' desires for social change. In reference to this development, Elaine Kim observes that this "novel is now viewed as a cornerstone in the Asian American literary tradition" (1990a, 155).

Cross-cultural (Re)presentation

Such a perception of the significance of *Eat a Bowl of Tea* has been rigorously resisted since the late 1980s by Asian American feminist critics who take issue with the novel's focus on male experience, with its inadequate—and often unconvincing—portrayal of women, and with its connections with Asian American cultural nationalism.[10] The novel clearly does not challenge patriarchy in ways that can speak to contemporary feminist concerns. But I would suggest, in light of my previous discussion of the political context of the novel's production, that Chu's emphasis on male experience in *Eat a Bowl of Tea* can be more fruitfully investigated if we treat such emphasis as a historically determined act of articulation, rather than see it through the lens of generalized gender politics. What is at issue is not so much what Chu as a male writer fails to address in his 1961 work as why he chooses to raise the issue of Chinese male immigrants' racial gendering at a time when Chinatown bachelors' social plight remained invisible to the American public and when self-representation of working-class Chinese immigrant women's lives was largely unavailable both to the ethnic community and to the cultural mainstream. From this perspective, Chu's 1961 novel needs to be seen as a reflection of his intimate knowledge of the social consequences of American anti-Chinese legislation since the nineteenth century and of his evaluative commentary on such consequences as a historically constituted speaking agent. In other words, even though female gender has indeed been an underprivileged category in Asian American social experience and literary representations in the period, Chu's attempt to tackle the issue indicates his recognition of and sensitivity to the complexities arising from the historical distortion of gender relationships in Chinatown, as well as his moral response, however undervalued by contemporary feminist perspectives, to the ramifications of such distortion as a male writer. To dismiss Chu's novel on the basis of its male perspective is therefore to miss the important political questions raised by its historical and aesthetic insertion into America's public discourse of the early 1960s.

In what follows I offer an analysis of Chu's novel which focuses on several issues frequently raised and debated by its readers: the arranged marriage between Ben Loy and Mei Oi, Wah Gay's relationship with his son, Ben Loy's impotence, and the bachelor community's reaction to Mei Oi's adultery. My reading aims to problematize some of the arbitrarily drawn parallels between the novel's meaning and contemporary ideological or theoretical assumptions (in particular, the tendency to equate the deformed cultural voices in Chu's work with the novel's actual possession of an innate capacity to oppress) and to highlight linkages that remain severed between the novel's textual signs and its contextual determinants. In trying to rehistoricize the novel, I intend not to reassert the central status once accorded to *Eat a Bowl of Tea* by the editors of *Aiiieeeee!* but rather to open up possibilities for this novel's further meaning-making toward transformative praxis from a more historical perspective. One important strategy for my reading, therefore, is to draw out the suppressed or potentially interventionary meanings from the text and to evaluate its cultural vision both in light of today's critical imperatives and in relation to the condition of its initial articulation.

Interpreting Chu's novel in these terms immediately raises the question of how to read cross-cultural signs in ways that are at once cognizant of the analytical power of contemporary theory and attuned to the textual and intertextual specificities of Chu's realist art. For example, critics typically read Chu's portrayal of the arranged marriage between Ben Loy and Mei Oi as an unambiguous novelistic manifestation of Confucian Chinese culture, as well as of its internal oppression. Although critiquing Chinese patriarchy is an indispensable part of discussing Chu's portrayal of the arranged marriage, to base such a critique on anthropological assumptions about the transparency of knowledge about Chinese culture can be problematic: it often leads to the predictable conclusion that the solution to the young couple's marital problem necessarily involves a rejection of both their parents and the culture they presumably represent; and it consequently forecloses a more revealing examination of the arranged marriage as a complexly coded rhetorical construct rather than as a sociological given. Within the intertextual register of Chu's portrayal, the arranged marriage reflects nothing more than the bachelor society's practical need to prolong its dying traditions and practices. Such a need is indicated partly in the awareness of Wah Gay, Ben Loy's father, that "each day makes the light of life dimmer" for him (42), and partly in the old man's fear that his son may end up marrying a *"jook sing"* girl—a United States–born, "heartless" Chinese American girl—and may therefore lose interest in preserving the traditional ways. Chu ironically contrasts Wah Gay's view of *jook sing* girls with the old man's "appreciation" for Lau Shee, the wife he has left behind in China for twenty-four years, but who, in Wah Gay's imagination, feels "no bitterness" but only "sympathy and understanding" toward his long absence from home, an attitude that he finds "lacking in *jook sing* girls" (45). Wah Gay's

reliance on a historically unwarranted practice of marriage for a presumably normative cultural renewal of the New York Chinatown bachelor community at a
time of drastic social change thus points up the inherent contradictions of his concern about his son's "proper" marriage, which, ironically, is largely shaped by his
concern for his own.

The novel provides, without explanation, historically significant dates for both
the father's and the son's marriages, the first being 1928, the year when Wah Gay
went back to China to marry Lau Shee, and the second being 1948, when Ben Loy
sails "home" to get his bride, the daughter of his father's friend Lee Gong. The intervening twenty years witnessed the adverse effects of a series of U.S. immigration
laws that profoundly affected the life of Chinese immigrants. The 1924 National
Origins Law established a permanent numerical restriction on immigration to the
United States from all parts of the world outside the Western hemisphere. Under
this law, also known as the "Second Exclusion Act," entry of Chinese students was
restricted, and Chinese wives of U.S. citizens were not entitled to enter the United
States. Such historical circumstances help explain why Lau Shee is "not alone in her
husbandless existence," but is one of the "hundreds and hundreds of women in Sunwei like her, whose menfolk had sailed the wide seas for the Beautiful Country and
never returned" (45). The National Origins Law, together with earlier legislation
such as the 1875 Page Law, the 1882 Chinese Exclusion Law, and various antimiscegenation laws instituted during the nineteenth century, accounts for the existence of a predominantly male society in New York's Chinatown. It was not until
the lifting of the National Origins Law in 1943 and the enforcement of the War
Brides Act in 1945 that Chinese spouses and children were able to come to the
United States to join their families. During the few years between 1943 and the
communist victory in China in 1949, 90 percent of Chinese immigrants to the
United States were women (Chen 1980, 141). Thus Ben Loy's visit to China in
1948 takes place precisely at a time of historical change in both Sino-American relations and the demographics of New York's Chinatown population.

For Wah Gay, what the twenty years of his "marriage" means is separation from
his wife, endless toil as a manual laborer in a racially segregated community, and
fathering the China-born son who does not join him in New York until the age of
seventeen. But Wah Gay ironically finds justifications for this situation through
the rhetoric of "duties": he declares it "a sacred duty" for him eventually to re-
unite with his wife in China, while praising her for selflessly taking care of his
family and "dutifully" waiting for his return. In a similar way, Wah Gay thinks
that it is the "son's filial duty" to let the parents decide on his marriage and to
agree to be sent back to China to get married, because it "mark[s] a solemn obligation dutifully discharged on the part of the parents" (44). Although the new
immigration laws allow Ben Loy to bring his bride to America, Wah Gay initially
"would rather see his brand-new daughter-in-law remain in China," for "she

would keep the mother-in-law company and look after her wants until, in a few years perhaps, she would pass away." The thought that Lau Shee "might find her loneliness more bearable with a daughter-in-law to share her tribulations" makes Wah Gay feel happy about his son's marriage (46). Despite Wah Gay's musing about his wife and his daughter-in-law, however, he never makes a serious effort to return to China to fulfill his own "duties."

Wah Gay's self-contradictory attitude toward familial obligations, as critics point out, may result from his financial difficulties, inertia, or a sense of guilt over failing to keep his promises (Kim 1982, 112–13; Hsiao 1992, 153–54). Yet these factors become insufficient explanations for Wah Gay's inconsistency in view of his longtime immersion in the culture and the social customs of Chinatown bachelor society. I would suggest that Wah Gay's failure to return to China despite his rhetorical endorsement of family values signals an implicit, though by no means natural, transformation in his own cultural identity. This transformation is marked by the breaking up of his family, his selective use of ancestral cultural values to make sense of problems arising from his struggle for survival in New York, his adaptation to and grudging acceptance of the only mode of life available to him in his adopted country, and his embarrassment, if not cynicism, about the incompatibility between the life he actually leads—loafing, gambling, and, in his younger years, whoring—and the idealized images of his life in America as entertained by his wife, who imagines him as "a happy and jovial man in a white linen suit" thriving in the Gold Mountain (45). Wah Gay's awareness of the contradictions in his life thus constitutes a tacit acknowledgment of the instability of his cultural identity. Maintaining separation from his wife, in this sense, allows Wah Gay to avoid facing the implications of his moral dilemma.

This perspective on Wah Gay's psychological complexity significantly contradicts the commonly held view of the old man's relationship with Ben Loy as one of simple cultural opposition. As we have seen from Chu's depiction, Wah Gay's insistence on shaping Ben Loy's personality and behavior according to "traditional" Chinese ideals, as well as on finding for him a "respectable" and "worthy" Chinese bride, is motivated not by his urges to control the young man's fate according to culturally sanctioned patriarchal needs but by his need to rationalize the adversity of his own experience in the United States, which deprives him of the kind of respectability he hopes his son could enjoy. In other words, wishing Ben Loy to be everything that he is not himself, Wah Gay assumes a form of parental control—by sending his son away from New York's "evil influences" to work in a small town in Connecticut—that is simultaneously ineffectual and self-deceptive. Springing from his life experience in Chinatown, Wah Gay's hope for his son's good future then reflects what the bachelor society is most lacking at this moment of transition—self-discipline, moral strength, virility, and the "potency" to reproduce itself in future generations.

Thus invested with Wah Gay's as well as other bachelors' values and illusions, the marriage of Ben Loy and Mei Oi naturally becomes a site of subjective motives and projective desires: rather than a culturally vital and effective strategy, the marriage arrangement becomes a wishful reconstruction of an inherited cultural ritual unable to carry the burdens of continuity and renewal that the split families and divided communities placed upon it. It is no accident that when the marriage disintegrates—and public knowledge about Ben Loy's impotence emerges alongside speculation that his past sexual history is to blame—it affects the older bachelors most. For Ben Loy's sexual and moral failures threaten to bring to light an unspoken history that the aging bachelors secretly shared among themselves: knowledge of Wah Gay as a frequent visitor of whorehouses when he was young, of Chin Yuen as the mentor of Ben Loy's indulgence in easy women and as (unsuccessful) seducer of his wife, and of Ah Sing as a lowly observer of women and sex. Such knowledge among the old bachelors not only prevents them from being realistic about Ben Loy's merits prior to his marriage, but also makes them unduly alarmed at the discovery of Ben Loy's impotence after the marriage begins to fail; for they realize that, rather than a figure of youth who can renew the old order, Ben Loy has turned out to be just another old man unfit for "real marriage," like themselves. Ben Loy's loss of sexual power clearly represents the old order's structural impotence: Wah Gay's comic efforts to exercise his role as parent and his "lip service" (Jeffery Chan 1979, 5) to his wife about family obligations can both be seen as emblems of the old bachelors' gradual but irretrievable loss of control over the younger generation in a failing community, and of these bachelors' ironic withdrawal from ordinary family life as a result of their prolonged entrapment in Chinatown bachelor life. Significantly, Ben Loy's impotence occurs only when he is confronted with memories of his sexual history on the one hand and his culturally constructed image of Mei Oi as an incarnation of the respectable "Chinese wife" on the other: "wife" is a category of women that he splits radically from the "other" kind he has known—the prostitutes of New York, Calcutta, and Hong Kong, with whom impotence had never been a problem. Ben Loy's failure to lead a married life thus becomes a generic metaphor for the consequences of Chinatown bachelors' social and psychological "disfiguration" by their adopted country, consequences that the bachelors try to ignore by maintaining the forms but not the substance of their culturally inherited male roles.

Male Voice and Female Desire

The most disruptive force in the marriage as a site for hopes is Mei Oi, whose behavior is instrumental in revealing the moral flaws reflected in both her husband's loss of sexual rigor and the entire bachelor society's social impotence. The subversive implication of Chu's creation of Mei Oi in a predominantly male but largely dysfunctional society tends to go unrecognized by critics because of the relative lack of development in her characterization. Such a lack, however, does not have to be seen as an indication of Chu's artistic deficiency or of his sexist view of women. On the contrary, I would argue that, Mei Oi's insufficient characterization can be see as a formal embodiment of the material truncation of early Chinese immigration to the United States and a way of revealing, either consciously or unconsciously, the specific mode of racial oppression experienced by Chinese males in the pre-1965 period.[11] Mei Oi's presence in a predominantly male society becomes in this sense a reminder of Chinese female immigrants' submersion by the visualization of time. Chu's portrayal of such a female character is therefore open, rather than closed, to feminist inflections: it invites a fleshing out of the residual traces of suppressed particularity of the Chinese female immigrant experience, as well as an imaginative constitution of the Chinese American female subject. Indeed, if we read Mei Oi not according to abstract standards of female agency but in relation to the changing historical contexts and shifting social expectations that surround her experience, her identity and her behavior in the novel can function transformatively. We recognize, for example, that, unlike her mother, Jung Shee, who is totally bound by traditions and obliged to sacrifice her own needs to the fulfillment of familial duties, Mei Oi belongs to a generation of young Chinese women who possess a small measure of self-determination through modest access to education and the possibility of travel, and she accordingly dares to entertain some hope of freedom from the drudgery of farm work, the impoverished life of a schoolteacher, and the emotional pain of being separated from her "gimshunhok" (gold mountain man) husband.[12] Significantly, Mei Oi's self-affirming attitude is directly encouraged by her mother, who often reminds her: "Mei Oi, I hope you will marry a *gimshunhok* and go to America with him. Then you will see him in the morning and at night" (65). Though stated in undramatic language, these words constitute explicit denials of Wah Gay's remark about the Chinese wives' "sympathy" for and "understanding" of immigrant husbands who never return, while they imply the existence of a degree of mother-daughter bonding among the women in Sanwei as a result of slowly changing social mores in a community fragmented by geographic distance.

Despite being frequently perceived as a construct of Chinese patriarchal oppression, Mei Oi is attracted to Ben Loy because he is framed, ironically, in terms of the "American Dream": she is prepared to see him as an embodiment of "youth. Dreams. The future. All that a girl from New Peace Village in Sunwei could ever hope for." In Mei Oi's imagination, a marriage to Ben Loy and the move with him to New York are not simply the fulfillment of a culturally prescribed duty; rather, they promise to open "before her a whole new panorama" in life (66). But soon after Mei Oi moves to New York's Chinatown, she is confronted with the limits of

America's promise: she finds herself stuck in a racially marginalized and dysfunctional community of bachelors, jobless, sequestered at home while her husband is
at work, out of touch with women who can provide her with solace or advice, and
deeply hurt by her husband's unaccountable "monk-like behavior" in the nuptial
bed (65). Such gender-specific portrayals of Mei Oi's sense of loneliness, displacement, and frustration underscore Chu's sensitivity to the problems that Mei Oi
faces as a female immigrant, as well as foreshadowing the alternatives that Mei Oi
later seeks out in the belief that "she was only human in wanting to be a woman"
(172). Key to Mei Oi's rebellion in the novel is her initiation of a process of demystification of her "feminine" self, the bachelors' "masculinity," and the New
York Chinatown community's seemingly resilient patriarchal control. The demystification process is carried out on two levels: first, through Mei Oi's presence as
a beautiful bride in the bachelor society, and second, through her affair with a
middle-aged Chinatown bachelor, Ah Song, which produces an illegitimate child.
In the novel, descriptions of Mei Oi's "innocent," culturally sanctioned beauty
(her ivory skin, her crescent-shaped eyebrows, and her small, cherry-red mouth)
stand in sharp contrast to the old bachelors' lewd talk about prostitutes in their
womanless life and to Ben Loy's "foolish, impetuous, stupid past" (12), a reminder
that is externalized and amplified into a collective panic among the bachelors as
they, too, react to Mei Oi's presence in a world in which the category of "wife" is
necessarily distinguished from the category of sexual partner. The panic among
the Chinatown bachelors is not so much about the young woman's moral "mis-
conduct" as it is about the demystification of their settled binary attitudes toward
women, attitudes that Ben Loy must examine in order to build anew his shattered
marriage in the last episodes of the novel.

Mei Oi's challenge to the bachelor society reaches a high point when she has an
affair and falls in love with Ah Song, and then becomes pregnant with his child.
Predictably, Mei Oi's image undergoes a transformation in the mind of the bachelors, from that of the innocent and virtuous bride to that of the seductive female
protagonist of *Gim Peng Moy,* the Chinese literary counterpart to D. H. Lawrence's
Lady Chatterley.[13] With her fall from the pedestal comes her increasing identification in the mind of the aging bachelors with *jook sing* girls, who are seen as
sources of moral pollution in Chinatown, who threaten the sexual and cultural
mores to which the bachelor society pays lip service. Mei Oi's insistence on having
an affair with Ah Song despite Chinatown elders' warnings, neighbors' gossip (including women's disapproval), and Ben Loy's physical punishment defies traditional social conventions and expectations about women's relations to male authority, and does constitute, in some senses, what Jeffery Chan calls a "comic
revenge" on Chinatown bachelors on behalf of all neglected wives in China (1979,
5). Yet Mei Oi's challenge to the bachelor society seems to have gone further: she
poses a threat to the political order of Chinatown by challenging patriarchal con-

trol at both familial and social levels. When Ben Loy asserts male "authority" by slapping Mei Oi for her relations with Ah Song, she responds: "You wife-beater, that is the only thing you know how. What kind of a husband have you been? Why don't you ask yourself that? . . . I didn't do anything wrong" (145). Mei Oi's retort to her husband is a significant moment both in the collapse of the marriage arranged by Chinatown's old men and in Mei Oi's positioning herself to renegotiate her relationship with Ben Loy by insisting that her interests and frame of reference be acknowledged. In a similar way, her stout denial of Ben Loy's charge that she "knitted a green hat" for him is not merely a refusal to admit that a woman is more culpable than her male lover in an affair; it is a declaration that she will not submit to a male discourse that constitutes the meaning of her behavior solely in terms of its relation to her husband's pride. It is from such a position that Mei Oi argues that a husband "can't force" his wife "to stay with him if she doesn't want to" because "sometimes the husband is in error too" (166, 168). Mei Oi's contestatory position involves a rejection of the bachelors' gender role assumptions, particularly their double standard which holds that "husbands are different. . . . They can go out and sleep with another woman and . . . women folks can't do anything about it. It's different with a woman" (168). That the essential foundation of the men's position was the need to maintain control over women is articulated by Chuk Ting, the president of the Wang Association: "Women cannot be trusted. . . . I've always told my boy to run his family with a firm hand" (137). Similarly, Chuk Ting thinks that Wah Gay should "bring up [his daughter] right" (198); and when Ben Loy fails to control his wife, he logically seems "a renegade" in his father's eyes (141).

In a novel that provides almost no background explanation, the task of constructing an understanding of the codes at work in the bachelors' lives is largely, if not wholly, an inferential one for readers. The New York Chinatown community's responses to Mei Oi's behavior, especially the way in which it protects the reputation of the family association, obviously reflects Chinatown's stratification of its social discourse predicated on patriarchal concerns, traditional gender bias, and hierarchical arrangement of everyday life. But such responses are also historically contingent and reflect practical considerations: they work to strengthen the primordial family ties in the ethnic enclave which must be cohesive enough to resist racial hostility from the outside. And as a way of maintaining such internal cohesion, the elders must channel the potentially explosive internal dispute over Mei Oi's affair with Ah Song through familial networks in order to achieve a peaceful, though obviously repressive, resolution, especially when viewed from a presentist perspective. The Chinatown leaders' harsh reaction to Ah Song's involvement with Mei Oi,[14] and later to his turning a dispute internal to the Chinatown community into an external controversy when he lodges a complaint with the police against Wah Gay (who catches him coming out of Mei Oi's room and chops off one of his ears), not only illustrates how gender, patriarchy, and resistance to racial oppression intersect, but also highlights the extent to which the New York Chinatown family association functions as what Sucheng Chan calls a "power broker" (1991, 63) in preventing external interference and ensuring Chinatown's political survival. Ironically, Ah Song's disrespect for families and Chinatown authority serves the ends of the leaders of the Wang Association: it helps fuel their rhetoric for mobilizing and uniting the bachelors against what they see as a potential threat to the political integrity of the ethnic community.

As in the case of the community's view of Ben Loy, who falls from perfection, irony undercuts condemnations of Ah Song's behavior, for the old bachelors secretly view his lifestyle with considerable envy. Wah Gay observes: "The women like him. He is a beautiful boy," while Lee Gong, though grumbling that "that sonavabitch Ah Song eats good, dresses good, and he never works," has to admit that "maybe he was born under the right stars" (18). In a sense, Ah Song is better adapted to Chinatown's bachelor life than the old men, who, because of their age and their concerns with prestige, can only indulge in talk about young girls. When both Ah Song's and Ben Loy's actual lives turn out to be not only similar to each other but also resonant with the old bachelors' past, unspoken experience, all the men in New York's Chinatown, married or unmarried, old and young, become multiple images of a male role that is mutually reflective and mutually transferable. Ah Song is simply more open about his "bachelor" behavior than the others, while Ben Loy learns in painful steps to abandon his binary attitudes toward women by accepting Mei Oi's position as a valid one. Although Ah Song's defeat by the Wang Association and his subsequent banishment from New York are signs of the persistence of Chinatown community tradition, both Wah Gay and Lee Gong are similarly obliged to go—Wah Gay to Aurora, Illinois, where his brother has a Chinese restaurant, and Lee Gong to his cousin's poultry market in Sacramento—by the logic of their concept of saving face. But their departure also emblematizes the disintegration of the old way of life in New York's Chinatown, as marked by the sale of the Money Come Club, Wah Gay's gambling den, which has been a haven for the downtrodden, homeless, and aging bachelors. When Wah Gay and Lee Gong say to each other, "See you again, grandpa," before they leave New York, they know that "in all probability, [they] will not see each other again" (231); yet, they have not faced up to the reality or significance of Mei Oi's bearing another man's child. Wah Gay still believes strongly that Ah Song's relation with his daughter-in-law is his "misfortune" (221), while Lee Gong curses the "no good daughter of [his]" who is "the cause of it all" (228–29). The two old men's farewell remarks make obvious how little they have recognized about themselves, and how firmly they cling to their illusions. With Wah Gay's and Lee Gong's departure from Chinatown, their awkward, formalized relations with their children come to an end, although it is clear that the substance of such relations was broken long before by geographic distance and adherence to empty rituals of parental supervision.

The shattered, demystified relationship between Ben Loy and Mei Oi is the ground on which the couple begin to rebuild their marriage. The creation of a viable marital relationship involves a painful mutual adjustment that proceeds without illusions on either side: Mei Oi has "risked disgrace to have an affair" with Ah Song because she finds Ben Loy "no good as a husband" (204), and Ben Loy finds himself "seething with resentment" at Mei Oi's (and his) status as "laughingstock of the whole town" even as he admits that his impotence has led to Mei Oi's affair (209). The importance of Chu's narrative strategy in the final episodes of this novel is easy to overlook because of various external factors and changes that appear to bring about a reconciliation between the couple. For example, in an effort to free themselves from their parents' interference, Ben Loy and Mei Oi decide to move from New York's Chinatown to San Francisco's, where the couple "enjoyed emancipation" from "the stern parental eye" (246), while their relationship is "nourished" by the birth of their child (247). In San Francisco, Ben Loy finally seeks aid for his impotence, which is apparently "cured" by the medical use of tea—an ancestral prescription provided by a Chinese herbal doctor.

To most historically informed critics, these changes in the conditions of the young couple's relationship unambiguously signify the crumbling of the old bachelor order, increased freedom for the new generation, and the beginning, in the restoration of sexual relations and the birth of the son, of a Chinese American community in the United States built around family life and children. But the changes in Ben Loy and Mei Oi's life are more provisional and ambiguous than they appear to be in such readings. For example, even after the young couple's move to San Francisco, Ben Loy still suffers an "inner torture" over not being the real father of the child, while Mei Oi still feels "terror and resentment" at the thought that her husband's "lack of manliness" may be permanent (246). And while the couple may feel that the move away from New York has freed them from much-dreaded "parental supervision," such supervision has been largely in name only. As we have seen, in spite of Wah Gay's careful plan to bring up his son in isolation from New York's temptations, Ben Loy has had no problem consorting with "loose women." Similarly, Lee Gong, for all his "fatherly" concern about his daughter's welfare, does not learn of Mei Oi's relationship with Ah Song until gossip about her questionable pregnancy reaches his ears. In fact, the two fathers give little more than lip service to parental roles: they do what is customary, but *only* what is customary, until trouble brews, and their children's behavior in New York seems little impeded by their supervision. Finally, contradictory implications can be drawn from the birth of Mei Oi's child, which indeed encourages "understanding" and "compassion" between the couple (247). But the child remains a constant reminder of Mei Oi's infidelity to her husband and of Ben Loy's sexual incapacity; its birth has as much potential to drive the couple apart as it does to bring the two closer together.

On Reading Formations

Most ambiguous is the power attributed to the healing agent for Ben Loy's sexual problem, the Chinese ancestral panacea of herbal tea, which Ben Loy invokes at a moment of deep emotional crisis in San Francisco. Ben Loy's final resort to ancestral force in hopes of solving his problems in the marital bed constitutes a significant shift in the novel's discourse—from that of realist portrayal to that of magical solution. The result of such a shift is equally significant: it suspends the novel's realist economy while opening up possibilities for what Paul de Man calls "referential aberration" (1979, 10; I will return to this aspect of the novel in the last portion of this chapter). In the existing studies of Chu's novel, critics have tended to ignore the intertextual implications of such a shift in favor of the symbolic meanings of tea. Hence Cheng Lok Chua observes that Ben Loy "gets a second chance" and "rehabilitates his sexual potency" by "accepting his wife's illegitimate child and by eating the brews of herbal tea concocted for him by a medicine man. Both are bitter draughts that he must drain, and the bitterness of the tea aptly suggests the gall of his portion. . . . Ben Loy's draining this bitter cup, his acceptance of the calvary of his cuckoldry, strengthens him to transcend and free himself from the dead weight of past traditional restraints and vengefulness" (1982, 45). In a similar vein, Elaine Kim also concludes: "Ben Loy must drink a bitter bowl of tea: he must make amends for the excesses of the bachelor legacy. He must accept his own mistakes, his wife's mistakes, and the child who, although illegitimate, will be his own. Ben Loy will be the father and husband Wah Gay was not, because he has chosen to face reality" (1982, 117).

In emphasizing the need for Ben Loy to accept responsibility not only for his own acts but also for the bachelor society's legacy in order to transcend the burden of history, such a reading overdetermines the tea as a symbol and neglects its more modestly inscribed meanings within the cultural milieu presented by the text. Throughout the novel the reader has been introduced to two kinds of tea—tea appreciated for its savory and aromatic quality, and tea used for medicinal purposes. The first kind is associated in the text with the Chinese ceremony of hospitality and, in a peculiarly metaphorical way, the rituals of sexuality. For example, the tea ceremony at the young couple's wedding banquet involves Mei Oi's ritual offering of tea to the male guests; the banquet is immediately followed by a bedroom scene in which the couple's attempt at sexual engagement is unconsummated. Later a white-enameled teapot and a lone cup of unconsumed tea on the table in Mei Oi's bedroom stand witness to the bride's initial extra-marital sexual encounter with Ah Song, which begins with a hospitable offer of tea that Ah Song transforms step by step into a seduction. Later still, Mei Oi's offer of tea to Chin Yuen, a visitor in her husband's absence, coincides with the latter's secret desire to take advantage of Mei Oi as a sexual object. Unlike Ah Song, he drinks the tea but does not make love to his friend's wife. Thus, in the textual system of the novel, tea is not so much an enabler of sexual potency as it is a ritual substitute for sexuality itself. Significantly, an early recommendation by an herb doctor that Ben Loy use tea as remedy for sexual incompetence does not yield results in New York (89–91), just as a medical doctor's recommendation that Ben Loy attempt to restore his sexual capacity by temporarily moving to a different location fails to effect any permanent change (84–85). The conditions for producing the desired result have been tried and found wanting. Is the difference in San Francisco primarily the result of Ben Loy's severing relations with "past traditional restraint" while accepting the "bitter" responsibility for the bachelor society's legacy? Does the tea carry this symbolic burden as the author's proffered "cure" for the ills of the United States' Chinatown communities? I would suggest that it does not.

The essential factor that transforms the demystified marriage site in San Francisco is not merely sociogeographical (Ben Loy and Mei Oi still live in a Chinatown), nor is it Ben Loy's "eating" of large quantities of bitter tea (although he does partially abandon his wounded indignant-husband discourse with Mei Oi, and of course male pride in any culture is often a bitter substance for men to swallow). Rather, the marriage is transformed because the gender obligations between the parties become matters under negotiation: Ben Loy does not abandon his fairly traditional male position as "active" decision maker and provider, but he does recognize that a relationship with his wife demands that he acknowledge and respond to Mei Oi's voice, rights, and sexual needs. Mei Oi makes similar adjustments in her bargaining with Ben Loy. The difference is subtle but clear: for the first time, Ben Loy "had willingly and, without ill feelings or reluctance, discussed his physical condition with Mei Oi," and, also for the first time, Mei Oi "felt both a desire and a responsibility of *sharing* her husband's problems" (242; italics mine). The impotence is now framed as a common issue, and the marriage relationship ceases to be a static "given" and becomes a construct that both parties build between them, in recognition of their past behaviors and assumptions and the pain they have caused each other.

The difficulty of interpreting *Eat a Bowl of Tea,* particularly for its contemporary readers outside of Chinatown communities, largely results from Chu's refusal to provide them with cultural translations of his carnivalized realist portrayal of the New York Chinatown experience. In refusing to do so, Chu's novel situates itself in ways that recall Mei Oi's bargaining position with Ben Loy: the text demands that readers enter into a relationship with it by working to understand its appropriation of "native" voices, its peculiarly structured speeches and vocabulary, and its specific frames of reference, and to negotiate the text's complexities by first abandoning ideas that privilege their own positions as superior to Chu's. This task, if undertaken, must necessarily disturb readers' own established cultural assumptions; indeed, the novel positioned readers in the 1960s to see another center of American society, one that established habits of perception and interpretation had effectively hidden from view. In addition, adopting a narrative mask that refuses a variety of "expected" roles (Chinatown tour guide, cultural ambassador, or deferential and informative host to strangers in a "foreign" land), Chu unostentatiously but radically resists the impositions of much American cultural discourse about Chinatowns. Just as the narrative events of *Eat a Bowl of Tea* assign no hierarchical "borders" between Chinatown and the majority society—through textually centering what is socially peripheral—so too does the narrator refuse to grant superiority to the cultural position occupied by the novel's potential readers, either by condescending to his materials or by deferring to his readers' implicit demands to translate those materials into available cultural or ideological equivalents.

This examination of *Eat a Bowl of Tea* demonstrates that what seems from a poststructuralist point of view to be the novel's essentialist cultural typology in masculinist terms can become, in a fully contextualized analysis, a property of the narrative that opens up rather than reduces the complexity of the Chinese American experience in the United States in a crucial period of postwar American immigration history. It has also shown that the novel's unity of meaning, its sublation of difference, and its construction of cultural "types" are in fact often produced precisely by its critics' refusal of referentiality in interpreting the densely textured Chinese American immigrant experience depicted in Chu's novel. For such refusal has the tendency to minimize the ideological and aesthetic challenge the novel poses both for its initial readership and for the reproduction of its meaning in contemporary American culture, as well as to suppress the performativity of the contradictions and differences inherent in the novel's realist representation. So rather than an allegory of "the master narratives" of generational conflict between "nativism" and "assimilation," Chu's portrayal of the family relationship is full of inconsistencies and contradictions, features that insistently cast the unresolved historical consequences of "emasculation" of Chinese immigrant males on a dialectical plane. Furthermore, Chu represents the two central characters of the novel—Wah Gay and his son Ben Loy—not as simple cultural opposites but rather as conflicted yet interdependent facets of a socially and economically produced temporality that at once affirms their selfsameness and throws them into crisis as a result of the continued tension between Chinese males' racial gendering and Chinese women's double social marginalization. The difficulty of fitting Chu's treatment of generational conflict in *Eat a Bowl of Tea* into pre-given theoretical categories thus emphatically underscores the need for theorists to record the resistance that theory encounters, to recognize that the notion of historicity does not by itself guarantee a historical perspective, and to attend with precision to who is making cultural translations, about what knowledge, and from which particular historical locations.

In adopting an authorial mask as well as using carnivalesque inversion as a form of ideological critique of both the deep-rooted racial prejudices in American society and Chinatown subculture's existential dilemmas, Chu's stance in *Eat a Bowl of Tea* is highly self-conscious. Such self-consciousness manifests itself, on the one hand, in Chu's attempt to negotiate the intertextual tensions surrounding the publication of his novel and, on the other, in his positioning regarding the differences between mainstream and Chinatown cultures and, in particular, between voices from different generations of Chinese immigrants. One such voice, Ben Loy's, seems related to, if it does not speak for, Chu's own. Like Ben Loy, the author was born in Canton, China, came to live in New York's Chinatown when young, served in the U.S. military during World War II, and visited China to marry before the communist victory in 1949. These parallels between the author's life and that of his interlocutor in the novel indicate that by the time Chu published his novel (at the age of forty-six), he had already had substantial contacts with China and Chinese culture, over thirty years of direct and indirect experience with New York Chinatown's bachelor society, and an understanding of the life of mainstream America. Such experiences enabled him to function both adaptively and oppositionally within and across the cultural and geographic barriers that tend to limit the self-perception of most first-generation Chinese immigrants in the period. Chu's unique position in the community thus explains his ability to offer penetrating portrayals of the mental world of Chinatown bachelors and the intricate gender politics of Chinatown organizations while maintaining a critical distance from them through a strategy (especially for mainstream readers) of seeming decontextualization. The novel's chronology makes clear the author's awareness of Chinese immigrants' historical and cultural burdens, and of America's historical responsibility for New York Chinatown's current situation. But he obviously chose to focus his satire on the Chinatown community, especially by critiquing how the patriarchal values of his ancestral culture had become an internal spiritual prop for its moribund bachelor society, whatever the mainstream culture's role in creating that society. It is through such a strategy that Chu's novel opens up a space of discursive contestation that places the authority of received representations and popular knowledge of Chinatown within the perspective of historical and cultural relativism. Despite charges against Chu's work as a fiction of surface, its complexity exceeds the novel's structure of representation, while its proliferation of concrete details refuses to fall victim to passive, monolithic reflections of the complex material world.

It would be an overstatement to suggest, on the basis of this analysis, that

Chu's portrayal of the relationship between Ben Loy and Mei Oi indicates the author's thorough understanding of the complexity of the issue of gender or that his reconstruction of Ben Loy and Mei Oi's marriage resolves the problems arising from the transformation of gender roles in the postwar Chinese American immigrant community in New York. On the contrary, Chu's attempts to portray Chinese immigrant women of the period, to problematize patriarchy, and to return to women their own voices, as critics point out, remain bound by the ideological limitations of his time and by his own limitations as a man. But we should also recognize that, in his dramatization of the compounding effects of the interrelated social ills of racism, sexism, and patriarchy, Chu, along with other Asian American writers in the immediate postwar period such as Monica Sone, Diana Chang, and Hisaye Yamamoto, rehearsed ideological battles that were still beyond the horizon of much Asian American literary representation in the 1950s and 1960s. In probing into these yet-to-be-contested grounds of postwar Chinese American realities, Chu subtly positioned himself in the chorus of the cultural dissent of the era and anticipated the more self-conscious articulations of these issues by Asian American men and women in the 1970s and 1980s. Although Chu's novel can in this sense be seen as implicitly participating in a process of transforming and recoding postwar Chinese American social relations, the effects of his participation are necessarily limited by the lack of public space for dissenting Asian American literary voices in the era, by the embryonic nature of Asian American feminist thinking, and by the existence of generic imperatives in the literary marketplace which tended to reduce the novel's subversive ideological potential to certain textual a priori. Recognizing such external and internal constraints on the production and reception of the novel alerts us to the dangers of judging this and other Asian American literary works as "self-sufficient texts" or of assessing the ambiguity of desire in them solely in terms of presentist ideological schemata.

The most telling site for assessing the ambiguity of desire in Chu's novel, as we have seen, is the author's invocation of tea as a magical emblem of Chinatown renewal. On one level, this invocation appeals to socially frustrated aspirations, that is, to the Chinatown community's attempt to recover itself from the consequences of genocidal discrimination and social, economic, and political disfranchisement—consequences that remain submerged in the overall cultural mystification of America as an "affluent" society on the eve of President John F. Kennedy's assassination. On another, it clearly suggests Chu's difficulty in visualizing a convincing social solution to Chinatown's problems and consequently his relocation, through the textual sign of tea, of the unresolved externality of his concerns to the realm of fantasy. Presumably, Chu's abstraction of his socially unrealizable desire would give him a certain creative autonomy within which he could deal with the physically and morally sick Ben Loy and the decaying New York Chinatown community, and thus provide a temporary textual resolution for the ideological tensions that he insistently invites the readers to foreground and come to terms with. The implicit political intent of Chu's use of tea is further emphasized by the central status the author grants the word, both in the book's title and in its climactic conclusion. Yet in using tea as a healing agent for the ills of New York's Chinatown, Chu is mobilizing a worn cultural icon incapable of serving as a site for ideological struggle between such real social issues as gender, race, and class.

Understandably, the sign turns most readers toward explanations of Ben Loy's revival of sexual power in terms of tea's symbolic connections with the internal—and presumably anthropologically based "cultural"—causes of Chinatown's externally created conditions and problems. Such an aesthetic closure performs important intertextual functions: it conforms to accepted formulaic patterns of plot development in a realist novel; it symbolically invokes the Chinatown community's repressed desire for stability, continuity, and inner strength at a crucial time of the community's transformation; and it offers an occasion for Chu to detach himself from the novel's spent (but not extinguished) economy of transgression while giving the book the appearance of a "finished" cultural product. Yet the calculated formal coherence of this novel provides only a provisional containment of the social dislocation suggested by the novel's content under the political climate of the early 1960s. During the Asian American cultural revival of the 1970s and its ongoing resurgence in the 1980s, not only does the adaptive potential that lies dormant in the novel's ambiguous desire for transformation receive fuller social expression, but the hitherto worn cultural icon of tea becomes enlivened into a zone of active ideological transcoding as well. In the context of post-1970s Asian American literary discourse, the prominence of "tea" ceases to be a mere suggestion of "oriental" cultural mystique; indeed, in my reading it becomes a sign that registers the nuances of the author's symbolic and actual struggles in his negotiations with the external forces and internal contradictions that informed and conditioned the novel itself.

At the beginning of this chapter, I mentioned an irony about the reception of *Eat a Bowl of Tea* in the 1980s and 1990s: that is, Asian American critics, while generally endorsing the book's canonization, tend to show little interest in close reading its text. This lack of critical attention, despite the text's seemingly secure status in Asian American literary history (even though no work should be secure in a productively provisional canon), shows, if nothing else, that the inclusion of this novel in the Asian American literary canon does not truly resolve the more complex issue of the work's readership. Today's reading situation for Chu's novel is particularly illustrative of how the audience's perception of the book is complicated by the widening distance between Chu's initial encoding of its meaning and its subsequent interpretation under circumstances where postmodernist and poststructuralist analytical approaches have become dominant. Contemporary theories in cultural studies and semiotics recognize that there is no necessary correspondence between encoding and decoding for the simple reason that interpretations impose new values on a given text that must be made sense of by the culture that receives it. Umberto Eco calls this characteristic of the reading process "aberrant decoding" (1976, 141–42), a term that not only alerts readers to the problematic character of reconstruction of authorial intentionality but also asserts that the meaning-making of a text depends ultimately on the codes available to its readers. Along the same line, Tony Bennett further suggests: "Different reading formations . . . produce their own texts, their own readers and their own contexts" (1987, 74). My interpretation of *Eat Bowl of Tea* recognizes the significance of aberrant decoding in its use of a set of interpretive strategies congruent with what I would call transformative reading. At the same time, my analysis also points toward an aspect of the reading process that was not foregrounded by Eco when he initially formulated the concept, that is, the burden of a literary text, as Edward Said observes, with the occasion or the plain empirical realities from which it emerged (1983, 35), and consequently with the textual and contextual constraints on what a text can do and can mean.

In reading Chu's novel in the current historical moment, we need to acknowledge both the inaccessibility of its principle of encoding and the limits of retrospective decoding. Yet we must also recognize, as Stuart Hall points out, the need for "some degree of reciprocity" between encoding and decoding in order to ensure "effective exchange" and to avoid reading merely random meaning into earlier texts (1980/1993, 100). Obviously, contextualizing an Asian American literary text such as *Eat a Bowl of Tea* involves more than acknowledging the relevant historical backgrounds of its production, a method that often fails to recognize that historical contexts are never "a set of extra-discursive relations" but "a set of inter-textual and discursive relations" (Bennett 1987, 74) mediated through textual signs that bear traces of social heteroglossia. Ultimately, the burden of interpreting Chu's text involves the critical and creative reconstruction of Asian American experience and the social and cultural conditions under which the author wrote his book as grounds for the novel's further meaning-making. This is not to suggest, as I indicated earlier in this chapter, that we embark on the impossible task of searching for some essentialized local knowledge or authorial intentionality; rather, it is to caution against ways in which injustice to an Asian American text can be done in the name of refusing to deal with referential immediacy and to call attention to the contradictions of critics' privileging some "traditional" Asian American works while dismissing others.

Louis Chu does not deny women in his realist depiction of New York Chinatown's bachelor society; on the contrary, women are denied by the economic, legal, and political suppression of Chinese immigration to the United States in the pre-1965 period. In misrecognizing the textual traces of such a denial in Chu's work as symptoms of his sexism, critics of *Eat a Bowl of Tea* are complicit with the

historical suppression of a collective Chinese immigrant agency in American culture, which depends on a greater suppression of Chinese immigrant women.
What I have shown so far in this chapter is that, at the very least, paying attention
to the historical specificity of *Eat a Bowl of Tea* helps to foreground the novel's unacknowledged significance: its exposure of the mutually defining relationship between race and gender by dramatizing the historical consequences for the pre-
dominately male Chinese immigrant communities in America, and its implicit
call for historical investigation and literary rearticulation of the lives of working-
class women in the Chinatowns of the period. No less important is how Chu situates the text of *Eat a Bowl of Tea* relative to prior literary discourse about Chinatown on the one hand and to different communities of readers on the other. In
both cases, I suggest, Chu used his novel to negotiate the tensions between the coercive influence of the dominant culture and his own urge to tell a "real" story
about New York Chinatown society, between literary figurations and actual social
existence.

In providing a sympathetic reading of Chu's realist depiction of late 1940s
New York Chinatown bachelor society, I do not intend to valorize realism as a
mode of representation necessarily more revealing than others. Nor do I wish to
confer on Chu's novel a representativeness it does not possess. The context of my
argument for the significance of Chu's realist intervention, as I argued at the outset of this study, is the overwhelming skepticism about the representational
power and relevance of realist narrative in current Asian American literary criticism. The kind of social engagement that marks the power of Chu's realist novel
is not its tendency to produce correspondence, condensation, or typification, but
rather its ability to expose the inadequate modernist representation of American
society in the period in question, to represent the limits of cultural denial of the
specificity of Chinese American social experience, and to bring to light its own
split historical referent and then to call for further narrative supplementation of
the reconstituted intertextual dynamics revealed by the novel's conjunctural—
but only conjunctural—realist "elucidation of difference" (Iser 1987, 225). As
Wallace Martin observes of the effect that plot cliché in a realist work can have,
"it shatters the credibility we had not just lent but given to the story, and we may
feel that the author has not simply made a mistake but betrayed our confidence.
In the best realistic narratives, we are startled into awareness of the real" (58). The
performativity of the realism of Chu's novel lies ultimately in our willingness to
tap the fictionality of his fiction and hermeneutically bring into play the novel's
signification as an enabling cultural and political signifier in a unique period in
post–World War II Asian American literary history.

In this chapter I have tried to show how Chu negotiates the relationship among
class, gender, generational, cultural, and diasporic issues through a narrative form

that embodies both the need for and the difficulty of effectively articulating pressing concerns about survival and regeneration in a dying community. Shot through
with multiple contradictions, the novel is thus inscribed in its own ambivalence—its awareness of both the majority society's hypocrisy in ignoring the social and economic plight of Chinatown communities, and Chinatown inhabitants'
own hypocrisy in paying lip service to family duties while entrapped in the bachelor mentality. Despite such ambivalence, however, Chu's novel finds strength for
sympathetically representing an immigrant community that suffers miserably
from the consequence of its historical deprivation of women even while it struggles to adjust to their "renewed" presence. The novel thus raises questions that go
beyond women's exclusion from Chinese immigration to the United States to signify the implication of their challenge—through their gradual increase in number
in the communities in the period—to the hierarchical arrangement of social life
that marked Chinatown life before the 1960s. Chu is clearly not an ideal agent to
report and represent working-class Chinese American women's subjectivity. But
his having to do so in the early 1960s reflects, among other things, the social and
political constraints on what working-class women could say about themselves in
a culture (both mainstream and communal) dominated by patriarchal values.
Registering the emerging politics of gender that would be given fuller articulation in Asian American literary representations and criticism in the years to come,
Eat a Bowl of Tea constitutes a symbolic act of trying to fill a "structural lack" (Laclau 1993, 284) in Chinese American social life in the early 1960s, foregrounds
the contradictions and controversies that are part of that life, and makes the most
significant attempt to force open the largely closed horizon faced by Asian American writers since the publication of John Okada's *No-No Boy* in 1957.

4

Performing the Margins

Ethics and the Poetics of Frank Chin's Theatrical Discourse

A given consciousness is richer or poorer in genre, depending on its ideological environment.
> —Pavel N. Medvedev, *The Formal Method*
> *in Literary Scholarship*

What I value most I guess is what I'm doing, trying to legitimize the Chinese-American sensibility. Call it my accident in
time and space and that all the talent, everything I have is
good only for this. Nothing else is any good until I get this
done or started. And if I can't legitimize it, or if Chinese-
American sensibility isn't legitimized, then my writing is no
good.
> —Frank Chin, quoted in Victor G. Nee and
> Brett de Bary Nee, *Longtime Californ'*

In the two previous chapters I argued that both *No-No Boy* and *Eat a Bowl of Tea*
are texts that challenge contemporary readers to negotiate their meanings and to
enact the political potential implicit in their content and form. This chapter explores two Asian American texts with a sharply contrasting strategy: they make
oppositional use of drama for open political engagement and force readers to reflect on their own relationships with the social issues foregrounded through the
form. I focus on Frank Chin's theatrical work in the early 1970s: *The Chickencoop
Chinaman* (1972) and *The Year of the Dragon* (1974). This analytical focus reflects
my assessment that more than any of his earlier or recent writings—short stories,
novels, essays, or political commentary—Chin's plays illustrates a productive convergence of his artistic individuality, his moral conviction, and his literary practice as part of a strategic action in the historical moment when he began his
writing career.[1] An elucidation of this convergence, in my view, is vital for under-

standing Chin as a complex writer and as a historically responsive social critic, as well as for evaluating the unique role that his theatrical art plays in a crucial moment of post–World War II Asian American literary history.[2]

In a 1976 letter to Michael Kirby, editor of the *Drama Review,* Chin retrospectively describes his impulse to become a playwright: "I write from links with the original whoremothers of our people and through my mother, ties to the most popular hero of the most popular novel and opera living with me. The Kwan blood from my mother meant I was chosen to write theater like making war, throw everything away and get even" (quoted in McDonald 1981, xxvii–xxviii).[3] Chin's rhetorical references to his being "chosen to write theater," to "war," and to "the Kwan blood" indicate not only his outrage at the mainstream culture's continued silencing of Asian American literary voices but also his idealistic view of the social function of the aspiring Asian American artist. Chin's concerns, as set forth in essays he wrote at that time, derive mainly from situations he finds detrimental to the development of an "Asian American cultural integrity." First is the perpetuation of stereotypical images such as Fu Manchu and Charlie Chan in American popular culture, a form of cultural racism that, in Chin's view, effectively excludes Asian Americans from "creative participation in American culture" and from operating in "the mainstream of American consciousness" (Chin and Chan 1972, 77). Second is Asian Americans' apathy toward the majority culture's acceptance of them in stereotypical terms, an attitude that, he argues, reflects a state of "self-contempt," self-rejection, and "self-destruction" in the Asian American psyche. These situations, according to Chin, give rise to the myth that Asians came to the American continent with neither a historical "vision" nor a written cultural tradition, and they consequently allowed "the details" of that heritage to be either forgotten or "euphemized into a state of sweet confusion," because "the men who lived through the creation are dying out, unheard and ignored." Deeply concerned about the perishing of Chinese American history under American linguistic and cultural domination, Chin imagines the fate of Asian America to be "simply a matter of growing old and dying" like "an extinct race" (1972a, 44, 60). It is out of an enormous sense of historical urgency that Chin takes upon himself the moral obligation to reinvent Chinese American history, to speak across generations about the density and intensity of his feelings, and to call for an open confrontation with the institutional wrongs done to Asian Americans historically. Kai-yu Hsu accurately captures the specificity of Chin's sense of historical mission:

> Frank sees himself in a unique position to transmit the truly identifiable Chinese-American experience because he is young enough to see through the stereotyped images with which many Chinese in America above the age of forty identify themselves, and yet he is old enough to remember what it was

like to be Chinese in the United States during World War II. As to the Chinese of the postwar era, in Frank's view, their Chineseness is being rapidly absorbed by the white-American values. And those young Chinese, either championing the cause of, or resisting the emergence of, a new China, are so busy fighting on the active front of politics that they unavoidably fall short of being fully sensitive to all the subtle pressures and forces operating on each individual. (1972, 47)

Chin's perception of a perishing Chinese American history and his self-assumed obligation of communicating to emerging generations of Asian Americans their unacknowledged cultural roots in America thus demands that he go beyond the mere textuality of writing and seek "a style of excess" (Chaney 1993, 22), a style through which he can not only disturb the immobility of Asian America that results from its internalization of racial inferiority but also force mainstream society to face its own complicity in creating such a situation. The literary genre that Chin finds most effective for realizing such an intention is the play in performance: it gives specular prominence to his political desire through a demonstrative use of oppositional gestures, languages, and imagery; it allows him to break out of Asian Americans' "self-effacing presence on the American scene" through boisterous resistance (Chin 1972b, 5); and it licenses open disruption and violation of social and cultural norms in a highly associative space of transgression. The imaginative sustenance of Chin's theatrical intervention is Kwan Kung (god of war and literature in traditional Chinese culture), a figure kept alive ritualistically by early Chinese immigrants to the United States through traveling Cantonese opera troupes in Chinatowns or mining and railroad camps (see McDonald 1981, xxvi–xxvii).[4] For those early immigrants, Chin would later explain, the theatrical image of Kwan Kung—which embodies the "impeccable, incorruptible, personal integrity" of "fighters" and "avengers" (1977, 43; 1982, 165; 1985, 120; Chan et al. 1991, 38)—provided a source of moral support and emotional assurance in the face of prolonged racial hostility, open violence, and discriminatory legal restrictions, just as the life experience of Ben Fee, a 1920s Chinatown labor organizer whom Chin met in the early 1970s and admired for his courage and ethnic pride, constituted a living example for the playwright of how Asian Americans could unite and fight for equality in their historical present (see Chin 1972b, 58).

Chin's theatrical mobilization of the performative potential of the ethnic community's cultural memory was strategically connected with the social "dramas" that he helped to script in the period: he co-sponsored the Combined Asian American Resource Project (1969); he founded the Asian American Theater Workshop in San Francisco (1971); he orchestrated a movement in California for redressing the grievances of Japanese Americans interned during World War II

(1974); and he headed a research effort aimed at recovering unrecognized, little-read, or forgotten Asian American literary voices (1970–76).[5] The symbolic dissolution of boundary in these projects between Chin's theatrical practice and Asian Americans' mounting drive for self-determination implies a strategy for maximizing the effects of the playwright's art. For Chin, the theater constituted both an aesthetic concretization of his action-oriented moral idealism and a symbolic extension of the outer limits of the evolving Asian American literary discourse, and thus allowed the textual struggle so far carried out by Asian American writers to take on a material and visual form through staged oppositional action. It is from this radically conjunctural yet deeply committed sociocultural space that Chin negotiates the tensions between the physical and cognitive temporalities occupied by the actors and audiences of his plays, explores the contradictory positions of his artist figures, and experiments with a heteroglossia made up of discourses embodied in the enunciated historicity of his characters' racial, cultural, and moral plight.

Language, Masculinity, and the Birth of the Asian American Artist

The Chickencoop Chinaman (1972) was Chin's initial attempt to use theater for negotiating his historical vision and his characters' conflicting voices relative to one another and to mainstream culture. Its plot revolves around a Chinese American filmmaker, Tam Lum, who has come to Pittsburgh to make a documentary film about the sports hero of his youth, a black boxing champion called Ovaltine Jack Dancer. One purpose of Tam's trip is to meet Ovaltine's father, Charley Popcorn, who allegedly trained the boxer and knows the details of the latter's heroic life. Tam's seemingly naive quest for recovering a heroic Asian American past through idolizing a black boxer linked to a mythic father (who turns out in Act 2 to be the manager of a porno movie theater) is fraught with ironic authorial intentionalities: rather than a simple reflection of Chin's rigid reproduction of the culturally affirming discourse of black nationalism of the 1960s, it serves as a comic-tragic reenactment of the playwright's perception of Asian America's helpless yet continuing slippage between its displaced present and its effaced past, as well as of his painful recognition of the Asian American artist's problematic dependence on borrowing mythologized histories from African American models in order to force a consideration of the consequence of a vanished Asian American historical referent.

Such a sense of crisis in historicity is effectively conveyed at the beginning of the play through Chin's construction of a surrealistic encounter between Tam and the Lone Ranger, the hero of the majority culture's popular westerns, before Tam meets Charley Popcorn. Through a dreamy interior monologue inspired by the

presence of an old-fashioned radio on stage, Tam relates to the audience his childhood fascination with the Lone Ranger—a masked, black-haired man—as an
Asian American hero with a mythic origin, the "thundering hoofbeats" of his
horse resembling, in the boy's imagination, the thunder in the Sierra caused by
the Chinaman-built train, a sound that his grandmother used to listen for in the
kitchen (31–32). But the Lone Ranger whom Chin then brings on stage is fat and
decrepit, a fraud who keeps his composure only with the help of Tonto, his "faithful Indian companion," who periodically injects heroin into his "master's" veins.
In his interaction with Tam and Kenji (a Japanese American friend with whom
Tam stays in Pittsburgh), the masked man proves himself a sad, bumbling white
racist who warns the two to "keep your asses off them long steel rails and short
cross ties" and to stop "looking for a train" or for "their place in the American
dream" (37–38). To reinforce the effect of its unmasking of the Lone Ranger, the
play makes a point of reminding the audience that Tonto's identity is but a white
mythic projection complete with a comic "Indian" dialect. In his exchange with
his master, Tonto twice slips out of his designated tongue, and twice the Ranger
comically fails to recognize him and orders: "Tonto. Be yourself" (34, 36).

The play's lamenting of a suppressed Chinese American heroic tradition associated with railroads—reinforced by Chin's inverted critique of American popular
cultural assumptions about rugged individualism—tends to be viewed by critics,
not without some compelling reasons, as evidence of the playwright's impulsive
endorsement of an American western myth predicated on violent and expansionist
impulses. But a serious participation in the economy of Chin's peculiar representation of the encounter between Tam and the Lone Ranger suggests that it is open
to more nuanced and less reductive constructions of meaning (although Chin's
tendency to embrace masculine valor does need to be critically examined within
its relevant contexts). Indeed, if we do not assume Chin to be so naive about the
efficacy of a simple reversal of the two competing visions he dramatizes, then the
significance of the railroad imagery called forth through these two figures'
metaphoric encounter lies not so much in its liberatory possibilities as in its ironic
questioning of the relevance of referential coherence within falsified historical discourses. The maintenance of such falsified historical discourses, according to
Chin, depends both on an effacement in American culture of the early contributions of Chinese immigrant workers to the construction of America's railroads
and on contemporary Asian Americans' refusal to acknowledge the mental and
physical strengths associated with such an endeavor as necessary virtues of their
own immigrant forebears. From this perspective, the railroad memory that Chin
invokes through the ironic clash between Tam's and the Ranger's visions—a
memory he would later call "railroad standard time" (the title of Chin's 1978 short
story)—can therefore be seen as performing a deeply subversive function in the
play's intertextual situations: it strategically splits the official "past" so that the

playwright can further comment, from within the differential temporality opened by his insistent railroad references, on the continued waning of Asian America's lived possibility of actively experiencing history.[6]

Chin's foregrounding of the illusory nature of Tam's childhood association of the Lone Ranger with the heroism of the Chinese immigrant fathers significantly anticipates Charley Popcorn's open skepticism in the next scene about Tam's search for a black boxer: the old man categorically denies his relationship with Ovaltine Jack Dancer and explicitly resists Tam's attempt to elevate him to the status of a mythically heroic father figure in the documentary. In a way, the referential discontinuity from which Tam suffers as a result of his rejection by the symbolic father figure he tries to emulate—Popcorn (and, invertedly, the Ranger)—shows some similarities with aspects of Lacan's appropriation of the Freudian notion of the castration complex (1919/1957, 231, 233–34). For Lacan, this complex involves a male child's frustration and anxiety about the rupture between the signifier (phallus) and the signified as a result of the father's threat of castration, and the child's latent desire to enter into the symbolic order defined by the prohibitive (as well as abstract) father with whom he strives to identify and to whom he thereby becomes subject (Lacan 1977, 167–69). What Lacan emphasizes is the ambiguous tension between a simultaneous lack and desire in the split subject, and between the subject's dependence on a lack for desire and its simultaneous refusal/inability to fulfill desire in order to maintain the elemental lack. Such a tension, as critics point out, does not automatically lead to a historical emergence of submerged subjectivity unless it is informed by a recognition of the materiality of the psychic irresolution.[7] In my view, Chin's play both presupposes the binary scheme of Lacan's original formulation and performs the function of disrupting it. And, as I will show, it is precisely from the contingency co-produced by radical alienation from the father and its attendant excruciating desire that Chin introduces the material modalities of Tam's emotional and existential dilemma and contemplates this character's historical emergence as Asian American subject.

Significantly, Tam's initial heroizing of the Lone Ranger and Popcorn is contrasted with his rejection of his own Chinese American father, "an old dishwasher" who wears underpants in the bath for fear that "old toothless goofy white ladies" will peek at his body through the keyhole (16–17). This image suggestively parallels a story that Ovaltine Jack Dancer makes up about Charley Popcorn's turning away from women when urinating by a car, as it does Tam's and Kenji's memory of urinating with the black boxer. The broader cultural and rhetorical contexts of Chin's parody of a self-contemptuous and paranoid "Chinaman" indicates deliberate irony at work, while the subtext of this image evokes issues of potency, reinforced by Lee, a Eurasian woman of Chinese descent, who comments on her Chinese American husband, Tom, that "he wasn't a man" (18).

It is Popcorn, the black father figure, who brings to both Tam's and the audience's awareness a different story about the filmmaker's father: he was a man who loved boxing and maintained a fierce sense of dignity; indeed, Popcorn says to Tam, "maybe I respect [him] more than you." Out of such respect, the "old Chinese gentleman" by whom Tam was obviously embarrassed had been given the name "Chinatown Kid" (46).

The vindication of a Chinese American father's dignity, as well as of Chinese American masculinity, through the voice of a cynical black boxing trainer tough enough to live without the kind of myths that young Tam (and Ovaltine Jack Dancer) need, provides insights into Chin's strategy for dealing with power transference, as well as into some of the implications of Chin's dramatization of his alter ego's search for a father figure. It is true, as critics point out, that Chin's search for an ideal father and for Asian American masculinity is problematically based on a patriarchal belief in measuring adequacy in terms of male aggressiveness and violence. And along this line, Chin polemically argues: "The blacks complain about being emasculated. The genius of white racism in regard to the Chinese is that they never granted them balls in the first place" (Nee and Nee 1973, 385–86). Chin's anger is clearly directed toward both stereotypical views of desexualized Chinese American men in mainstream culture and what he perceives as the absence of a "legitimate" Asian American cultural voice, an anger that he expresses through the lewd, loud, and lawless Tam. But it should also be recognized that Chin does not make Tam an idealized figure for the Asian American artist: Tam avoids accepting his own father and recognizing the strength and dignity underlying his appearance; as a father himself, he is deeply ambivalent about his own children; and his filmmaking fails to address directly his own plight as a Chinese American man in order to celebrate the "warrior" heritage passed down by a black father/trainer. Tam's struggle clearly symbolizes the difficult emergence of the Asian American artist self-conscious about the historical and cultural limitations of his own position. The tortured, voluble Tam thus highlights the connection that Chin sees between the lack of a male-oriented Asian American heroic tradition and the invisibility of Asian American cultural production, a situation that Chin describes in strongly gendered terms: "Without a language of his own . . . [the Asian American] no longer is man" (Chin et al. 1974, xlviii). For Chin, the crisis in masculinity is bound up, ultimately, with the crisis in language facing the artist; from this perspective, Tam is but a mediational figure who invokes not only the idolized ancestral Chinese American male who built North America's railroads but also the Asian American artist who must not only envision and connect with an Asian American heroic tradition as well as fight to make his voice effective in the present. The key issue that Chin's play explores is the complexity of Asian American consciousness, which is largely but not wholly embodied in his artist figure's anguished voice. Tam's limitations, in other words, only partially mask the heroic myth of Chin's ideal of a cultural awakening and of community empowerment, even as they display the difficulties that pursuit of such an ideal can pose to the individual artist.

Throughout much of the play, Tam, unable to envision a heroic history for Asian Americans, frequently runs into obstacles that not only distort his immediate vision but also prove it false. Tam's sense of his "language" difficulty—his inability to enter into the symbolic order named the Father in Lacanian terms—is elaborately conveyed through the conflict between Tam's and Kenji's voices (see also Li 1991, 215–16; 1992, 323), and through their angry interchanges with Lee and Tom, conflicts that make the stage an extremely demanding site for Chin's projections of the kind of painful negotiations that confront the emergent Asian American artist. The voices of Tam and Kenji involve systematic inversion and negation of the structures and semantics of a variety of available linguistic discourses: their exaggerated imitation of Helen Keller's halting utterances, their frequent switching to black accents, and their deliberate, repeated insertion into the already mixed and multiaccented English discourses the mocking chicken sounds "Buck Buck Bagaw" (simultaneously echoing a rooster's call, the cry of earlier generations of "Chinamen" in place of "giddyup," and a remembered graffiti on a "crapper" wall in "Old Oakland") are all signals of Chin's consciousness of the ideologies of America's many communities. The interplay between and among polyphonic, bastardized voices on stage presents a specular plurality of unmerged and unobjectified thoughtworlds, while it puts to the test the abiding expectations of a majority audience thrust into a highly polemical encounter with an anarchy of resistant, traditionally submerged voices suffering from ethnic "defects" (7). This encounter clearly was a troubling one for reviewers, who complained, for example, that Tam's monologues were "hot air, disguised as poetry," or that the playwright failed to demonstrate in the play his own capacity as a "master rhetorician" (see McDonald 1981, xv), because many failed to recognize that Tam's carnivalesque display of words is in itself a symptom of the plight of the artist that the play addresses. In the rhetorical and linguistic maneuvers between and among the characters of different cultural backgrounds, we sense the presence of an author fully aware of the nature of his characters' problems and adept in moving between cultural production and reception, verbality and performativity, spectator and spectacle, and visual appeal and auditory experience.

One verbal strategy Chin uses effectively to enhance the contested relationship between his own discourse and those of his characters and of his audience within the enunciative-receptive format of the play is the deliberate shifting of illocutionary acts, a strategy described by Roger Fowler in his linguistic appropriation of Bakhtin's concept of dialogism. According to Fowler, in a (counter)hegemonically designed communicative situation, the speaking agent assumes the role of an audience ideologically opposed to the author: the author presents the addressee's position as false by making the speaking agent act on the audience's beliefs, and the addressee cannot refute such a relationship because his or her own position is structurally implicated in the given communicative arrangement (1981, 88). In the play, Lee and Tom, who can both speak a "standard English" familiar to the audience, play precisely the role of the speaking agent described by Fowler. For example, Lee scolds Tam in words that implicitly raise the very questions the play's audience might have in mind:

> I knew you hated being Chinese. You're all chicken! Not an ounce of guts in all of you put together! Instead of guts you have . . . all that you have is . . . culture! Watery paintings, silk, all that grace and beauty arts and crafts crap! You are all very pretty, and all so intelligent. And . . . you couldn't even get one of your girls, because they know . . . all about you, mama's boys and crybabies, not a man in all your males. (24)

Lee's confusion about Tam's deliberate switching of voices in her presence is a similar voicing of the audience's concerns about Tam's "ragmouth" imitations as possibly demeaning gestures of "making fun of blacks" (13). Thus, Lee comments: "He's talking in so many goddamn dialects and accents all mixed up at the same time, cracking wisecracks, lots of oh yeah, wisecracks, you might think he was a nightclub comic. What'sa wrong with your Chinatown acka-cent, huh?" (24). In reply, Tam produces the rhythmic sounds "Buck Buck Bagaw" that mock deep-seated prejudices against Chinese Americans.

The most ironic critique of audience positions in the play is carried out through Chin's construction of Tom, an assimilated Chinese American and Lee's former husband. The play portrays Tom as conforming to almost every given cultural perception of Asian Americans as a "model" minority. He knows his place as a "Chinese" and feels content about his present opportunities. He says to Tam:

> Maybe you don't like being Chinese and you're trying to prove you're something else. I used to be like that. I wondered why we didn't speak up more, then I saw we don't have to. We used to be kicked around, but that's history, brother. Today we have good jobs, good pay, and we're lucky. Americans are proud to say we send more of our kids to college than any other race. We're accepted. We worked hard for it. I've made my peace. (59)

Because of Tom's obvious acceptance of mainstream attitudes and values, he finds Tam unrealistic about his racial identity: "I can call you 'Chinaman' and insult you, 'Americanized Chinese' and insult you. 'Chinese' and insult you, 'American' 'Chink' 'Jap' 'Japanese' 'white' and insult you, 'black' and insult you" (63). But Tom's complacency is immediately subverted by Tam's forcing him to see that Lee is not the white woman he thought he was married to: "Look at her. Go on up and get a good look, fella, and you tell me who's prejudiced against Chinese. You want a white girl so bad, so bad, you turned her white with your magic eyes. You got that anti-Chinaman vision" (60). Tom's misconception of Lee as white and non-Chinese is ironically reinforced by Lee's view of him as her "Chinese husband"; Tom's passing remark that "in American eyes we don't appear as he-man types" suggests that he is more troubled by stereotyping than he admits (59), while Lee's earlier comment that "he wasn't a man" implies that Tom's embrace of the promises of assimilation may be an act that has "unmanned" him. Only by reject-ing Tam's acute sense of his anomalous cultural position can Tom feel secure in his ideologically designated place in American culture as a successfully assimilated minority. By defining Tam's aggressiveness and anger as idiosyncratic, as rooted in "personal" problems (60), and by seeing Tam's refusal to be pigeonholed into the mainstream culture's slots as a lack of courage in facing the reality of his being "Chinese," Lee and Tom pose an accusatory question regarding Tam's identity: "Who do you think you are?" (13). This is precisely the question that might be raised by the audience confronted by an alienated self as disturbing as Tam.

It should be stressed that Lee's previous multiracial marriage, her children re-sulting from different racial combinations, and her own ambiguous racial identity parallel Tam's and Kenji's deliberate cross-racial accents, and likewise render her efforts at clear-cut, either/or definitions of ethnic identity simultaneously absurd and ineffectual. Similarly, Tom's claim that he knows, through his marriage to Lee, the difference between a "Chinese" and a white woman indicates that the mainstream culture's willful blindness toward standards for ethnic identity are naive at best, racist and self-serving at worst. Since Lee and especially Tom are designated to speak for mainstream opinions that are represented as false, the question they pose in regard to Tam's identity—"Who do you think you are?"—forces audiences not only to face Lee's and Tom's, hence their own, problematic positions regarding Asian American identity, but also to see that the categories they use to understand Lee, Tom, Kenji, and Charlie Popcorn are equally arbitrary constructs. Thus a shift in tension occurs: from that between Tam and Tom/Lee on stage to the interstage cultural spaces in which the majority spectators are left dis-turbed and disoriented. Chin's introduction of multiple voices in the play and his conscious deployment of devices such as transference of voices and ironic juxtapo-sition of identities thus implicitly critique the hegemonic discourses of racial identity and strategically test the ground for bringing about multiple readerships through performative strategies.

Equally significantly, the "lumping" together of radically hybrid characters with mixed racial features and behaviors on a single stage confronts the audience with a polyphony of the new minority voices in the United States social arena of the 1960s and 1970s and thus indicates the author's recognition of an unprece-dented disturbance of traditional racial and class lines in that era. Chin's satiric vi-sualization of such interracial and multicultural dynamics poses serious challenges to hegemonic attitudes and values, as does his subversive critique of such influential signifiers of consumer society as the figures of the stewardess, the Lone Ranger, and the black boxer (as an example of black militancy in American sports of the 1960s). Indeed, the crossing of racial identity lines in Chin's play creates a panorama of confusion and fragmentation, confronting mainstream audiences with the instability and decentering of an early 1970s' postmodern culture characterized by the absence of a synthesizing vision and a hypnotized whole. (I further discuss Chin's plays in terms of the postmodern later in this chapter.) The sense of fragmentation that Chin foregrounds in his play invites the audience to witness the collapse of the totalizing structures of American culture's racial constructs; and the erratic, angry, foul-mouthed, many-voiced Tam at the "center" of Chin's disrupted stage world is emblematic of both the fact of that collapse and the plight of the marginalized artist seeking a ground and language for his vision when so many are blind to its sources.

The last act of *The Chickencoop Chinaman* prepares for the emergent Asian American artist-subject, albeit one who remains undefined and with an unclear sense of purpose. Such an emergence is simultaneously contrasted with the play's demystification of Tom as "Asian American" writer, author of a "cookbook" that Tam ironically derides as *Soul on Rice.* Although Tom insists that this book is about Chinese American identity and thus implicitly about Asian America, it is treated in the play as nothing other than a recipe from the dominant culture's archive. In the initial staging of *The Chickencoop Chinaman,* the same actor played the roles of both Tonto, the Indian companion to the Lone Ranger, and Tom, the "fake" Chinese American writer who implicitly celebrates the role of faithful subordinate to the dominant white culture. Such double casting reinforces the point that the roles played by both Tonto and Tom are defined by the majority culture in ways that do not disturb the historical dominance of Euro-Americans. In this sense, Tom (bearing a name recalling "Uncle Tom") is not only a recipe offered by traditional American culture for the "model" minority but also a perfect embodiment of the book he himself is writing. Viewing Asian American identity through cultural biases that he has internalized—biases that include a homophobic reference to Asian American males as "queer" and "willowy," a reference that Chin fails to resist in his theatrical critique of cultural racism—Tom reminds Tam that his cynicism about the mainstream culture's treatment of Asian Americans is "oversensitive" (58–59). Tam answers bluntly: "Tom, you! Your whole soul, man, has been all washed out, treated, your nerves all taped up and packed away, like mummies in the monster movies, man." About his own position, Tam cries: "I knew better. I must've been known better. My whiteness runneth over and blackness . . . but people still send me back to the kitchen. You know what I mean?" When Tom again asserts, "You're oversensitive. You can't be oversensitive" (60), Tam's reply marks a climactic, though no less ambiguous, attempt to clarify the difference in their position:

You're right. I can't be oversensitive. It's like havin too much taste. But that's me oversensitive. And I like it. I am not going to dig up the Dancer, mock his birth, make a fool of him just to make a name for myself. That's the way it is with us Chinaman cooks! Dat's the code of the kitchen, children. Anybody hungry? (63)

Tam's switch from condemnation of Tom to ironic replacement of him in the kitchen as a "cook," a preparer of "recipes" for Asian American identity, signifies the initiation of a process of cultural emergence for the ethnic artist by self-appropriation of the margin rather than, as is commonly observed, merely by reaction to oppressors outside the self and the ethnic group. Early in the play, Tam's language marks the kitchen as a cultural site of origin in discourses on the "birth" of his kind of "Chinaman": "I am the result of a pile of pork chop suey thrown up into the chickencoop"; "the chicks of the coop" are "created," "no more born than nylon or acrylic. For I am a Chinaman! A miracle synthetic!" (7–8). The role of cook and the site of the kitchen are implicitly where traditional American culture locates the figure of the Chinese American male. Tam's final move to the kitchen recalls the play's title, as well as its central figure: the chickencoop Chinaman. Figuratively, the chickencoop evokes images of Chinatowns and similar urban ghettos as sites for "breeding" of the Asian American as an invented species of the mainstream culture. Tam's talk about his "motherless bloody tongue" strongly underscores his sense of Chinese Americans as cultural "orphans" in the country's history. Tom, by contrast, can be seen to epitomize the consequences of embracing the orphan status and fleeing from his Chinatown "origins," from the kitchen, with his "cookbook," his "standard" English, and his parroting of mainstream culture's prejudices against Chinese Americans. Tam, also a product of the chickencoop, is a figure who can still be categorized among the "promiscuous and criminal birds" that are "too lazy to shape up a proper pecking order," and "grooved on running their fool heads off together, making chicken poetry after Mad Mother Red" (7). While Tam's voice remains the raucous, rooster-like cry "Buck Buck Bagaw," Tom's "orphaned" voice is that of a passive chicken sold for consumption to his "producers."

Chin's negotiating position is clearly not absolutized through the series of events concerning his protagonist's displaced search for the Chinese American hero, his unsuccessful effort to disrupt the complacency of Tom and Lee, and, particularly, his ambiguous articulation of alternatives to imposition of Asian American identity from the cultural margin dramatically imaged by the kitchen site. Significantly, the kitchen from which we see Tam speak at the end of the play is also the one in which, as a young boy, he listens to radio programs about the Lone Ranger, imagines the masked man to be an Asian American hero, and hears his grandmother tell stirring stories about Chinese American men's feats in building the railroads. A climactic moment in the final kitchen scene comes when Tam seems to hear, without the mediations of either the Lone Ranger or his grandmother, the sound of a train that recalls the memory of "granmaw's pa coming home" (65). But Tam is only on the verge of identifying with his symbolic father and of (re)possessing his imagined heroic Asian American past through the possibilities that lace his self-conscious struggle to keep the present disjunctive. For the kitchen site where he finally reasserts himself is the same cultural margin of his social deprivation, a site that remains fought over by conflicting ideologies and subject to the confounding effects of diverse inscriptions. As a multiply coded metaphor—which simultaneously evokes ethnic minority racial status, servitude, cultural enslavement, ethnic identity politics, and implicit gender valuations—it thus prevents Chin's artist figure from immediately realizing the desire to become a historical subject and frustrates the viewers' attempt to draw clear-cut conclusions about what they see on stage.

Chin's linguistic-political construction of Asian American subjectivity is thus continually problematized by the materiality of Tam's "birth defects" (11) and his opposition to cultural dominance constantly displaced by the social conventions that insistently speak through his ethnic subject-in-the-making. Chin's emergent Asian American artist remains tentative, unstable, and forthcoming, one who speaks from the kitchen site in a voice at once disruptive and incoherent, while refusing to deliver messages of acceptance and gratitude that the majority culture expects to hear from those it defines within those boundaries. Like the anxiety-ridden Lacanian male child, Chin's Chinese American male subject continues to be divided from its own contradictions and ambivalence. But this division is also something on which Chin depends for securing a relational temporality in which he can revitalize his desire to fill the cultural void that defines his subject's struggle and in which his frustrated Asian American artist is stimulated to renewed ideological productivity.

Commercial Culture and the Burden of Representation

The pains that Tam experiences on stage in trying to legitimize a Chinese American language in *The Chickencoop Chinaman* find a parallel in the frustrations that Chin himself went through in the early 1970s in trying to publish his co-edited anthology of Asian American literature *Aiiieeeee!* According to Chin and Shawn Wong, before the book's final publication by Howard University Press in 1974, it had been repeatedly rejected by white publishers for its allegedly excessive "ethnic" content and its unwillingness to "mold" its differences "to enrich the society" defined by the majority culture (1974, vi, viii).[8] For Chin, the difficulties he and other editors had faced in cultivating a public Asian American literary voice reflect not only the rigidity of an unyielding cultural establishment but also the need for Asian American artists engaged in such a struggle to perform an additional role as custodians of a fragile Asian American cultural identity. Such a perceived need was given full expression in Chin's second play, *The Year of the Dragon* (1974), in which he addresses with great satiric energy the agony and absurdity that the Asian American artist must negotiate in his relationships with family and community under the penetrating influence of capitalist commercial culture.

In a way, Chin's shift of attention from invoking the birth of the Asian American artist in *The Chickencoop Chinaman* to grappling with the burdens of representation faced by that artist in *The Year of the Dragon* was shaped by several developments that surrounded the latter's opening production.[9] In the era, for example, various anti-poverty programs exposed the long-standing problems of low income, unemployment, poor housing, and crime that had beset Chinese Americans, and highlighted Chinatown's continued isolation as a subordinate community. Such a development is directly reflected in the play in Chin's use of a cramped apartment and its tiny kitchen and bathroom as centers of family activities and in the character Johnny, the gun-bearing younger brother of the play's central character, Fred, who symbolizes the emergence of a generation of antisocial Chinese Americans. For Chin, the economic subordination of Chinatown and its inhabitants was but another manifestation of the cultural deprivation he exposes in *The Chickencoop Chinaman.* One grave consequence of such mutually reinforcing oppression, Chin emphasizes, was that many young Chinese Americans had developed intense self-hatred, which in turned led to the desperate attempt to escape their fate by abandoning the ethnic community, an attitude he finds symptomatically reflected in Chinatown's social demographic changes and marriage patterns in the period (see Chin et al. 1974, xxi). It is perhaps no accident that Chin makes the marriage of Fred's sister Mattie Eng to a white husband, Ross, a highly controversial issue in the play.

Chin's simultaneous concerns about the existence of Chinatown as an emblem of racism and its disintegration as a result of the younger generation's eager absorption into the mainstream reveal a profound ambiguity in his perception of the role of the Chinatown community in his project of ethnic formation. Such ambiguity, as we have seen, is partly reflected in his first play in Tam's simultaneous rejection and endorsement of the kitchen site that is open to both positive and negative associations. As we have also seen, Tam's frustrated struggle for a living Chinese American historical vision is sustained not through his ability to change the social reality faced by Chinese Americans but rather through his attempt at radical temporal reorganization of that reality by a strategy of doubling. The productiveness of Tam's existential ambivalence, in other words, depends crucially on his access to historical memory. In *The Year of the Dragon,* however, Chin seems to

suggest that maintaining such a precarious balance has become increasingly difficult in the face of the pervasive commodity reification in contemporary American
culture. Despite Chinatown's status as an urban ghetto marked by poverty, Chin
notes, the community has been effectively commercialized and abstracted into an
alien cultural spectacle, a quaint tourist attraction that travelers visit on streetcars
or on guided tours. For Chin, such commercial objectification of Chinatown poses
the greatest threat to the emergent Asian American literary voice: it corrosively
transforms—through external cultural falsification and internal reproduction of
falsified consciousness—the community's limited signifying capacity into a passive reflection or, in Jameson's term, a "blank parody" of mainstream culture's orientalist desire; and it threatens to erase the last vestiges of a Chinese American
historical memory by depriving the emergent artist figure of his "capacity actively
to extend its pro-tensions and re-tensions across the temporal manifold and to organize its past and future into coherent experience" (Jameson 1991, 17, 25),
hence making such memory no longer available to the upcoming Chinese American generations. Chin's reference to "the year of the dragon" (i.e., 1976) in the
play's title—an occasion for celebrating the richness and longevity of the community's cultural tradition—becomes in this sense the playwright's calculated satire
on Chinese America's cultural depthlessness as a result of the depletion of Chinatown's symbolic power through commercial culture.

From this perspective, Chin's play can be seen as centrally engaged in resisting
the effects of commercialism's growing penetration into Chinese American life
and exposing various forms of perceived complicity with the perpetuation of such
effects both within and across the ethnic community. The play's ultimate purpose
is to reinscribe, without certainty and compromise, a version of Chin's notion of
"cultural integrity" for the emergent Asian American artist confronting commercial culture's relentless appropriation of Chinatown as a possible source of political
resistance. Chin's efforts are realized mainly through the struggle carried out by
the play's protagonist, Fred, who suffers a fractured sense of selfhood: publicly he
is a Chinatown tour guide, a role forced on him by his own father, Pa Eng,
"mayor" of Chinatown and owner of its booming Tour'n'Travel business;[10] pri-
vately he is a Chinese American writer who has difficulty both publishing his
novels and being recognized for his literary talent. This duality of Fred's function
in the play is at once subversive and confining. On the one hand, his access to the
two conflicting roles enables him to manipulate the performative distances between the play's actual and potential audiences for these roles, while it allows
Chin to try out multiple positions, commenting on or responding to the range of
options available both to himself and to the play's mainstream viewers. On the
other hand, Fred's access to these roles is simultaneously curtailed by the constant
tension between his resentment toward his imposed social identity and his anxiety about his unrealizable aspirations. The play dramatizes this tension through

Fred's double voice: he adopts a phony, deferential "Chinese" accent when directly addressing the audience, and a vulgar and angry voice when talking with members of his Chinese American family. In this way, the play forces the audience not only to experience the discrepancies in Fred's divided self but also to see that their own tourist-like perception of Chinatown is based on a self-serving delusion: that is, they must recognize the naiveté of believing that the cultural other on which they depend for making sense of themselves can truly satisfy their curiosity about things "Chinese" simply as a result of the tour guide's performance. The play's demonstration of Fred's self-division thus illustrates commercial culture's tendency to falsify, conceal, and totalize, while it retaliatorily problematizes the seeming innocence of the audience's gaze by returning that gaze back to its source—a task that the play dramatically accomplishes through its satiric treatment of Ross, Fred Eng's white brother-in-law.

As a middle-class liberal white, Ross genuinely respects Chinese culture and loves the Chinese American family of which he has become a member. Yet, as the play suggests, his enthusiasm serves only to expose the orientalist nature of his liberal choice. For example, to show his appreciation for Chinese culture, Ross greets Pa Eng with "Gooh Hay Fot Choy" during their first meeting, a phrase that immediately angers Fred, who uses it only when he pretends to be a "Chinese" tour guide—a role that Ross unintentionally naturalizes by implicitly acting like a tourist. As the play proceeds to show, Ross is also prone to interpret what he cannot understand in the Chinatown family either as an indication of "normal oriental hospitality and restraints" (84) or as a sign of "the superiority of Chinese culture" (128), without realizing that his identification with the Chinese American family is ironically based on his simultaneous denial of their being his coequals. Fred's ruthless taunts at Ross's compliments about Chinese culture or Johnny's rude reaction to the Chinese cultural cliché with which Ross glibly misinterprets Chinese American family relations is designed to disturb mainstream audiences: the play does not invite sympathy for the frustrations Ross experiences in comprehending his Chinese American in-laws but rather harshly critiques almost everything he assumes regarding his relation with the Chinese American community. Mainstream audiences are initially invited to identify with the good-hearted, polite, and easygoing Ross and with his efforts to immerse himself in the Chinatown family. By placing this white character in direct confrontation with the objectified ethnic group he has married into, Chin exposes the superficiality of the majority culture's sense of justice toward the cultural other it sympathizes with and implicates the spectators as part of the folly by symbolically involving them on the stage. As the mainstream audience witnesses the Eng family's disturbing responses to Ross, it not only finds its assumptions about cultural identity turned into an object of satiric scrutiny but also discovers the unstable nature of its own position as the audience space itself becomes a staging of the tourist locale.

Because of the existence of large numbers of consumers of commercial constructions of Chinatown, Mattie's marriage to Ross, as well as the Chinese food business they operate, logically represents a kind of cultural transaction packaged and accomplished in terms of a cultural cliché the play satirizes—"a blend of the best of the East with the best of the West" (99). Indeed, Mattie herself is in many ways Chinatown sold to the mainstream, a delivery prepared through her collaborative staging of cultural identity by having competed when young for the title of Miss Chinatown USA under the sponsorship of Pa Eng's Tour'n'Travel, and having worn falsies in the swimsuit event in order to succeed. Mattie's urge to live up to the majority culture's tourist desire and Ross's well-intended condescension are most ironically compromised by their mutual acceptance of and appreciation for Chinatown as a simultaneously transparent and opaque commercial signifier.[11] Their married relationship thus becomes an allegorization of the postmodern tourist's abandonment of a search for cultural meaning and that tourist's acceptance of both the superficiality and the limitations of late capitalist culture's commercial abstraction of race relations in American society.[12] Mattie's rigorous cultural imaging of her self-identity thus reflects, according to Chin, her unconditional acceptance of tourist definitions of Chinatown, while Ross's unquenched thirst to "know" Chinese culture through interracial marriage reveals the self-mystifying effects of his indulgence in imagining the cultural other in tourist terms. Implicitly, the Mattie-Ross relationship serves as Chin's commentary on his vision of the dangers facing a new generation of Chinese American artists under the pressure of commercial objectification, and contrasts with the playwright's own effort to negotiate the social space he occupies as an Asian American writer by dramatizing Fred's struggle to find a position without compromise, without collapsing differences, and without denying the difficulties that Chinatown poses.

If the Mattie-Ross relationship illustrates how late capitalist culture effectively transforms Chinese American social relations into commercial forms, then that transformation foregrounds the interdependence between consumer values and orientalism, an interdependence that in turn requires collaboration between the consumer and the supplier of commercial goods, who can, hypothetically, manage the spectacle for gazing. In the play, Chin clearly designates Pa Eng, the China-born family head and owner of Tour'n'Travel, as performing such a function through inverted orientalist commodity fetishism. As we have seen, the father figure in *The Chickencoop Chinaman* is a recoverable image of the dignity and heroism of the Chinese American past and symbolizes both physical and cultural power. The father in *The Year of the Dragon,* however, stands for patriarchal tyranny, narrow commercial values, and, as we shall see, the divided consciousness of Chinatown as cultural colony and racially marginalized slum. The way Pa Eng decides Fred's future—by forcing him to drop out of college and to stay with him as a Chinatown tour guide—for example, is consistent with his perception of his own patriarchal privileges in the family (he made such an arrangement after realizing that he would soon die of a lung disease) and with his role as both a guarantor and an enforcer of commercial interests within the community. Accordingly, the most useful employees in his tour business are obedient tour guides who can market an "exotic" Chinatown to the mainstream culture for profit, whereas in his Chinatown family, the only "reliable" members are those who can preserve the "Chinese" family tradition. Logically, he makes Fred the top guide in the tourist business, while expecting him—his eldest son and heir to his tour business—to promise him, in ways that reflect his patriarchal commercial taste, that "Chinatown always house" (108).

Pa Eng's patriarchal commercial operation is ironically sustained by a sense of racial inferiority toward white Americans, an attitude manifested in a dubious mixture of Charlie Chan–like deference and mistrust, punctuated with comic assertions of patriarchal will. This feature of Pa receives biting satire in the play during his various encounters with Ross: he is "all smiles and giggling charm" before he learns that Ross is his son-in-law, yet once he realizes that Ross is a family member, he rudely interrupts him and calls him "Bok Guai Lo" (white devil) to his face (93–94). Similarly, although never convinced of Fred's talent for writing, Pa feels no hesitation to ask him to ghost-write his Chinatown New Year speech before Mattie's white husband arrives on the scene, after which he asks the latter to rewrite it for him. In Ross's presence, Pa refuses to let Fred even touch the notes he was asked to prepare: he shoves them at Ross, blurting out to his son: "What you know? No college graduation? Him Merican. Know da Engliss poofeck. You Chinese!" (104). Pa obviously thinks of Fred's writing skills as he thinks about his own English: "No good he ting I Englis too stupid. Better he ting Sissy Pa be somebody spesual" (108). Pa's exploitation of Fred's writing skills for his cultural exchange with Ross, as well as his disdain for Fred's ambition to become a Chinese American writer, is ironically juxtaposed with his excitement about the speech that Ross couches in racist cliché, a speech that the old man eagerly rehearses in the bathroom while noisily relieving himself.

The play's dramatization of Pa's enactment of "either/or" positions relative to mainstream culture's perception of Chinese Americans grows particularly intense when, under the belief that he should die the Chinese way, Pa brings into his Chinatown family the wife he has left in China for over forty years. Pa's insistence on keeping China Mama threatens to split the Chinese American family in ways analogous to those that Chin protests against in both *The Chickencoop Chinaman* and *Aiiieeeee!*—that is, the maintenance of Chinese Americans' invisibility by subsuming them to an ancestral culture to which they relate only imaginatively. The absurdity of such cultural erasure is further problematized in the play through Fred's painful realization that he is actually the biological son of China Mama, a fact that the latter insists Fred recognize by bringing him food and offering to wash his feet. Chin's portrayal of a culturally alien Chinese mother invading a Chinese American family should not be read too readily as a simple reflection of the playwright's anti-immigrant attitude or his motivated antagonism toward women; rather, it can be more profitably investigated as the playwright's peculiarly strategized critique of the superficiality of the majority culture's assumptions about Chinese Americans' cultural identity, as well as of his cynical resistance to the pervasive cultural dichotomy that effectively prevents Asian Americans from either conceptualizing their subjectivity or articulating their difference.

It should also be pointed out that Fred's rejection of China Mama is not without its global, geopolitical connotations, particularly in view of the implications of the normalization of U.S.-China relations in the era, which was marked initially by unofficial "Ping-Pong diplomacy" in 1971 and then by a visit to China by President Richard Nixon in 1972. This revival of interest between the United States and China, which would in due course lead to an official recognition of each other's political sovereignty, coincided with Chin's painful realization of the irresolvable duality in the Asian American cultural identity, as well as his bitter resentment about the majority culture's continued ignorance of the historical and cultural specificities of Chinese America. Chin's ambivalence is reflected in the play partly in his willful—and stereotypical—construction of a contemporary China Mama saturated with Confucian family ethics and partly in his polarized juxtaposition of Ross with China Mama as two powerful ideological forces that invidiously hail the cultural emergence of Chinese America. It is no accident that Chin cynically observed shortly before his second play was staged that "the Chinese-American, well, schizophrenia. That I'd been playing a kind of Ping Pong game, you know. Now I'm Chinese, now I'm American" (Nee and Nee 1973, 383). By parodying the dualistic cast of Western thinking, Chin's remark invokes Jameson's diagnosis of postmodernism as a "schizophrenic disjunction" ("écriture") in late capitalism, which mystifies the social consequences of its breakdown of the signifying chain, as well as of its displacement of historical affects with simulacral passivity and difference (1991, 26–31). Such a diagnosis constitutes an ironic but fitting structural embodiment of the Asian American social experience portrayed in Chin's play.

Chin's contrast of Chinese with Chinese American cultures is further highlighted in the play by Fred's remark: "Just because we're born here don't mean we're nobody and gotta go away to another language to talk. I think Chinatown Buck Buck Bagaw is beautiful" (116). The echo of the "language" that Tam celebrates in *The Chickencoop Chinaman* should not be ignored: the issue of Chinese American identity raised here does not merely contrast with Mattie's naive belief in the possibility of leaving Chinatown and becoming a "free" individual; it underscores the radical break that Chin proposes for his largely linguistic-cultural

construction of the ethnic identity from both Euro-American and Chinese traditions. The play is clearly very tough-minded about insisting that such splits are
not easily "negotiated." By including an alien China Mama and a patronizing
white liberal male in the dramatic exchange, Chin implicates the audience in
these two characters' positions; he reveals the absurdity of equating Chinese
Americans with the Chinese, and exposes the distortion of white America's osten-
sible "respect" for Chinese culture as a disguised assault on Chinese American
identity and history. Pa and China Mama's reunion in Chinatown in this sense
also constitutes an inverted critique of the marriage between Ross and Mattie:
both implicitly mock tourist perceptions of Chinese American culture. The play's
mainstream audience is framed by the dramatic structure as a body of naive
tourists who are forced to see the absurdity of "typical" tour-guide versions of Chinatown and Chinese Americans.

The tensions that have built up in Fred as a result of his repeated frustrations
with the effects of commercialized tourist constructions of Chinatown ultimately
sets him in direct confrontation with his father. The play reaches its climax when
Pa savagely slaps Fred across the face for insisting on being taken seriously as a
writer, for refusing to hear him deliver the New Year speech, for resisting playing
the role of dutiful son, and for denying his verdict of him as a failure (unlike other
sons of Chinatown businessmen who become doctors, lawyers, engineers). Fred's
open negation of the role that Pa has assigned him signals a loss of balance in
Fred's hitherto nimble verbal games, which have sustained his double performance and his precarious dialogue within the Eng family and with the viewers of
Chin's play. Pa's sudden death, as a result of his exertion in attacking Fred, ultimately provides the latter with a chance to voice his anger with the father whom
he has been "expecting . . . to die for so long" (86): "He's a flop! Couldn't even
make your stupid speech without hanging onto me, couldya? You flop! 'Mayor of
Chinatown' Flop" (140). Pa's death within the house is ironically accompanied by
the New Year celebrations on the street and by the voice of a tour guide announc-
ing the parade in a phony accent: "Lady gennuhmans . . . dere it's are! Dah
worl's famous, worl' longes' really Chinee Dragger inna wor'l Ache hunner feet
longs . . . dah boy runnings inna anna outta dragger feep it go dong dah strit
once a year" (141). The counterpoint here between Pa's death and the public display of the dragon for Chinatown tourists underscores the profound irony of how
the Chinese Americans' suffering as a result of the social and psychological consequences of their position remains hidden behind the glamorous tourist facade.

At one point, seeing no way out of the contradictory world of Chinatown, Fred
advises his younger brother to marry a white woman and leave the community for
good (123). Even he himself thinks of moving out before Pa dies because he is so
tired of telling the tourists stories about a Chinatown that is not there. But he
also recognizes, as he tells Mattie, that once out of Chinatown, "we'll become no-

body," but "here we're somebody" (116, 117). Rejecting his sister's strategy of dealing with Chinatown by flight from its decay, Fred hints that he has to find a way to "protect" himself from the influence of Mattie's example and from the family's expectations for him. Fred's positioning here extends to his role as a writer and constitutes Chin's major negotiating strategy with regard to his notion of the Asian American artist. Realizing that "no one gonna read the great Chinese American novel," Fred has announced, tongue in cheek, that "I'm going to write the great Chinese American Cookbook" because, as he adds ironically, "food's our only common language" (83, 85). In this playful exchange with Mattie, the cookbook becomes a mock figure for "a new literary form" for Chinese Americans. The fact is that Fred rejects both the role of writing what he calls "food pornography" and the role of Chinatown tour guide (86)—both equivalents to the Chinese food business. What he tries to do instead is to live in Chinatown without lying about it; to negate mainstream culture's deceptive views of Chinatown with his angry "Buck Buck Bagaw" without losing sight of Chinatown's internal contradictions. With Pa's death, the Chinatown Eng family formally disintegrates, while Fred angrily claims his Chinatown "home" in all its contradictory ugliness and ambiguous relation to a mainstream culture which is imaged at the end as spitting drool in which Chinatown's inhabitants must swim.

The ending of the play projects a very uncertain future for Chin's artist figure, whose painful balance between his urge to fill in the gap left by the makeup of his own subjectivity and his repeatedly deferred entry into conscious performance of that urge is constantly displaced by his increasing psychological tendency toward stasis, implicitly the result of capitalist culture's structural essentialization of Chinatown according to the principles of commodity production and orientalism. One of Johnny's remarks to his brother during the last scene of act 2 seems to capture Fred's raw awareness of the dilemmas facing him: "You're the one told me . . . living in Chinatown's an art, man. Well, dig it, punk, I'm an artist" (130). The angry and agonized Fred, whose cynicism is deliberately couched in hipster talk, black humor, and rhetorical overkill, suggests an artist who is trying to find his own discourse in a place where no shared language is provided and where only a cultural space defined by contradiction is available as a site from which to speak. A central strategy of Chin's dramatization of the nature of his male protagonist's inner struggle involves Fred's capacity to reveal the multiple tensions that actively shape the double self of the Asian American artist-in-the-making: the dominant values of the community, the family, the "tourist" audience, and the publishing market that buys only what does not disturb mainstream assumptions. And the play's structure forces the audience to hear and experience Fred's contradictory voices, and to face the merging of them in the final scene. Such doubleness in the play must have been particularly disturbing to the mainstream audience of the 1974 opening of Chin's play off-Broadway in New York, because it both invaded their evaluative systems and required them to enter the ironic world of the stage without a secure frame of reference. In a sense, Fred's contradictory voices at the end of the play are a logical outcome of what Chin perceives to be the burden of representation on the artist of the Asian American "dual personality" defined by the commercial culture: the character angrily expresses the brew of contradictions and anguish that are ordinarily hidden to make the differential "tour guide" voice palpable to the mainstream.

The problems faced by such an artist are obviously as much personal and cultural as they are intellectual and social. Chin's portrayal of Fred as an artist bound by multiple contradictions in his cultural and historical situation but refusing to admit defeat clearly establishes a contrast, as he argues in *Aiiieeeee!,* to a recent generation of Asian American writers who tend to ignore such problems and consciously or unconsciously engage in what he sees as a devastating cultural sellout of Asian American identity. Such writers are satirized in Chin's characterization of Mattie as a performing collaborator in the play—as opposed to Fred as a self-consciously subversive performer—and named by the editors of *Aiiieeeee!* in their attacks on Jade Snow Wong, Virginia Lee, and Betty Lee Sung (Chin et al. 1974, xxii–xxiv, xxviii–xxxi).[13] A common characteristic of these writers, the editors assert, is that they perpetuate the stereotypical image of Chinatowns and Chinese Americans according to the concept of the dual personality. The editors conclude that this false view of dual personality explains not only Asian Americans' lack of political presence in American society, but also the commercial success of Asian American literary discourse that is complicit with white culture. Chin and his fellow editors claim that these writers accept the dominant culture's rules, discourse, and frames of reference—a position that gives up any possibility of "bargaining" that demystifies the dominant culture's hegemony or demands acknowledgment of Asian American vision in the process of the exchange. The seriousness with which Chin assesses the situation faced by Asian American writers clearly reflects his sensitivity to the realities concealed by the evolution of the Chinese American "model minority" image in American popular culture up until the early 1970s, and his calculated selection of that historical moment for strategic intervention. But his blanket attack on the Asian American writers he considers "assimilationist" also indicates his rejection of a range of less contestatory positions, a rejection that once again testifies to the radicality and moral urgency of his theatrical enunciation, while it points toward the problems inherent in his attempt to regulate and control the oppositional energy he helps to vitalize through his plays.

Audience and the Politics of Negation

In *The Chickencoop Chinaman* and *The Year of the Dragon,* Chin explores representational strategies that disrupt dominant codes of meaning through a type of cultural engagement that is intense, argumentative, and self-consciously ironic. Such strategies, especially in the voices of his protagonists, express at the formal level the raw vigor, toughness, pain, and masculinity that Chin believes should characterize Asian America's resistance to the linguistic homogenization and cultural deformation of a distinct Chinese American experience that he tries to legitimize. If mainstream drama tends to assert formal control over the eruptive desires for social change that it represents in its conflicts, Chin's off-Broadway and San Francisco productions were interventions into a form of history production that had never before included the work of an angry Asian American playwright. These plays in this sense also express the author's demand for cultural space from American theater and other hegemonic institutions that had heretofore refused to acknowledge the existence of Asian American artists, expression, and history. But the significance of Chin's theatrical experiments derives not so much from its attempt to construct alternative dramatic conventions as from its questioning of the existing process of meaning production through invoking a repertoire of insurrectionary politics associated with the dramatic genre. At the same time, the plays' dramatization of a suppressed yet living form of "Asian American myth" marked by participation in the opening of the American West and heroic feats of railroad construction constitutes Chin's aggressive (though not unproblematic) engagement with the American canon in its own terms and his affirmation of Asian Americans' contribution to laying the material and cultural foundations of the United States. Part of Chin's efforts in this period, as I noted earlier in this chapter, were directed toward recovery of Asian American literary writings that had been lost, ignored, or misclassified, or had gone out of print, writings that include Bulosan's *America Is in the Heart,* Diana Chang's *Frontiers of Love,* Okada's *No-No Boy,* and Chu's *Eat a Bowl of Tea,* all of which, as I have argued, accumulatively, though nonteleologically, exposed the sociopolitical conditions that Chin's artist-protagonists probe in their angry "Buck Buck Bagaw" and that his theatrical discourse richly explores.

The vision that emerges from Chin's theatrical discourse is not predictable or uniform—it does not equate rhetorical desire with political efficacy or promote Asian American counterimages according to rigid representational types. On the contrary, Chin's plays register multiple forces at work and engage complex operations of doubling. One issue of representation that poses a particular challenge to Chin in this process is how to convince the viewers of his plays of the limitations of conventional cultural perceptions of Asian Americans as foreign while at the same time suggesting to them, at least with some degree of clarity and coherence, that the Asian American counterimages he has created in their place are viable cultural options. The paradox here is that Chin's ridiculing of cultural stereotypes and his forcing into view what mainstream cultural representations ignore depends simultaneously on his unintentional visual preservation of the cultural other[14] and his deliberate construction of opaque and inarticulate Asian American subjects—strategies that intentionally simulate for his audience Asian America's sheer inaccessibility to history. Aware of the contradictions in fashioning an effective, one-directional oppositional strategy, Chin makes a characteristic postmodern move by multiplying both the sites of cultural disruption and the number of Asian American images and voices in his plays in order to display the multiple sources of his artist figure's plight. Chin's self-conscious use of a strategy of "disruptive complicity" (Federman 1988, 1156) through cross-cultural ventriloquism and role playing in his theatrical participation in the social movements of the era thus makes his plays multiply performative. Indeed, the discontinuous point of view of the plays and their hybridization of binary opposites discourage any coherent grasp of the protagonists' subjectivity and prevent the audience from identifying with any one subject position as fully valid or meaningful. The crude, highly self-contradictory voices of the protagonists in these two plays thus testify to the complexity of the playwright's positioning toward Asian American history and identity that he at once constructs and problematizes.

Reviewers' initial response to Chin's plays took the form of a mixture of admiration and revulsion. One mainstream reviewer of *The Chickencoop Chinaman* found Chin to be a "natural writer: his language has the beat and brass, the runs and rim-shots of Jazz." Another thought that "a Chinaman [who] was 'loud, violent, sexually aggressive' was imitating blacks because 'loud, violent, sexually aggressive' was stuff that really stunned most Chinese." A Chinese American writer commented on a performance of *The Year of the Dragon:* "It was an outpouring of bitterness and hatred mouthed through lengthy monologue after monologue. Not that it was Randy Kim's fault [the lead actor] but it was Frank Chin showing through" (quoted in McDonald 1981, xiv–xv). Such confusion about the meaning of Chin's plays, I would suggest, reveals several issues regarding the tactical implications of the confrontation-bargaining process that Chin initiates through his openly combative theatrical work. First, although Chin's rowdy defiance of the conventional cultural treatment of Asian Americans by the mainstream is morally sound, the amount of aggressiveness with which he directs such defiance against the audiences for his plays in the early 1970s and the self-questioning responses he constantly demands of them reveal Chin's problematic attribution to the audience of his plays of an ideally participatory and politically homogenized spectatorship. In positioning his audience as uniformly ignorant and uninitiated, Chin apparently confused contemporary theatergoers more than he prepared the ground for their conversion. The various reviewers' responses to Chin's plays indicate that there was still no socially recognized grammar or vocabulary for decoding the cultural and ideological symbols introduced by his plays. Although Chin idealistically constructs historical meaning in his plays as natural and demands that mainstream society recognize that its own views of Asian American history are false, his obliquely recoded signs of the Kwan tradition and Chinese American history

are not explicitly connected to the social and political context of his plays' signification. As a result, the meaning of his angry protest and privatized adoption and
revision of cultural symbols was apparently lost on a significant portion of his audiences, perhaps because the arbitrariness of an ideologically revised relationship
between signifier and signifieds demands simultaneous and willing adjustments
of conceptual distinctions, adjustments that may be possible for close readers but
beyond the power of theatergoers experiencing a performance like this for the first
time.

Second, the poor runs of Chin's plays in their first productions raises the question of how dissenting Asian American voices can deal with the complex entan-
glements of established literary forms with various affiliative or oppositional constraints, with the tactical limitations of waging wars only on the basis of a
self-conscious attempt to be counterhegemonic, and with the practical problems
of how meaning can be effectively communicated to audiences who do not necessarily share the same assumptions. Chin's response to these contingencies is
marked by the tendency toward didacticism in his theatrical art, despite his apparent openness to certain aspects of postmodern experiments. Such a tendency is
exemplified in the playwright's repeated expression in *The Chickencoop Chinaman*
and *The Year of the Dragon* of mistrust of positions taken by commercially successful Asian American writers, an attitude that frequently gives rise to charges
against Chin of moral policing or even cultural tyranny. In light of my analysis of
the historical specificity of the plays' production, I would suggest that Chin's
polemical attacks on "inauthentic" Asian American creative activities were primarily motivated not by those impulses but rather by his refusal to abandon
"truth." In other words, he insists on giving his audiences a concrete idea of what
is "true" and what is "false" about Asian American identity and on ensuring that
they not mistake one for the other. But Chin's efforts to (re)construct audience attitudes are made with such arbitrariness and hostility toward what he distrusts
that his artist protagonist, a personification of Chin's own theatrical style, characteristically ends up like a tragic Faust figure: he exhausts himself in the impossible task of shaping the public perspective on Asian America according to his
ideals; he forces the audiences of his plays to ideological and emotional extremes
by relentlessly confronting them with the plays' unresolved contradictions; and,
because of his intense negativity, he draws attention from his artistic production
to his own moral self.[15]

Postmodernist Theatrical Art

In his 1986 essay "Ethnicity and Post-Modern Arts of Memory," Michael Fischer
suggests that Chin's early literary work exemplifies postmodern modes of repre-

sentation and finds that the following "modalities of postmodernist knowledge" figure especially prominently: "transference, dream-translation, talk-story, multiple voices and perspectives, and highlighting of humorous inversions and dialectical juxtaposition of identities/traditions/cultures, and the critique of hegemonic discourses" (202). While Chin uses all these techniques in his plays, the association Fischer makes raises questions that seem to go beyond the conceptual framework within which he defines and applies postmodernism to the analysis of Asian American literary works. For example, in framing postmodernism largely in terms of styles, Fischer invokes but does not explain the entangled relationship between modernist and postmodernist aesthetics, while in emphasizing the representational power of indeterminacy and fragmentation in Chin's minority literary practice, he touches on but somehow evades a crucial distinction between postmodernism as a form of artistic expression and postmodernism as a social condition in America's late capitalist culture.[16]

The latter condition has received provocative analyses by commentators such as Stuart Hall (1986), Cornel West (1987), bell hooks (1990, 23–31), José David Saldívar (1990), and Phillip Brian Harper (1994), who, despite their different intellectual positions and critical assumptions about postmodernism, all emphasize the need to resist imagining the fate of people of color by replicating simulacral heterogeneity, the need to draw out the socioeconomic dimensions of any particular postmodernist aesthetic, and the need to redeploy postmodernist politics through reworking its basic assumptions and categories.[17] Although these efforts to contextualize postmodernism have obviously shaped my own analysis of Chin's plays in this chapter, they are relatively silent about the aesthetic issue evoked by Fischer. A careful examination of this issue, I would suggest, is essential to understanding the specific political location of Chin's theatrical art, a location that is deeply implicated in early American literary postmodernism's shifting concerns and changing frames of reference.

According to Paul Bové (1995, 4–9) and Patricia Waugh (1992, 4–5), one significant historical moment in which to locate the critical formulation of American literary postmodernism is an aesthetic debate in the United States in the late 1950s and the early 1960s. In this period a new generation of American writers set out to define, against their differing artistic and political persuasions, the existence of a literary mode of "replenishment" (Barth) characterized by sensuous immediacy, discursive proliferation, parataxis, or multiperspectivism.[18] An important rationale that critics have advanced for such literary experimentation is that, as an art of surface, it was the era's reaction against modernism's complicity with consumer capitalism in its evoking a "negative liberty" for artistic freedom (Jay 1984, 122–31). Such "negative liberty"—emblematized in the modernist defiance of commercial culture through surrealist techniques of fragmentation and unexpected juxtaposition—ironically fetishized objects in a way that stimulated, rather than subverted, capitalist consumerist desires (McGowan 1991, 11). "Post-modernist" artistic form, in making itself opaque and resistant to interpretation through its effective silence, then refused consumption, even as it partook of a culture of consumerism (Waugh 1992, 4). Within this context, postmodernist art is seen as contesting capitalist commercialism in areas where the system is found most actively operating on the deformation of culture (Baudrillard 1983, 41–43). But since early American literary postmodernism relied on the archive of its own time for intellectual, imaginative, and political inspiration (Bové 1995, 4–5), it established itself mainly through a reversal or rearrangement of the high-modernist reification of unified art while adopting a similar set of linguistic strategies and philosophical positions (North 1994, 32–33, 208). The political power of early American postmodernist literature thus lies mainly in its subver-sive appropriation of late modernist aesthetic assumptions, as well as in its self-conscious reengagement with the issue of social morality through the act of "writ-ing," of "narration," and of "composition" (Federman 1988, 1143).

Such a view of postmodernism has drastically changed since the early 1980s, when American literary postmodernists began to draw on insights from French theorists. (Note that Jameson's "Postmodernism and Consumer Society" was pub-lished in 1983; Lyotard's 1979 *The Postmodern Condition* became available in En-glish in 1984.) Thus Waugh observes, obviously in reference to a Jamesonian view of the postmodern:

> "Postmodernism" now expresses the sense of a new cultural epoch in which distinctions between critical and functional knowledge break down as capi-talism, in its latest consumerist phase, invades everything including the aes-thetic, the post-colonial world and the unconscious . . . leaving no re-maining oppositional space. At this point, the term becomes inflected with a kaleidoscope of meanings drawn from those human sciences variously en-gaged in the production of a theoretical palimpsest where the specific *aes-thetic* origins of the term are almost entirely obscured. (1992, 5–6)

Along with this theoretical shift away from an emphasis on the aesthetic, the critical discourse of postmodernism has expanded, often in a totalizing fashion, both the terms and the scope of its earlier concerns to wider social and political domains. Such an expansion characteristically involves a more thorough critique of the assumptions of the Enlightenment and its "grand narrative" (Lyotard 1984, xxiii) and a greater awareness of the speaking subject's being "within a way of thinking," a condition that disallows "the comfort of absolutely naming the terms" of the subject's overdetermined existence (Marshall 1992, 3). In a sense, recent conceptualizations of postmodernism differ from its earlier versions in their marked rejection of the residual humanistic visions which their predecessors in-herited from modernism, and in their heightened cynicism and relativism toward the capacity of human agency to act historically and to effect real social change within America's late capitalist culture.

In light of this briefly drawn trajectory of the shifting contexts and the evolving concerns of American conceptualizations of postmodernism, I wish to register several caveats about discussing Chin's work in relation to the term. First, as the foregoing examination suggests, "postmodernism" signifies not one but several positions and functions: a practice of aesthetic styles, a theoretical discourse, a way of talking about popular cultural forms, and a variously defined historical condition, with each connected to but different from another. Absolutely positing one dimension of postmodernism against the perspective of another leads to omissions of important constituent details of the "postmodern" features in Asian American texts such as Chin's plays. Second, the recent theoretical rearticulation of postmodernism, including some of its materialist reformulations, contains one paradoxical tendency—its relegation, as Bové points out, of the literary to a marginal status—which makes much careful study of literature today suspicious of "cultural conservatism" or of "reactionary effort to reestablish literature's old ideological privilege and academic position" (1995, 3). This tendency, as I will argue in the closing chapter of this study, inappropriately downplays both the need and the difficulty of working through and winning control over aesthetic modalities from America's late capitalist culture, while simplifying both the nature and range of cultural critique. Third, Chin's plays, if seen as "postmodernist" in technique, necessarily belong to an early phase of the phenomenon, a phase in which postmodernist works tend to exhibit both a greater degree of overlap with late modernist concerns and a lesser degree of the theoretical self-consciousness characteristic of recent postmodernist developments. In light of my analysis in this chapter, the postmodern experimentalism in Chin's plays might best be seen as the product of a writer who oscillates between modernist and postmodernist affiliations within an increasingly postmodern Western culture, one marked by a new phase in commodity fetishism, a profusion of subcultural styles, the emergence of a plurality of power and/or discourse formations, and a generalized recognition of but insensitivity to race, gender, class, and other local differences.[19] From this perspective, the shared stylistic features that Fischer identifies between Chin's work and existing definitions of postmodernist art do not affirm the universality of canonical postmodernism but rather instance how the limits of any given postmodern theory are disclosed by its encounter with particular examples of Asian American experimental works.

Overall, the readings in this chapter suggest that Chin's plays occupy an aesthetic location that at once registers modernist and postmodernist concerns, and resists absolute divisions or oppositions between them. As we have seen, Chin's theater offers a space where competing ideological tendencies and diverse social and cultural accents are allowed to interact or clash, its in-betweenness and open-endedness explicitly disruptive of the "closed circuits" of traditional dramatic representation premised on the notion of a self-sufficient text. The permeability between Chin's theatrical operation and the live social issues it actively signifies works to disrupt—particularly through the plays' "vulgarized" use of language and cultural codes—the modernist tendency to separate the aesthetic from the social, the high from the low, and the act of cultural consumption from that of its production. By the same token, the plays' awareness of the social and economic consequences of how dominant linguistic and cultural conventions speak for Asian America can also be seen as the playwright's active engagement with the discursive power of discourses on racial, sexual, and cultural marginalization, as opposed to the early modernist preoccupation with the crisis of language per se.[20] At the same time, Chin's engagement is essentially motivated by a conscious search for suppressed forms of knowledge about Asian America's past, a search that contrasts significantly with the familiar postmodern critique of origins as well as with its characteristic lament for a total loss of the oppositional space in late capitalism. Also illustrative of the ambivalent aesthetics of Chin's theater is the role that he assigns both to art and to the artist figure: by presupposing the effectiveness of an oppositional use of the theater and an agonistic persona, Chin departs from postmodernism's general skepticism about the transformative and critical power of art, as well as from its implicit acceptance of the self-consciously dissolving subject, whose meaning can be understood only through the overdetermination of ideologies or discourses.

With regard to Chin's artist figure especially, this character, as we have seen, is fully comprehensive of the nature of Asian Americans' social predicament and alert to the pitfalls underlying their seeming social acceptance, a consciousness vividly displayed in his anxiety, pain, and cynicism. Unable to act in the face of the paralyzing effect of his existential dilemma, he resorts to shocking his auditors through unconventional representational strategies, but without abandoning a desire to construct a unified individual identity against overwhelming adversities. What gets foregrounded through such resistance is what John McGowan calls "the primacy of the will" (1991, 11), a legacy from high romanticism which, I would suggest, is implicitly embodied in Chin's notion of "Asian American cultural integrity." In emphasizing the autonomous self and its ability to maintain moral heroism in the face of irresolvable social contradictions, this dimension of Chin's artist figure quintessentially emblematizes the playwright's commitment to the humanist assumptions associated with modernism. Such a commitment also underlies this artist figure's adamant resistance to any perceived threat of political "merger" (Hebdige 1993, 75)—a seemingly postmodern gesture toward open-endedness—which, as I have shown in my textual analysis, turns out to be an individualistic stance that at once denies totalization and demands uniformity. Indeed, in his insistence on the undesirability of internal fragmentation of Asian American political forces at the historical juncture of his plays' production and in his simultaneous underestimation of the particularities of the diverse voices suppressed by such insistence, Chin obviously redeploys modernist politics in a changed social context. At the same time, his deliberate, and often instinctive, reaction against the ideological power and the ahistoricism of the dominant literary and cultural practices of his time also shows both his receptivity and his creative contribution to the force of an evolving American postmodernist cultural critique.

In short, Chin's plays are neither unambiguously modernist nor explicitly postmodernist in general senses of the term. Rather, they exhibit signs of conscious or unconscious negotiations with these positions and tactical or pragmatic crossing of their shifting, inadequately defined—and often undefinable—boundaries. It is amidst such movements between modern and postmodern spaces that Chin provocatively split what was Asian America's discursive present in the early 1970s through the performativity of his drama, an approach that deconstructed the authority of given representations of Asian America and pointed to alternative relational positions.

The alternative position that Chin's plays opened was clearly unintentional. In particular, his theatrical works were received with ambivalence within the ethnic community that he aimed to mobilize, especially by women who were repelled by his boisterous male self-representation predicated on sexist assumptions. Women readers in the community became increasingly disturbed by Chin's attribution of the absence of Chinese American history, identity, and language in American culture to a femininizing displacement of the masculine center, a view that leads the playwright to an obsessive construction of the male subject as the only possible site for reinscribing Asian Americans in the nation's historical consciousness. Chin's ready use of women, as one critic complains, as "foils for tough-talking males" in his plays (Sucheng Chan 1991, 184) constitutes a dramatic illustration of the "remarkable oversight" about women in early postmodernist critiques of totalization in general (Lacan 1982, 87) and in Chin's literary representation in particular.[21] Indeed, despite Chin's best efforts to avoid any transcendent positioning of his subject, the critical hermeneutic of his plays remains partially enveloped in an ideological and highly gendered meta-narrative. As a consequence, his theatrical problematization of racial inequality has failed to enlist many of the potential allies from the community for which he tried to speak. Instead, it has triggered intense, unpredictable debates within that community over the issue of women's agency eclipsed in his skewed theatrical enunciation.

Homi Bhabha observes: "Once you release into the present of any culture this kind of agonistic, differential moment, then really it opens up an endless possibility for different conjugations of time and space and meaning—different uses of symbology, different kinds of social metaphor, different practices"—because those suppressed differences occupy exactly the same cultural space of the pronounced adjuration and articulation (1990b, 84). Robert Stam similarly points out: "Social diversity is fundamental to every utterance, even to that utterance which on the surface ignores or excludes the groups with which it is in relation. All utterances take place against the background of the possible responding utterances of other social points of view" (1988, 130). As we shall see in the next chapter, Chin's assertion of "Asian American cultural integrity" through a tough-talking male voice and his unintentional reproduction of male domination within the community paradoxically became an obstacle and an invitation to Asian American women's rearticulations of their differences on their own terms. Such female reinscription of gender differences, which culminated in the 1976 publication of Maxine Hong Kingston's autobiography, *The Woman Warrior,* signals a dialectical relocation of the Asian American subject constructed by Chin.

Finally, the interdependent relationship between Chin's male-oriented theatrical protest against cultural domination and Asian American women's resistance to the continued suppression of their voices from within and across an emergent Asian American literary discourse highlights both the strategic and practical value of what Stuart Hall calls "arbitrary closure," a dialogic process that, according to Hall, inheres in many counterhegemonic practices. In using the term, Hall suggests that a radical, one-sided assertion of cultural difference in a hegemonic process is often knowingly or unknowingly constructed by underrepresented, marginalized groups as communicative closure because, by constructing the former's limitations as natural and permanent, the latter can justify counterstrategies for overcoming their disadvantageous situation in a radically oppositional fashion. Yet because the former's arbitrary assertion of power is exposed to the infinite semiosis of sociocultural processes, Hall further observes, the meaning it suppresses cannot be effectively sealed off. Rather, the dialogic process continues to unfold not only beyond arbitrarily installed boundaries but also in defiance of any rationally conceived goals of struggle implicitly aimed at by the former (1990/1994, 397). Despite its "remarkable oversight" about women and its polemical efforts to confine "Asian American cultural integrity," Chin's use of the theater remains viable and productive, its significations open to heterogeneous possibilities, as well as to ideological revision, rearticulation, and rearrangement.

5

Maxine Hong Kingston's Remapping of Asian American Historical Imagination in *China Men*

To name it now so as not to repeat history in oblivion. To extract each fragment by each fragment from the word from the image another word another image the reply that will not repeat history in oblivion.

—Theresa Hak Kyung Cha, *Dictée*

The reason why the issue of 'female emancipation' seems to disappear from all the public agenda of nationalist agitation . . . is not because it was overtaken by the more emotive issue concerning political power. Rather, the reason is in the refusal of nationalism to make the women's question an issue of negotiation . . .

—Partha Chatterjee, *The Nation and Its Fragments*

In this chapter I examine Maxine Hong Kingston's 1980 work of nonfiction *China Men* in relation to the controversies that surrounded the production and reception of her 1976 autobiography, *The Woman Warrior*. Within this ground of inquiry, I see *China Men* as Kingston's implicit response to the consequences of her first book's exertion of ideological difference both in mainstream culture and in Asian American literary discourse of the mid-1970s. My reading of *China Men* stands in tension with two existing assessments of the book's significance: that it signals an act of retribution and compensation for the suffering experienced by early Chinese male immigrant laborers, suffering Kingston valorizes through her portrayal of their tragically heroic feats (e.g., Sledge 1980; Kim 1982, 207–13; Wang 1988); and that it reflects the author's balanced treatment of Asian American men's and women's causes through its simultaneous critique of racism in American society and the sexism in the Chinese immigrant community (e.g., Li 1990; Goellnicht 1992, 194, 205). The difference between my position and these assessments is partly determined by the analytical framework I use to interpret *China Men*. But it also stems from my attempt to avoid an overemphasis on Kingston's famous 1980 remark about her purpose in writing *China Men,* an overemphasis that characterizes most prior assessments of her work. In that remark, Kingston says:

> What I am doing in this new book is claiming America. . . . That seems to be the common strain that runs through all the characters. In story after story Chinese American people are claiming America, which goes all the way from one character saying that a Chinese explorer found this place before Leif Ericson did to another one buying a house here. Buying that house is a way of saying that America—and not China—is his country. (Pfaff 1980, 1, quoted in Kim 1982, 209)

The problem of reading *China Men* through the lens of this assertion lies not so much in the kinds of hermeneutic results yielded by the process as in their underlying assumption that the meaning of Kingston's 1980 work bears a full contractual relationship with the author's publicly—and thus rhetorically—declared goals for her artistic creation.[1] This assumption, I argue, can interpretively reduce the web of social and cultural forces through which *China Men* is shaped and articulated to an authorial agenda little troubled by the contradictions and unevenness of the book's production. Not heeding such contingent elements, Linda Ching Sledge sees *China Men* as "an overwhelming heroic account of sojourner family life" (1980, 13), while Donald Goellnicht regards Kingston's approach in *China Men* as an unambiguous "act of reconciliation" and a "pure gift" to what father figures lack historically, despite his caution against reading off meanings associated with the book's contextual constraints (1992, 205).

My disagreement with such privileging of the correspondence between *China Men*'s textual articulation and its authorial intent forms the polemical basis of my analysis. Specifically, my examination posits two alternative views of the cultural work it attempts to enact: first, that it subverts, rather than gives credence to, the "claim on America" as a self-limiting impulse that simultaneously depends on and works to perpetuate a concealment of canonical history's erasure of Chinese male immigrant laborers' subjectivity; and second, that it extends, rather than totally or partially suspends, Kingston's project of critiquing masculine ideals in *The Woman Warrior*—a project I see as only half finished—in full recognition of the crisis of making such a critique within the temporality of Western modernity. Such a narrative purpose in *China Men* is achieved through Kingston's double displacement of two interrelated linear meta-narratives informing the Asian American identity politics of its era: that of Western historicism and that of a male-oriented Asian American nationalist imagination precariously (but only precariously) affiliated with its teleology. Recognizing these various levels of cultural and ideological negotiation at work in *China Men* is necessary for both understanding and reinstating the specificity of the book's historical vision, which is at once disruptive of given assumptions about history and resistant to fixation of excavated historical knowledge. In my view, *China Men* marks a uniquely self-reflexive moment in post–World War II Asian American literary history: it not only signifies upon various earlier and subsequent Asian American literary voices but also foregrounds a host of extant yet inadequately articulated issues that Asian American writers and critics would interrogate with greater critical energy and theoretical awareness during and after the mid-1980s, issues that include postnational and diasporic concerns.

The Debate over *The Woman Warrior*

The publication of Maxine Hong Kingston's autobiography *The Woman Warrior* in 1976 was a landmark phenomenon in postwar American literary history: the book self-consciously injected a dissenting Asian American feminist perspective into the largely male-dominated Asian American literary discourse; it enjoyed immediate commercial success with mainstream publishers and widespread institutional recognition; and, because of the book's ambivalent relationships with both the evolving Asian American social movement of the 1970s and a seemingly accommodating yet suspiciously "expansive" literary establishment capable of misappropriating the autobiography ideologically, it generated vigorous, uncompromising debates within Asian American communities with regard to the nature and social function of their literary practices in contemporary America.[2] Frank Chin, it is well known, has advanced perhaps the harshest critique of *The Woman Warrior*. In his various comments on Kingston's autobiography, Chin suggests that the book achieved its success mainly through the author's "selling out" of Asian American interests, either by misrepresenting Chinese culture as inherently "anti-individualistic" and thus morally inferior, or by caricaturing Chinese American males as "cruel" and "misogynistic" sexual perverts (e.g., 1985, 110, 130; Chan et al. 1991, 9, 27, 28). Numerous counterarguments have been made since the early 1980s that challenge Chin's critique of Kingston's book, his implicit attempt to impose a single standard on the polyphony of Asian American literary expression, and his insensitivity to the social and cultural inequalities suffered by Asian American women both historically and in their contemporary experience (e.g., Sledge 1980, 70; Sau-ling Wong 1988, 23–25; Cheung 1990; Kim 1990b, 75–80; Lim 1993, 576–78). Despite these and other efforts to direct attention to the historical specificity of Kingston's autobiography, the controversy has shown little sign of abating. For example, Chin has recently reaffirmed with undiminished seriousness his commitment to reviving a masculinist Asian

American heroic ideal, as well as his lack of sympathy for critical efforts to address gender inequality through both community activities and academic criticism (Chan et al. 1991, 7–8). At the same time, some Asian American feminist critics continue their impassioned exchange with Chin, mostly in reaction to the obviously simplistic aspects of his position, with the aid of analytical tools available from posthumanist discourses of the late 1980s and 1990s.

The hardening of Chin's stance toward *The Woman Warrior* is, without a doubt, an unfortunate turn of events. But the context of Chin's solidification of his attitude merits some critical attention for the simple reason that there is a difference between Chin's angry endorsement of ethnic essentialism and Asian masculine ideals through rhetoric, and the actual fulfillment of his declared goals in a material sense. In making such a distinction, however, I do not intend to sever the relationship between Chin's aversion to *The Woman Warrior* and the entrenched patriarchal thinking and practice in American society in general and in Asian American communities in particular. Nor do I wish to downplay the consequences of Chin's continued refusal to acknowledge the impact of women's contribution to the development of Asian American literary discourse from the 1940s to the present. On the contrary, as I have argued elsewhere, Chin's contestatory invocation of an Asian American masculine ideal as a corrective to the historical "emasculation" of Asian men in America is useful only when such a critique is capable of revealing how race, gender, class, and national identities are entwined in the construction of Asian men's sexuality in American culture and of self-consciously accepting its inevitable dissolution into more self-reflexive counter-hegemonic positions (1997, 318–19).

What I wish to suggest beyond the general agreement on the limitations of Chin's approach is that the hardening of his position has also been affected by a gradual shift of critical attention in the debate from the social and cultural forces that surround the feminist position in *The Woman Warrior* to Chin's uncompromising self. Such a shift clearly reflects Asian American critics' recognition of the overwhelming success of *The Woman Warrior* as a firmly established ethnic/feminist literary text in the American canon, a fact that makes Chin's polemical approach to the autobiography stand out even more negatively. But at the same time, this shift is accompanied by two problematic tendencies among Chin's critics after the autobiography's canonization both by the literary establishment and by the ethnic community: the first is to view the established analytical frameworks for reading the feminist message in *The Woman Warrior* as somehow definitive and the second is to reproduce discursively gained initial insights about the debate despite new developments that point toward the need to rethink the book's intertextual significance. As I suggested in the foregoing chapters of this book, Chin's suppression of Asian American women's voices is undeniable, but it is neither wholly intentional nor successful, and his unidimensional critique of racism and his narrow definition of Asian American identity in the 1970s promoted an oppositional consciousness that dialectically facilitated Asian American women's efforts to voice their concerns in their own terms. Such critical appropriations and revisions of Chin's oppositional strategy by Asian American women indicate that new social formations have taken place. If we recognize the substantive progress that has subsequently been made both in Asian American social life and in its academic discourses, then we should also agree that insistence on using some of the obviously thoughtlessly articulated aspects of *Aiiieeeee!*'s and *The Big Aiiieeeee!*'s positions as the only point of reference to advance new arguments about gender becomes inadequate in itself. For such an approach continually elides the immediate political contexts of the publication and reception of *The Woman Warrior,* including those of Chin's and his critics' engagement with one another; it makes Asian American critical practice less demanding by reproducing only the familiar and the predictable; and it turns the Asian American critical gaze away from sites where emerging problematics in ethnic critical practice demand new and creative answers.

In the analysis that follows, I examine some of the ideological complexities that have been neglected in prior analyses of the reception of *The Woman Warrior* through a recontextualization of the debate. My contention is that the controversy does not have to be seen as a purely negative turn of events. As a terrain where vital issues concerning Asian American subject formation were contested and negotiated, it has also served as a necessary precondition for renewed transformative articulations in Asian American literary creation and criticism.

Most discussions of the debate have so far focused on the limitations of Chin's view that the literary establishment's misappropriation and adoption of *The Woman Warrior* for its own purposes reflect nothing but the motivated urge for assimilation on the part of Kingston. It is equally problematic, I would add, to regard Asian American male writers' and critics' negative responses to the autobiography's canonization as merely sexist reactions against Asian American women's artistic freedom or as manifestations of an implicit male desire to maintain control over women. Rather, these varying responses need to be viewed as illustrations of how the articulation of Chinese American women's oppression is caught up with that of Chinese American men's, and how the reception of *The Woman Warrior* reflects both the epistemological and the ontological difficulties posed for a woman writer of color, whose ability to speak—and whose chance to be heard—was severely limited by given racial, gender, and class power structures. Chin's negativity toward *The Woman Warrior,* as critics point out, arises partly from his failure to see the entanglement of the socioeconomic oppression of Asian men in America with their own cultural oppression in terms of sexism (Cheung 1990, 234–36; Kim 1990b, 75–79). When Asian American women seek to expose anti-female prejudices in their own ethnic community, he and others not illogically feel "betrayed" by attacks that appeared to line up with the majority culture's positions. As is also well known, from the mid-1950s until the publication of *The Woman Warrior* in 1976, most writings by Chinese American women did not feature explicit critiques of racism and sexism in American society.[3] The overtly oppositional literature produced by Chinese American male writers such as Chin in the early 1970s strategically raised Asian America's angry voice publicly, a development of Asian American cultural identity congruent with and partly shaped by the black protest and counterculture movements of the era. If this emergent Asian American sensibility was at a fledgling or, in the words of the editors of *Aiiieeeee!*, "delicate" stage (Chin et al. 1974, ix), it was also little informed by Asian American women's urgent social demand for gender equality. With the publication of *The Woman Warrior*, Kingston virtually started a revolution within a revolution.[4] Shortly after the formation of a narrowly defined counterhegemonic Asian American literary discourse represented by Chin and other editors of *Aiiieeeee!*, Kingston's Chinese American feminist discourse defiantly branched out from the largely community-based Asian American literary revival and drew support from the mainstream feminist movement. This formative moment created a context ripe for perceived betrayal. More important, it revealed the complex internal and external constraints on these almost simultaneously emergent, unavoidably conflictual, yet ideologically interdependent discourses within a restrictive cross-cultural space of self-representation.

As a product of this historical moment, Kingston's articulation of oppressed Chinese American women's voices in their male-dominated community could scarcely have been free from reactive impulses, and it was understandably done without full control over how it might intersect with the social construction of gender and sexual politics at a time when the social history of Chinese American women's oppression was largely ignored. In an era in which practitioners of a male-oriented Asian American literary discourse saw it as a newborn vehicle for cultural identity and worked hard to cultivate a sense of ethnic pride and solidarity, a previously submerged Chinese American feminist discourse challenged the sexism in Asian American communities in striving to make its voice heard and to subvert established gender hierarchies. In fact, Kingston was quite sensitive to the cultural risk and the multivalent nature of her injection of a Chinese American woman's voice into a discourse characterized by a male ethos. Immediately after the publication of *The Woman Warrior*, for example, she recognized that her book "was one of only heroines. Men are minor characters. It seems an unbalanced view of the world" (quoted in Taylor 1976, B1). On another occasion, Kingston reflected that although she intended to write about women's and men's experiences as an "interlocking story," because of her fear that the men's story was "anti-female and would undercut the feminist viewpoint," she decided to write about women's issues "separately" in *The Woman Warrior*—her "selfish book" (quoted in Kim 1982, 207–8). Kingston's concerns here obviously were not unique to her own position of enunciation but would be shared by other women writers of color in an era when women's claim on the ethnic community's interests, as Elaine Kim persuasively argues, became inseparable from their claim on female self and subjectivity and when women's interpretation of their own experiences as women could hardly be made without simultaneously "airing the 'dirty laundry'" (1990b, 78, 81).

It is against the historical background of such an emotionally and ideologically charged moment of cultural emergence that we can better understand, for example, Kingston's using in *The Woman Warrior* of "the female *I*" in Chinese culture as an interchangeable word for "slave" in English (1976, 47). Unsuspecting critics tend to read Kingston's reference in strictly anthropological or sociological terms in order to affirm her feminist position in *The Woman Warrior.* Yet a cross-cultural reader may recognize that Kingston's usage is in fact her literal translation, as well as her deliberate misappropriation, of a gender-inflected Chinese female self-reference used among dynastic ruling classes to acknowledge status (奴 meaning "my humble self") into the English word "slave" (which corresponds to a different Chinese word 奴隶).[5] Such an appropriation of the Chinese language by Kingston seems to have derived its rhetorical force from two interrelated cultural contexts: first, it echoed an important argument made by "mainstream" American feminists in the late 1960s and early 1970s for consciousness-raising— that is, women's oppression is a form of enslavement—an argument that emphasized the moral urgency of women's liberation through evoking scenarios of American slavery.[6] Second, it was entwined with the deep-rooted orientalist assumptions about "Chinese despotism" in American popular imagination, assumptions·that, within the context of Kingston's deployment of the analogy, problematically designated Chinese culture as the ultimate source of women's oppression. Kingston's cultural appropriation thus conveyed a mixed message: on the one hand, it effectively differentiated and enhanced Chinese American women's plight by appealing to existing systems of Western knowledge; on the other, it partially decontextualized her critiques of partiarchy by obscuring how the racial element in Chinese American women's social oppression was inextricably entangled with Chinese American men's. In my view, it is mainly against such an orientalized or dehistoricized dimension of Kingston's feminist critiques of Chinese American patriarchy that Chin and others direct their strong criticisms—criticisms that, unfortunately, are often made within unexamined patriarchal and even sexist frames of reference (I return to a discussion of the implications of Kingston's cultural strategies in Chapter 6).

As a consequence, Kingston's appropriation of the Chinese language in *The Woman Warrior* occasions, along with other similar strategies she uses in her book (e.g., the episode on the "No-Name Aunt"), the well-known rupture of her autobiography's discourse from that of other dissenting Asian American voices. Thus, the conflict between Chin's valorization of Asian American manhood and Kingston's inscription of the Chinese American woman warrior becomes illustrative of what Mae Henderson calls the "discursive dilemma" for the simultaneity of oppression and articulation of ethnic writers of both sexes (1989, 24–30), a dilemma characterized by these writers' manipulations of available cultural symbols, their different degrees of dependence on discourse reversal, and their conscious or unconscious misuse of self-affirming terminologies.[7] In fact, Chin admits when looking back at the era that "rhetoric[s] counted for a lot . . . [but they] were no substitutes for real knowledge" (quoted in Abe 1991, 3–4). Similarly, Kingston embraces images associated with "war" in writing *The Woman Warrior* despite her well-known stance against violent resolution to ideological differences. Evidently, the Asian American *man* and *woman* that were constructed in this era with an explicit purpose of disrupting the often unidimensionally perceived cultural domination remained problematic for both authors in their implicit suggestion of gender opposition as a permanent feature of Asian American social relations.

The Woman Warrior's rupture with some of its potential allies in the Asian American community along with its disruption of patriarchal domination is clearly historically contingent. On the one hand, the rupture reflects inevitable collisions and disruptions between and among various oppositional forces that simultaneously articulate submerged concerns from the same community; on the other, it calls into question romanticized views of individual Asian American writers' or critics' utterances at given moments of cultural formation as capable of merging harmoniously toward shared goals or of transcending irreconcilable ideological differences. The challenge that faced Kingston, one may speculate, was how to carry out the task of articulating Asian American women's concerns and still locate common grounds with Asian American men's interests, and how to strengthen rather than weaken an evolving Asian American cultural voice through women's interventionary moves that could at the same time also be culturally rigorous and politically constructive. In particular, Kingston seemed to realize that Asian American feminist discourse was faced with the need to determine where its interests overlap or contradict the interests of mainstream feminism, and how its inscription of Asian American feminist sensibility would affect its relationship with both the Asian American community and the predominantly Euro-American mainstream culture. But Kingston obviously also came to see, in view of the intense ideological contestations that surrounded the reception of *The Woman Warrior,* that a simple reconciliation of the exposed ideological complexities obviously would not be a solution; for it would cast in greater obscurity the fundamental issue she raised in her first book, an issue that had been effectively overshadowed by the community's heated debate over her appropriation of Chinese culture, that is, women's continued marginalization in a community whose project of social emancipation remains locked in masculinist assumptions. The question for Kingston then became a somewhat different one: how to continue her feminist endeavor without embracing a reductive and culturally problematic paradigm of gender difference and how to transform the community's debate over Asian American identity politics in ways that both reveal its epistemological limitations and open themselves to greater interventionary possibilities.

It is my contention that *China Men* directly and indirectly reflects, first, Kingston's recognition of the need for post-disruption reassessment of her autobiography's impact and, second, her attempt to respond to existing and newly arisen cross-cultural polemics exposed by the controversy. Such an effort obviously involved the author's renewed dialogue with Asian American feminists, Asian American men, and a mainstream literary establishment that tended to interpret works by ethnic writers stereotypically. But the key element of Kingston's undertaking was to tackle the continued power imbalance between Chinese American men and women through a narrative form that could embody both the formal and the ideological complexity of the enunciative position from which she carried out her renegotiating project.

Claiming America?

Although the controversy over *The Woman Warrior* is highly complex, the issue that lies at the heart of the debate is essentially one of history, particularly how to deal with two central concerns of Western historicism: its construction of historical origins and its conceptualization of historical subjects. In *China Men,* Kingston implicitly engages with these concerns by problematizing the ideological foundation for Chinese male immigrants' claims on subject status through "claiming America," that is, the Asian American heroic tradition as envisioned by the editors of *Aiiieeeeee!* partly according to the assumptions of Western historicism. Growing out of the revisionist need to counter the totalizing Eurocentric American historiography and to assert early Chinese immigrants' roles as movers and shakers, rather than mere passive victims, of United States history, such a radical rewriting of American history, as I mentioned in Chapter 4, justifiably legitimizes the hitherto submerged Asian (especially Chinese) immigrants' participation in the making of America—their construction of railroads, cultivation of Hawaii's plantations, and opening of the American West—as the basic plot of an alternative history that Asian Americans can claim to be their own. Such emplotment of Asian American history fundamentally revises the content of most institutionally sanctioned histories of the United States, even while it confirms the ruling assumptions of that history: rugged individualism, masculine valor, and social progress wrought through technological achievements (see also Kim 1990, 76–77; Sau-ling Wong 1993, 148). As a consequence, while this heroic vision symbolically redeems the historical belittlement of early Chinese immigrants in America, it also continually conceals what the American grand historical narrative has erased in order to maintain its coherence—its violent incorporation of Chinese male immigrant labor into the social fabric of American society, as well as its arbitrary omission of women's contribution to the making of Asian (especially Chinese) ethnic communities, despite their repeated exclusion from entry into the United States as qualified immigrants.

This double concealment, inherent in any unqualified heroic account of the Chinese American collective epic, reveals an unintentional participation by the proponents of such a vision in the acts of historical erasure through silence about selective aspects of their own immigrant experience.[8] Thus, the significance of Kingston's feminist renegotiation in *China Men* lies crucially in her fashioning a strategy not only to expose the structural interdependence between institutionalized American history and the Asian American heroic imagination, but also to allow a reassertion of women's perspective that subverts the logic of Western historicism. It is in this process of simultaneous exposure and rearticulation that Kingston makes the female narrator of her book a truly enabling agent who reveals the political nature of China men's silence (from this point on in my analysis, I will use the term "China men" in lieu of "Chinese male immigrant laborers" in conformity with Kingston's usage in her book), tells stories that available history is unable to tell, and strategically disrupts the linearity and predictability of a form of historical imagination predicated on male heroism.

Specifically, Kingston's renegotiation in *China Men* is carried out through her setting in motion and subsequent manipulation of two narrative movements in the book—the historical and the mythic—with an implicit purpose of problematizing the telos of both.[9] At the level of the historical, she introduces a story line that emphasizes China men's pioneering efforts in the United States, efforts highlighted by the author's use of a traditional Chinese seal design bearing the words "Gold Mountain Warriors" on the book's cover and on its six section title pages. Corresponding to the seals are geographic and moral monuments of China men's achievements in American history: the labor that produced the nickname "China-man's Hat" for Mokoli'i Island (88), the granite railroad tunnel in the Sierra Nevada Mountains that China men pounded through by hand after three years of hard toil (135), the "crossing steel" with which these "binding and building ancestors" of the United States "banded the nation North and South, East and West" after the Civil War (146), and the Chinese immigrant railroad workers' strike in 1867, which resulted in a four-dollar raise in their monthly salary from the Central Pacific. At the level of the mythic, Kingston inserts at the crucial junctures of this storyline ten short interchapters made up of mythic tales on themes such as emasculation, gender reversal, sexual repression, loss of identity, and disillusionment.

Punctuated by these interchapters, the narrative of historicist memory about China men's heroic experience resists efforts to grant it an independent continuity and coherence. Instead, the interchapters call attention to another narrative center traceable to the chapter titled "The Laws." Most criticism sees Kingston's inclusion of this chapter in the middle of the book either as the author's explicit attempt to redress the wrongs of historical erasure of China men's contribution to nation building or as her ironic commentary on their loss of subject position. Despite the obvious relevance of these readings, they tend to treat the chapter more or less as an accident within the book's signifying systems rather than an occasion to investigate its function as a documentary intrusion at the center of its narrative design. What is often overlooked is the fact that these laws, while an often effaced element in "official" historical narratives of the United States, are a similarly unwelcome component in the construction of an "Asian American heroic tradition." The central position that Kingston grants this doubly marginalized aspect of Chinese immigration history thus serves several important rhetorical purposes: the chapter on laws (along with the chapter titled "Alaska China Men") connects the ten interchapters symmetrically arranged on its two flanks, and together they constitute a recurrent yet inadequately recognized subtext of the work's palimpsestic narrative (see Figure 1). Structurally, these interrelated short chapters systematically interrupt and splinter the regularity of the heroic narrative of Chinese immigration history into heterogeneous fragments, while they demand a full excavation of the breadth and specificity of this narrative's submerged stories. Such a deliberate structural subversion of unmediated history problematizes Kingston's invocation of "Gold Mountain Warriors" inscribed in the traditional Chinese seal as innocently celebratory, and provides the ground for the female narrator to tell untold stories about China men in her own terms. From this perspective, the complexity of Kingston's book lies primarily in her telling a woman's story about men through a men's story about themselves, and in her doing so with a keen awareness of the storyteller's/writer's role in demystifying the coherence of received history and in historicizing myths in ways that allow the emergence of perspectives that defy the telos of both history and myth.

Kingston's ironic treatment of these two conflicting narrative movements serves to underscore her telling of "untold" stories within the epic frame of the book. For example, BaBa comes to America by hiding in a sealed crate on a smuggling ship en route from Latin America, starved, dying for air, and fearful of being caught whenever the ship is in port. In an alternative account, he arrives legally at Angel Island in San Francisco Bay, where a white doctor pokes him in the ass and genitals, forces open his mouth, and pulls his eyelids with a hook. In parallel, Bak Goong, the Great Grandfather once described as standing on top of Sandalwood

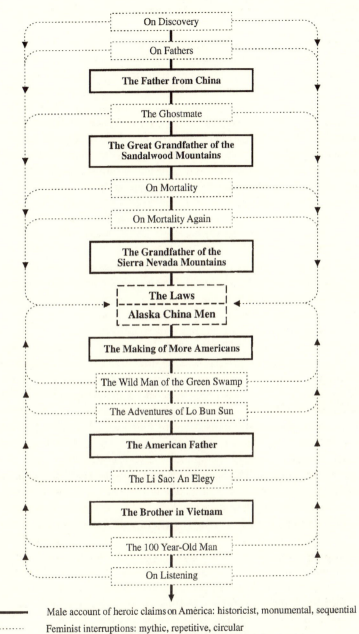

On Discovery

On Fathers

The Father from China

The Ghostmate

The Great Grandfather of the Sandalwood Mountains

On Mortality

On Mortality Again

The Grandfather of the Sierra Nevada Mountains

The Laws
Alaska China Men

The Making of More Americans

The Wild Man of the Green Swamp

The Adventures of Lo Bun Sun

The American Father

The Li Sao: An Elegy

The Brother in Vietnam

The 100 Year-Old Man

On Listening

—— Male account of heroic claims on America: historicist, monumental, sequential

·········· Feminist interruptions: mythic, repetitive, circular

– – – – Doubly marginalized Chinese American history that thematically connects the ten interchapters and critically reorganizes the book's narrative economy

Figure 1. The Narrative Structure and Movement of Kingston's *China Men*.

Mountain in Hawaii and singing "like the heroes" (98), is tricked into a "slave labor camp" by recruiters, fined for talking, cheated out of his salary, and whipped for disobedience (101–2). In other historical accounts woven into the text, white miners in Alaska forcibly ship out Chinese laborers for fighting with Indian miners, and, during the Treadwell Mining Company strike, white workers walk China men at gunpoint to the harbor to be shipped out again because ninety Chinese scabs took the white strikers' jobs (160–62). Even the Chinese railroad workers were not allowed to ride on the railroad they had built; once construction ended, they were killed, hunted down, or forced into flight like fugitives. Such humiliating experiences, Kingston suggests, are what the fathers would keep to themselves. Not accidentally, the female narrator comments, with regard to BaBa's illegal entry into the United States, "I think this is the journey you did not tell me," a comment that leads to her next ironic remark: "Of course, my father could not have come that way. He came a legal way" (53).

Kingston further shows that both institutional history's concealment of China men's contribution to the making of America and China men's self-concealment of their sacrifices and humiliations in order to maintain their moral pride have both produced problematic results. First, the epos of Asian American heroic tradition becomes easily assimilated by or dissolved into the grand American historical narrative of nation building because the latter tends to recognize only those identities it authorizes while it separates, abstracts, and ignores elements deemed external and illegitimate to its assumptions.[10] If, as a consequence, the content of China men's epic story has been rejected by the grand narrative's projected historical march, which privileges only white men's heroism, the employment within it of a structurally similar Chinese American epic can ideologically reinforce the same institutionally sanctioned historical chronicle it aims to revise.[11] Second, Kingston implicitly recognizes the resonance between the telos of the grand American national history and the epos of Asian American heroic tradition on the basis of their common denigration of women, a resonance mirrored in the former's oppression of Chinese men in America by means of social "emasculation" and the latter's protest against racial oppression of Chinese immigrants by using the same single-gendered metaphor of "emasculation," a strategy that doubly marginalizes Asian American women's experiences, concerns, and right to speak in their own terms.

Kingston makes nuanced comments on the consequences of the fathers' selective memory of their experiences in America in two interchapters, "The Adventures of Lo Bun Sun" and "The Wild Man of the Green Swamp." In the former, the author appropriates features of Daniel Defoe's *Robinson Crusoe* which parallel her text's accounts of China men's humiliating experiences as immigrants: Lo Bun Sun comes to an uninhabited island far from home, where he is forced to "toil" like a "naked," "sexless animal" and to suffer from "need of human company," a need reflected in his contemplation on a human footprint on the beach (226, 229). Kingston makes a point of stressing his textual rendering of his experience:

> After physical labor, he wrote in his diary, with which he kept his spirits up. He would leave a record. He ruled a page down the middle and listed the advantages and disadvantages of his island life. The two columns were entitled "Evil" and "Good." One of the Evils was the desolation; that he had not drowned was the balancing Good. Other Goods were food and water and the tropical weather that made up for his dearth of clothes. An Evil was that he had no one to talk to. His Good list outstripped the Evil list; Good may always preponderate in his method of reckoning. (226–27)

Kingston then offers Lo Bun Sun's rationalization of his unbalanced account: "from the start, he worried about using up his ink and paper, so he decided he would record only 'the most remarkable events of my life,'" that is, "Miracle. Miracle" (226–27). But, as Kingston quickly shows, Lo Bun Sun's unwillingness to record "the evil" in his life does not guarantee his status as the "king of his island" (229). For "evil" occurrences soon change the idyllic nature and the pristine state of his habitat: the island is invaded by "black demons," dominated by "mutineers" and "savages," and attacked by inhabitants of other islands with which it is at war (233). Eventually, Lo Bun Sun is forced out of the island refuge he has built with his own hands, resigns from the history he chronicles, and ironically returns to the place where he was born.

This theme of participating in the construction of miraculous history, of submitting to its necessities, and in turn of being erased by that history finds a ready echo in the interchapter about the wild swamp man, a metaphoric contemporary parallel to China men's Gold Mountain experience. The chapter tells of a Taiwanese who, out of economic needs, abandons his family and sails to the United States on a Liberian freighter. Tortured by homesickness during his voyage, he is anxious to go home but refuses to leave when, upon landing, the captain and his shipmates buy him a plane ticket to China. Judged to be insane, the man is sent to a mental hospital in Tampa, from which he escapes into the green swamp, reportedly surviving on alligators and the like. But after he is caught by a posse and put into jail, where his "illness" is treated, he kills himself. Read as an example of how "rational" historicism can hide private history, this story is particularly illuminating. The insanity of the Taiwanese in fact reflects the cultural blindness on the part of the captain and his shipmates toward the political division between mainland China and Taiwan, the man's actual place of origin. In offering to send him home to "China"—which synonymously invokes "Guangdong"—they not only obscure this geopolitical difference but also conflate two different Chinese immigration processes, a reductionism that the Taiwanese instinctively resists (note that Kingston does not refer to him as "Chinese").[12] By escaping into the swamp—thereby freeing himself from an external imposition of identity—he is able to survive the most inhuman conditions. But when ultimately placed in the government jail where he can no longer avoid the regulatory power of empirical scientific inquiries in the form of news media and official releases, he kills himself, perishing physically, along with his side of the story. Official history's capacity to erase the cultural specificity of the Taiwanese is comically paralleled by Kingston's mention, toward the end of the chapter, of a bizarre event in her neighborhood in Stockton, California, where white police perpetually searched for an ever-present black man whom they were unable to "see" among the Chinese Americans.

Kingston's problematizations of the reductionism of unidimensional history show, on the one hand, the tendency of such history to hide meanings and to misrepresent identities, and on the other, the epistemological difficulty of telling suppressed stories within the framework of traditionally accepted wisdom about historical order and rationality. For Asian American writers who find the recovery of a heroic tradition empowering, Kingston suggests that an awareness of the dangers of linear historical thinking is particularly important, because approaches to Asian America's past are obviously full of moral and epistemological contradictions not easily overcome. To treat the heroic deeds performed by China men in America's past as precious sources of present dignity and pride threatens erasure of other traces of what has been left of China men's past. And if the articulation of an Asian American heroic tradition must rely for rhetorical unity on the suppression of humiliating aspects of personal and collective experiences, then the act of reconstructing such experiences can be misread as disclaiming the heroic tradition per se or as weakening the political force of contesting the historical negation of Asian Americans' social and cultural significance to the United States. In positioning herself with regard to these issues, Kingston seems to take it as her task to show the contradictions in conflating rhetorical uplift with actually lived experience, the enormous moral price of refusing to face these contradictions, and the naïveté of embracing versions of counterhegemonic politics and desires that fail to acknowledge the complexities of China men's experiences in America. Despite the central position of the chapter on laws, the interchapters of *China Men* are not so much about history per se as they are about what history is able to conceal, about how a legitimation or naturalization of such concealment prohibits Asian American men from recovering their sexually and racially suppressed subjectivity, and about how the "orality" of Kingston's story can both disrupt the certainty of historical concealment and reconfigure the Asian American historical imagination through radical narrative contingency.

Probing the Gold Mountain Myth

Kingston's problematization of sententious historicism and traditional emphasis on temporal linearity, however, does not render history irrelevant. On the contrary, it makes way for the emergence of submerged historical knowledge that is vital and necessary for her feminist reworking of the content and form of the existing Asian American historical imagination. Thoughtful study has been done of Kingston's manipulation, at the outset of *China Men,* of the "emasculation" of Tang Ao, the protagonist-poet of the eighteenth-century Chinese classic *Flowers in the Mirror,* as an illustration either of the author's transgression of arbitrary gender boundaries or of the structural identity of gender oppression and racial discrimination (e.g, Rabine 1987; Li 1990; Goellnicht 1992; Cheung 1993, 100–108). What has been little examined, in view of Kingston's problematization of the Asian American heroic tradition, is how the author uses Tang Ao's experience typologically to foreground the contradictions of constructing a continuous Asian American subject and to emphasize, by dramatizing this subject's inability to verbalize his problems, the historicity of the book's feminist consciousness. Kingston creates a succession of such frustrated figures as Tang Ao, each, in his own way a failed father-artist: the young artisan Tu Tzu-Chun, Lo Bun Sun, and Chu Yuan (on the mythic level); and Ah Goong, Ba Goong, Kao Goong, and BaBa (on the historical level). Emblematic of Kingston's political intent in juxtaposing these figures, I would suggest, is her manipulation of the life of Chu Yuan, a banished minister-scholar of the State of Chu (one of the seven warring states) in ancient China. A symbol of righteousness and honesty in Chinese culture, Chu Yuan is portrayed in the book as yet another Gold Mountain China man, a "naked roaming saint" in "the barbarous lands," cynical about being caught in a situation in which "escape and return were equally impossible" (256, 258) and increasingly rigid and unrealistic about the world he is facing.

The satiric force of Kingston's treatment of Chu Yuan is best revealed in a dialogue between him and a fisherman at a time when Chu is deeply humiliated by his fall from the status of a prince to "nothing" and by his inability to make people around him understand his plight. He says: "The crowd is drunk; I alone am sober; I alone am clean, so I am banished. The world has gone mad. Even the reliable orchid has changed." The fisherman answers: "Why should you be aloof? When the water's clear, I can wash my tassels, when it's too muddy for silk, I can still wash my feet" (259). Unable to accept his reality or the less-than-ideal actions that it demands of him, Chu throws himself into the river. Implicitly, Kingston suggests that Chu Yuan's ways cannot serve as a model for the Asian American writer. His proud, moralistic, and detached discourse fails to acknowledge the inescapability of the harsh world he must not only face but also work to change, just as it fails to take into serious consideration the concerns of those who never had the privilege he complains about losing—including implicitly those of women, whose voices remain unheard or rejected within a cultural tradition that produces privileged male scholars as the only speaking agents in the realm of literary creation. By telling the story about Chu Yuan, Kingston seems to suggest that the female narrator of her book, as a woman writer, is the heir to this kind of tortured, inarticulate, and ultimately self-effacing male Chinese scholar.

Kingston's symbolic transference of the power of narration from the father figure, who silently endures suffering, to the daughter filled with urges to enter into the father's world is further thematized in two parallel accounts from the daughter's perspective: that of BaBa's failed career as a scholar both in China and in America, and that of Ah Goong's sexual frustration while toiling in the Sierra Nevada Mountains as a railroad builder in the 1860s. Early in the book the narrator calls attention to BaBa's youthful failure to get the top honor in a Chinese imperial examination and his becoming a village teacher, a respected yet humble position for a scholar. But, as the narrator quickly reveals, BaBa is unsuccessful even in that capacity: he is frustrated by the students' loss of interest in study as a result of the increasing commercialization and erosion of traditional emphasis on scholarship in his Cantonese village; and, like his students, he too becomes fascinated by tall tales about California's gold-cobbled streets, a fascination that leads to his taking passage to America in 1924 under the conviction that his diploma would earn him legal status (45). Not until he is detained at the immigration station on Angel Island does BaBa recognize the end of his career as a scholar. For the walls of the detention room are covered with poems written by educated immigrants like himself, poems that protest the jailing of new immigrants, unfair laws, and a Chinese government too weak to protect them.

Though surviving his detention, BaBa goes on to a life in America as troubled as his frustrating experience in China; eventually he loses his New York laundry, his savings in the bank, his two-story house, another house with a back porch, and finally his gambling job. BaBa's failed career as a scholar both in China and in the United States makes him taciturn and bitter, a change of personality that highlights, from another perspective, what Kingston tries to make her readers recognize—that is, the silencing of the poetic voice of those who (like Chu Yuan) fail because their aspirations and the world they must face are so disparate. It is in this sense that BaBa's mention to his daughter of Kao Chi, a Chinese poet who had been executed for his politics, is significant, for he cites an artist at odds with his world, an echo of the omission of BaBa's own poetic voice in the Chinese examination process and his problems with disrespectful students. Similarly, BaBa's experience in America, which is shaped by racial and economic exclusions that lead to the silences he occasionally breaks with screams and curses, can be considered a kind of "execution" of his poetic and scholarly aspirations in the new world.

While this silence is inadequately broken at home in abusive behavior toward his wife and daughter, he, like Kao Chi, also leaves a more positive legacy. The latter was "famous for poems to his wife and daughter written upon leaving for the capital; he owned a small piece of land where he grew enough to eat without working too hard so he would write poems." The narrator thinks of her own father's planting of "luffa and grapevines," of vegetables and fruit trees, as parallel: even if he was a poet in exile, he nevertheless was planting "trees that take years to fruit" (255)—and his daughter's own work, the text suggests, was part of the harvest.

Equally significant is the narrator's account of Ah Goong's silent suffering from a life without women: in the quiet of the night, he watches for the imaginary yearly reunion of Altair with Vega (which, according to Chinese folk tradition, represents a brief meeting between two forcibly separated young lovers, the Cowherd and the Girl Weaver); the watch leaves him staring at his own penis and "wondering what it was that it was for, what a man was for, what he had to have a penis for" (144). During the day, the narrator records, while riding a basket being lowered like a "plummet" into a valley that needs to be cleared for the base of a trestle, Ah Goong is suddenly seized by sexual desire, masturbates, and "squirted out into space," murmuring, "I am fucking the world" (132–33). Metaphorically, Ah Goong's explosive yet vain expression of his socially suppressed sexual energy parallels the thwarted creativity which Bak Goong (Great Grandfather) experiences, according to one of the narrator's accounts, in being forbidden to speak on a Hawaiian plantation and, with no other recourse, talking into a hole dug in the ground (115). The narrator, by speaking the forbidden—the never directly transmitted memory—is taking up the role of the artist unfulfilled by her male ancestors: symbolically, in doing so, the narrator is fertilizing the world with words.

Such are a few of the "secrets" of China men's spiritually vulnerable and disenchanted anguish, secrets that they tend to separate from the external physical sufferings they endure—their loss of ears and toes during blizzards or the destruction of their flesh in dynamite accidents (136-37)—suffering that they construct as a sign of their actual participation in the grand scheme of American history. After such sacrifices, the narrator implies, it was especially humiliating that China men were dismissed once the Transcontinental Railroad was completed, only to be excluded subsequently from other forms of labor. The narrator catalogues other instances of America's forcible denial of China men the rights assumed by other groups: the Los Angeles and Rock Springs Massacres, the Boston Arrest, and the drivings-out from Tacoma, Seattle, Oregon City, Albania, and Marysville (148–49). In light of such large-scale violent acts of exclusion, Ah Goong gives up his original plans to "walk along the tracks to review his finished handiwork, or to walk east to see the rest of his new country" and becomes a fugitive, "good at hiding" and "disappearing" (146). A highly ironic moment of Ah Goong's flight occurs when he escapes into a Chinese theater in San Francisco to watch an opera that celebrates Guan Goong (Kwan Kung):

> Ah Goong recognized the hero, Guan Goong; his puppet horse had red nostrils and rolling eyes. Ah Goong's heart leapt to recognize the hero and horse in the wilds of America. Guan Goong murdered his enemy—crash! bang! of cymbals and drum . . . Ah Goong felt as warm as if he were with friends at a party. . . . Guan Goong fought the biggest man in one-to-one combat, a twirling, jumping sword dance that strengthened the China men who watched it. (149)

But such an experience does not stop the discrimination and violent exclusion of Chinese immigrant labor outside the theater: eventually Ah Goong is forced to return to China; later, driven back to the Gold Mountain a second time by financial needs, he becomes homeless, shiftless, dirty, and jobless—a "Fleaman," in the family's words, who must be brought back to China by his eldest sons. (149–51)

Kingston's perception of the father/scholar figure in *China Men* is clearly not a simple one. As much as other Asian American writers, including the harshest critics of *The Woman Warrior,* Kingston explicitly acknowledges the achievements of the early Chinese male immigrants to the United States during a crucial period of the country's development. At the same time, she also points out the often devastating effects of China men's precarious social existence during their violent incorporation into America's socioeconomic processes. As the chapter on laws makes explicit, the fact that the exclusion proposals could make it through Congress and into federal law indicates that the story of Chinese immigrants' "coming to claim America" in the second half of the nineteenth century cannot be told as a story of heroic migration succeeding against overwhelming odds. While an idealized vision of Asian American history might offer multiple incarnations of Guan Goong, it could not change the fate of the author's fathers, who bear physical and psychological scars from their struggles, which their successors, according to the daughter-narrator of *China Men,* must recognize and understand. Her feminist account of male silence in *China Men* is complex, nuanced, and often debated. One fundamental difference between this treatment of early Chinese male immigrants' suffering and recent poststructuralist theoretical critiques of early Asian American projects as instances of totalizing nationalism is that the latter seldom or never bother to enter into dialogue with the men's experience the way Kingston does.[13] Thus, in recovering a submerged history and breaking the silence of Chinese male immigrant laborers through the heteroglossia of her narrative, Kingston not only turns a romanticized past into a disruptive prologue for the emergence of alternative histories and narrative subjects but also redirects the intertextual dynamics that surround the community's debate over its identity politics.

Kingston's problematization of the Asian American historical subject troped in "Gold Mountain Warriors" reveals its full complexity in the last section of *China Men,* where the narrator relays a Filipino scholar's implausible story about a group of Mandarin Chinese men who came to look for the Gold Mountain in the Philippines in March 1603. In ways strongly suggestive of the narrative structure of the book, the Filipino scholar's story develops in a nonlinear fashion. For the knowledge he passes on is highly equivocal, inviting questioning both from the female narrator of the book, who drives at exposing the inconsistency of his language and "facts," and from a group of Chinese American male listeners, who feel encouraged to share their no less implausible tales about Chinese gold diggers. With each interruption, not only does the original story get reorganized and retold, but the positions of the speaker and the listener become reversed as well. The skeptical narrator performs an especially instrumental role in this process by intervening at every critical juncture of the exchange between the Filipino scholar and his audience, and in doing so critically facilitates the surfacing of the underlying ironies of the Gold Mountain tale. For example, the narrator's first question about the scholar's story forces the latter to admit the possibility that the Chinese may only have been looking for a gold needle in the mountain rather than the Gold Mountain itself. This admission is immediately confirmed by the narrator through a second interjection, in which she tells readers that "looking for the Gold Mountain was [indeed] like looking for a needle in a haystack" (307). Her third interruption—this time to salvage the scholar's voice from being drowned in the diverse Gold Mountain tales zealously offered by the Chinese American listeners—enables him to proceed, but with an entirely different story: on their way to the Gold Mountain, the Chinese had already built roads and railroads and cities, filled swamps, had children, and in fact created their own "gold." And the narrator's last intervention—in which she asks about the possibility that the Chinese were tricked by the Filipinos, since the former took home nothing but dirt— drives home a point Kingston makes consistently throughout the entire book: that the Gold Mountain myth is but a fiction.

E. San Juan, Jr., accurately captures this aspect of Kingston's nuanced treatment of Gold Mountain when he observes:

> "Gold Mountain" is the mythical name given to the United States by the Chinese in China to symbolize familial aspirations for wealth, freedom, happiness, etc. But in this playful exchange, the rubric "Gold Mountain" becomes detached from the aura of myth owing to the pressure of painful, dehumanizing experiences undergone by generations of sojourners and settlers from the 1860s on; it becomes a floating signifier, a charisma-laden mana, which then can be fixed to the Philippines, Mexico, Spain, or to wherever the imagination or Eros cathects its adventurous utopian drive. (1992, 112)

Furthermore, I would suggest, the exchange between the narrator and the Filipino scholar unfolds a process of ironic shifting of intertextual dynamics: the author shifts the position of reader as participant in the debate over Asian American cultural politics to that of critical listener; and she further shifts the reader's attention from the authority this move grants the narrator's questioning to the problematization of the authority of any "maker" of history. In the conclusion of "On Listening," the narrator signals these shifts when she says, after the Filipino scholar dodges her question, "Good. Now I could watch the young men who listen" (308). The young men the narrator refers to are the Chinese Americans who gather around the Filipino scholar and occasionally venture their own versions of Chinese experiences with Gold Mountains elsewhere in the world. Here, Kingston makes specific assumptions about her audience's ideological preparation for *China Men.* For what the narrator wants to "watch" for in the young men, who implicitly stand for the community of male readers and critics of Kingston's *Woman Warrior* and *China Men,* is what lies at the very root of Asian American identity politics during the 1970s: the problematic of seeing the Gold Mountain both as a crucial historical referent for early Asian immigrants' suffering in the United States and as an indispensable political anchor for ethnic empowerment, something that needs to be defended in order to refute continued institutional denial of Asian immigrants' relevance to the history of the United States. Kingston's interrogation of the contradictions of such a vision of Asian American identity involves demystification of both the cultural sanctity of the Gold Mountain myth and the idealized vision of Asian American heroic tradition rhetorically resonant with that myth—a rhetorical stance that cannot stand the full test of history.

Kingston's demythologizing of the Gold Mountain myth goes beyond merely undercutting the American dream of success through a systematic scrambling of the relationship between the signifier and its assumed referent. For it functions, along with the chapter listing discriminatory immigration laws against the Chinese, to define a (re)negotiating stance in *China Men* that takes into account the negative consequences of using insufficiently historicized knowledge to carry out debate over ethnic identity. Kingston's positioning here reminds us that an ethnic writer of color can consciously assume authorial responsibility to prepare an (uninformed) audience for a specific vision of history, and that such choices can involve significant political decisions relative to the pressures of his or her historical situation. Kingston's depiction of the female narrator in her book as inheriting the plight of "failed" male scholars and, as we shall see in the analysis that follows, her reflections on the problematic character of the relationship of Chinese Americans to their connections with China, on the racial underpinnings of America's war in Vietnam, and on the renewed Chinese quest for the Gold Mountain in the post–World War II era, all reflect positions responsive to the external demands she faces as a history-conscious writer. Kingston's deployment of different narra-

tive strategies in *The Woman Warrior* and *China Men* suggests the risks that an ethnic writer must take to engage in an unfolding sociocultural dynamics: misread-
ings may abound, both in a mainstream audience ignorant of the history of its
own assumptions and domination of others, and among ethnic community readers who have little sympathy for a writer whose cultural politics departs from its
norms, as was the case with Kingston's feminist mythologizing in her first book.

Identities and Positions

Kingston's reengagement with various cultural and political voices through displacements of the Gold Mountain myth and its related beliefs reveals its full critical potential in the last portion of the book, in which she consciously entwines
the community's debate over its identity politics with multiple axes of globality.
This complication of her position is effected through two interrelated strategies:
her making the female narrator reflect on the immigrant fathers' ambiguous relationships with their ancestral land and her problematization, through the narrator's American-born brother, of the boundaries between Asian Americans' "civil
war" and America's involvement in international geopolitical struggles, between
racism on the home front and U.S. imperialism in Asia. Such a development in
China Men's narrative preemptively disrupts the teleological tendency latent in
framing debates over ethnic identity as solely a domestic issue, a disruption that
intertextually anticipates more self-conscious articulations of the complexities of
Asian American cultural politics in the late 1980s and 1990s.

The argument for Asian Americans' emotional and cultural alienation from
Asia was a major rhetorical component of the "Asian American cultural integrity"
proposed by critics such as Frank Chin, Jeffery Chan, Lawson Inada, and Shawn
Wong in the 1970s. In the final major chapter of *China Men,* Kingston seems to
engage directly with this argument, not by outrightly dismissing its relevance to
Asian American life at the time but rather by teasing out its suppressed ideological implications. In a chapter titled "The Making of More Americans," Kingston
tells a story of Say Goong, the deceased fourth grandfather and the narrator's "railroad grandfather's youngest brother." Say Goong's ghost keeps showing up in the
family stable shed in Stockton, California, where he used to play with the narrator
and bring in the horses after work with his brother Sahm Goong (the narrator's
"third grandfather"). The author contrasts Sahm Goong's ordering the ghost of
his brother to "go home"—to China where he was born—with the ghost's persistent yet silent reappearance in the shed. It soon becomes clear that this stable shed
and the tottering house in Stockton have become the "ancestral ground" for the
various descendants of both Say Goong and Sahm Goong (171), descendants who
come to visit the place from across the United States. Implicitly the United

States, not China, is "home" and thus "ancestral ground" for the narrator's family, a ground that the narrator's mainstream readers often denied her in their responses to *The Woman Warrior*. In a reversal of the Say Goong story, Kingston constructs a tale of a Chinese mother-ghost's coming to haunt her son in America. The mother-ghost insists that her son, Mad Sao, an established U.S. citizen, fulfill his filial duty by returning home to take care of her despite the son's argument about realistic limitations to such obligations. Unable to drive her away, the son spends money for a trip on which he lures the ghost back to China and to her grave there. After placating the ghost, according to the narrator, he "hurried back to America, where he acted normal again, continuing his American life" (179).

If the story of Say Goong emphasizes a newly emergent sense of United States origins among Chinese Americans, then the story of Mad Sao (which recalls Chin's construction of China Mama in *The Year of the Dragon*) underscores the identificatory difficulties that often beset Chinese Americans in a culture that tends to see them as perpetual cultural aliens. The question that haunts the narrator of the book is then not simply one of cultural identity unsettled by immigration and cultural rejection in the United States; it is also one of Chinese Americans' uncertain desires caused by their awareness of the contradictions between their actual cultural allegiance and America's insistence on seeing them as national other because of their race. With the return of Mad Sao's mother-ghost, Kingston suggests that contemporary Chinese Americans are constantly forced to grapple with their ambiguous connections with a largely imagined ancestral home, connections symbolized in the female narrator's awareness of the "gaping, gaping spaces" between Kuao Goong (183), her aging Great Uncle in America, and the wife he has left in China for several decades and decided not to return to.

In exploring spaces that may be too painful and too deep to fathom yet ideologically too important to transcend, Kingston shows not merely the process of the father figures' cultural transformation as they make their claims on America but also the ideological consequences of America's institutionalized racism on Chinese Americans' attempts at self-definition. Relevant here is the comic story in "The Making of More Americans" concerning Uncle Bun (Uncle Stupid), who goes back to a postrevolutionary China he idealizes because of his frustration with American cold war domestic politics—ironically portrayed by the author as his obsession with wheat germ, communism, and white oppressors' plotting. Again, this story illustrates the "unfathomableness" of space, memory, hearsay, and reality in the family's "China connections," while it problematizes not only available knowledge of China in America but also Chinese Americans' quest for self-identity through uncritical reliance on such knowledge. Kingston's multi-angled positioning toward the issue of ethnic identity is motivated by a deliberate design "to compare China, a country I made up, with what country is really out there" (87), a comparison that informs the chapter's examination of the tensions that come to surface when Chinese Americans attempt to engage with a contemporary (revolutionary) China in the process of normalizing its relationship with the United States throughout the 1970s. One such comparison actually leads to a decisive choice for I Fu, the husband of the narrator's young Auntie, who, after a great deal of wavering between living in China, Hong Kong, and San Francisco's Chinatown, finally chooses the "China" in America. Another important choice between different "homes" is made by Kau Goong's aging wife, who, no longer able to bear separation from her husband, manages to be smuggled out of mainland China to Hong Kong, where she expects her husband to join her from the United States so that the two can settle down for the rest of their lives. When Kau Goong chooses to stay in California, she decides that she is not going to spend the rest of her life "alone in a strange city" and accordingly returns to China (184), again through smuggling.

Kingston's use of a China in transition as a point of historical reference in probing the question of Chinese American identity politics serves several important rhetorical purposes in the book: she highlights the historical constellations of different immigrant experiences and generations in the Chinese American community of her own time; she constructs a nonessentialized "Chinese American perspective" that is multivocal and problematic in relation to its "roots" in China; and she reintroduces the Chinese diaspora as an indispensable cultural frame of reference for her community, whose historical imagination tends to be limited by a narrow domestic interpretation of the "Gold Mountain" dream. Through her speculations about and comparisons between the different perspectives around the "unfathomable" spaces that both separate and join Chinese America and China, Kingston turns the identificatory liminality faced by Chinese Americans within American racial and cultural hierarchies into a useful site for fashioning counter-hegemonic strategies more answerable to the demands of new historical conditions. Kingston clearly implies that the Chinese American community cannot make full sense of itself without an adequate grasp of its relationship with its ancestral culture because of America's overall failure to incorporate Asian Americans in its body politic on equal terms. A full understanding of Chinese American identity would in this sense inevitably involve a perspective that not only can interrogate prevailing assumptions about ethnic identities in the United States, but also can acknowledge both the connections and contradictions between domestic and global dimensions of their construction.

The narrator's American-born younger brother Joe, whose name means "bridge" in Chinese, becomes in this sense the most significant character in the book's final chapters, particularly for his grudging participation in the Vietnam War. The complexity of Joe's meaning can be understood on three different but interrelated levels. On a general level, he obviously performs the symbolic function of a cultural agent who negotiates a variety of positions within the unfathomable psychological and geographic spaces that have made clarification of Chinese American identity difficult; as such, he climactically displays Kingston's own recognition of the complexities of the cultural and political processes that both constitute and are constituted by the ideological ambivalence of *China Men*. On a more specific level, the brother's opposition to the Vietnam War when he is drafted functions as Kingston's implicit commentary on the problematic tendencies in ethnic and gender conflicts within her own community. This authorial concern is reflected in Kingston's portrayal of the brother as a "Champion Complainer" in a recruit training camp and his eventual return from Vietnam "without being killed" but also "without killing anyone" (288, 304). Critics generally regard the brother's refusal to comply with the war authority and war principles as either an index of Kingston's own political convictions or as an indication of authorial belief in pacifism (Kim 1982, 174; Cheung 1990, 243; Li 1991a, 249). Within the intertextual dynamics of *China Men,* however, Kingston's construction of the antiwar brother can be interpreted in historically more specific terms. Significantly, while the brother dreads participating in the war in Vietnam, he is haunted by nightmares full of ethnic concerns (see Amy Ling 1981, 76; Kim 1982, 212). One bad dream involves his contradictory role as a member of a "rescuing army" while he is on board an aircraft carrier heading for Asia:

> He walks through a castle into the dungeons. Going down the stairs, he sees at face level—bodies hanging, some upside down, some brown and dried up, black hair and arms swaying, feet turning this way, then that, bodies with black hair in their middles, corpses with sections missing and askew, but mercifully all dead, hanging by hooks and ropes. Laundry tubs drain beneath the bodies. The live women and children on the ironing tables, the last captured, are being dissected. . . . He takes up his sword and hacks into the enemy, slicing them; they come apart in rings and rolls. . . . When he stops, he finds that he has cut up the victims too, who are his own relatives. The faces of the strung-up people are also those of his own family, Chinese faces, Chinese eyes, noses, and cheekbones. He woke terrified. (291)

In specifying "Chinese faces," "ironing tables," and "laundry tubs" as the background of the scene of horror, the brother's dream implicitly invokes the condition of intra-"family" violence that the war situation forces on those with Asian ancestors, a condition that coincides with his second dream of family warfare in the kitchen:

> He dreamed that he was a barkless dog tied to a table leg in a kitchen equipped with a sink, oven, and operating table. Families—mother, father, and one child—are in kitchens like this all over the world. A voice came over the loudspeaker: "Children, take up your knives; women, forks; men,

spoons." The fathers take the children's knives and stab them quickly. Then with their arms around one another, the wife picks up the fork, and the husband the spoon. The loudspeaker says for them to kill themselves by forking and scooping. "Spoon, knife, or fork?" the loudspeaker asks the barkless dog, who knows that if he took the sharpest instrument, he would deprive someone else of a quick death. (292)

The brother's behavior during military service is based on efforts to avoid participating in the vision he experiences in nightmares. For example, while in the army, he turns down the opportunity to go to the Monterey Language School to be trained as a spy, as an interrogator of the Vietnamese, because he finds the Vietnamese people "disturbingly similar to Chinese." He recalls that

the Vietnamese call their parents Ba and Ma; *phuoc* means "happiness," "contentment," "bliss," the same as Chinese; *lan* is "orchid," the same as his mother's name; Vietnamese puns are like Chinese puns, *lettuce, life;* they probably also bring heads of lettuce home on holidays. *Study, university, love*—the important words the same in Chinese and Vietnamese. Talking Chinese and Vietnamese and also French, he'd be a persuasive interrogator-torturer. He would fork the Vietnamese—force a mother to choose between her baby with a gun at its belly and her husband hiding behind the thatch, to which she silently points with her chin. (300–301)

Kingston's juxtaposition of the narrator's "vision" of the "actual horror" of large-scale wars (264)—World War II, the war against Japan, the communist revolution in China, the Korean War, and the Vietnam War—against the brother's nightmares about the irrationality of "local" wars fought within one's family or community suggests that the term "antiwar," as a characterization of the brother's attitudes and behavior, carries specific contextual overtones in *China Men.* Among them, I would suggest, is an allusion to the "war" of ongoing ideological differences and controversy within the Asian American community over artistic creation and identity politics—conflicting ways of interpreting and positioning Asian America in its equally conflictual relationship with mainstream culture in the United States.

Elaine Kim suggests that the brother's antiwar attitude can be associated with his immigrant forebears in terms of their "Chinese heritage" and with "their refusal to be victimized, and their mutual claim on America" (1982, 212). Yet within the intertextual relationships signaled by his dreams, the connections of the brother's antiwar attitude with his American ethnic community is clearly stronger, at least for that segment of the audience conscious of the cultural and historical codes the author is using. For example, in an apparent allusion to the "war" of words over *The Woman Warrior* and its title figure, Kingston describes the consequences of a war breaking out on the Gold Mountain, where "Fa Mu Lan

bled from sword wounds until her armor was soaked red" and the arms of her
male transfiguration, Nogk Fei, "were tied behind his back, and the blood
squeezed out from the wooden collar around his neck" (268). The wounding of
these metaphorical warriors in an imagined war on the Gold Mountain, and the
suffering of a prototypical Kingston Grandfather who was "bayoneted in the head
for patriotically withholding information from a Japanese soldier" during World
War II (268), highlight the significance of the text's treatments of "pacifism": the
undesirability of "war" not only as a means of resolving conflicts over geographic
territories abroad but also as a way of conducting cultural politics and dealing
with ideological differences within and among the ethnic communities making
up American society. In this sense, the interpretation of the brother's life experience can be seen as Kingston's deliberate attempt to re-vision the "interlocking
system" of war to which "everything was connected" as a negotiated process
(284–85). Such a process of going to "war" while attempting to resist violence
transforms the ethics of "war of maneuver" into that of "war of position" and helps
sharpen the brother's sense of self-identity: in military service, he becomes keenly
aware of his connection to Asia, an awareness that makes him feel that his whole
life "suddenly made sense"; at the same time, the way the Taiwan and Hong Kong
Chinese react to him reminds him of his "Americanness" (294), an identity that
gradually takes shape and prevents him from "rid[ing impulsively] into China"
just across the Hong Kong border, even when he is gazing at its "valley and dis-
tant hills covered with wild vegetation" (302).

A third level of meaning for Joe's antiwar attitude and his imaginative encounter in Vietnam is perhaps the most significant in revealing the ideological
thrust of *China Men*. For Kingston's description of the brother's dreams of ethnic
massacre points to the author's implicit recognition of the racial nature of
America's imperial wars in Asia as well as of the connections between America's
continued construction of racial others domestically and its active engagement in
the violent destruction of its ideological other in Asian countries such as Vietnam.
The racially inflected war images of brutalized men, women, and children con-
jured up through the brother's dreams therefore become a powerful commentary
on America's unequal treatment of racial minorities, including Asian Americans,
as other within its own national boundaries—a situation that, Kingston implies,
renders the community's persistent yet rigid arguments over identity politics not
only counterproductive but also ideologically confining.

As if reflecting on the issue of raising such perspectives with her readers,
Kingston describes the brother's teaching experience as an unsuccessful form of
addressing the audience: as a high school teacher prior to being drafted into the
army, the brother tries to convince his working-class students of the "atrocities"
and "wrongness" of war, but his objections in the classroom are resisted as "communist" propaganda or met with defiance by students' "dropping out" to enlist

and fight in the war (278–81). The brother's frustration with students who refuse to think and question the war effort, though similar to the narrator's father's trouble with disobedient students in the Cantonese village school, drives home a point that Kingston attempts to make throughout her deliberations: relationships between authors/speakers and resistant, ill-informed readers/listeners are necessarily problematic. Unlike BaBa, Joe, the teacher-scholar, is clear-minded, purposeful, and articulate, but he still fails to connect with students/audiences who are confused, defiant, and indignant at being lectured at in "Remedial Reading" (279). In thus imagining her own concerns about addressing the community's internal conflict through Joe's voice, however, Kingston does not collapse her feminist agenda into her brother's male perspective. Nor does she suppress the radicality of her critiques of masculine ideals that underwrite both U.S. nationalism and the Asian American heroic tradition. Rather, the strategy she adopts acknowledges both the tactical value of gender ventriloquism and its ability to expand the terms of previous ideological debate over identity politics; and it insists on the importance of women's voices in that debate by the act of telling stories in *China Men,* including that of the brother, through a woman's voice. What emerges from her representation of Joe's mental struggles about Vietnam, China, and his own identity is an open-ended and multidimensional scenario for the Asian American writer's negotiating position from which Kingston herself addresses the reader in her own nuanced voice, a scenario that at once foregrounds ideological indeterminacy and historical specificity in her relationship to her materials, to her comparative frames of reference, and to her multiple audiences.

In *China Men,* Kingston uses a narrative strategy that is ideologically, culturally, and aesthetically complex. This complexity reveals itself, as I have attempted to demonstrate, through the author's successful (re)negotiation of the need to fulfill her unfinished feminist project, to stake out her position beyond the limits of given perspectives on ethnic and gender identities, and to write a woman's story about men both through and against the pervasive mythology of the "main/*male*stream" (West 1987, 19). As the center of consciousness, the female narrator does not simply problematize the claim of representativeness or the idealized "search" for a coherent Asian American past. Rather, her storytelling acknowledges the contradictions of remembering while refusing to lament the contingencies of memory, and it avoids endorsing essentialized identities while insisting on naming the specificity of its politics. Such a narrative strategy unfolds accounts of diasporic experience in *China Men* both centrifugally and centripetally, revealing the depth and scope of the female narrator's perspective that privileges neither endless sliding of the signifier nor fixation of the referent of the narrator's utterance. At the same time, it allows the author to comment on China men's crisis both inside and outside the trope of Gold Mountain. Kingston obviously aims to produce a text that is able, in Edward Soja's words, to "re-entwine the making of history within the social production of space" (1989, 11). In spatializing the political geography of China men's often discontinuous experience of the diaspora in America, she not only breaks down the linear temporality of Western historical thinking but also redraws the boundaries of the cultural space available to the Asian American literary imagination of the late 1960s and the 1970s. In textualizing the incommensurability as well as the interdependence between various Asian American social experiences, political imperatives, and strategies of resistance, *China Men* ultimately negotiates issues extending well beyond its generic boundaries: it blurs the distinction between the discourses of theory and of literature by creating a "paraliterary space" for subversive operation;[14] it counterposes and conjoins the interests of Asian American men and Asian American women; it presents readers with a multifaceted narrative signifying contrapuntally on key postwar concerns in Asian American literary and cultural history; and it experiments with a narrative form that supplements various modes of discourse elected by earlier Asian American writers while requiring further supplementation of both prior and current use of them. And most important, in fundamentally problematizing two interrelated meta-narratives—U.S. nationalism and the male-oriented heroic account of Asian American immigration history—*China Men* risks misinterpretation while demanding that its multiple communities of readers reassess their conscious or unconscious reliance on these debilitating narratives.

6

Critical Negotiations

Issues in Asian American Cultural Studies

> It seems to me that this is the gravest menace to theory today:
> its professionalized simulacrum, well ensconced in the system
> of knowledge, usurping the voice of the Other while silencing
> it and the practice of resistance that is genuine theory. The ap-
> pearance of a professionalized conception of theory would
> mark the advent of a total culture of literacy, in which theory,
> far from challenging the system of the posthistorical state,
> would be content to flourish in the sphere that was assigned
> to it.
>
> —Wlad Godzich, *The Culture of Literacy*

> The purpose of theorizing is not to enhance one's intellectual
> or academic reputation but to enable us to grasp, understand,
> and explain—to produce a more adequate knowledge of—the
> historical world and its processes; and thereby to inform our
> practice so that we may transform it.
>
> —Stuart Hall, "The Toad in the Garden"

In my readings I have foregrounded the positioning of particular authors and texts from the perspective of their negotiated relationships with various readers at given historical moments, and sketched out the intertextual processes that emerge from such a perspective. In this concluding chapter, I return to broader critical concerns with a focus on three persistent interpretive questions that have con-fronted Asian American critics during the 1970s and after: the extent to which particular Asian American literary works confirm or challenge hegemonic or cul-tural assumptions; the nature of ethnic authenticity invoked by Asian American writers in their self-representation; and the issue of political responsibility faced by Asian American writers and critics. Explorations of these questions among Asian American critics can be traced to the publication of *Aiiieeeee!* in 1974, to Elaine Kim's landmark study *Asian American Literature* in 1982, to numerous anthologies, books, and articles produced in the wake of these two inaugurative works, and to exchanges at national Asian American Studies conferences held since 1975.[1] These activities mark Asian Americans' ongoing concern with the social and political relevance of their creative practices, a concern that has in turn energized the community's critical construction of a multivalent Asian American political agency as a dynamic and dialectical process: it has engaged in exchanges, contestations, and adjustments with a national and international archive of theoretical perspectives, and moved Asian American literary discourse toward transformative praxis through shifting sites of cultural production and multiple axes of identities and differences.

Hegemony: The Case of Jade Snow Wong

Critical assessments of Jade Snow Wong's *Fifth Chinese Daughter* (1945/1950) provide a logical site for examining how Asian American literary criticism has debated the nature of its founding assumptions and the extent to which such assumptions still reflect the essential characteristics of Asian Americans' experiences in contemporary society. The editors of *Aiiieeeee!* and Elaine Kim set out the terms of the community's initial assessment of Wong's autobiography as an embodiment of assimilationist compromise; they find that *Fifth Chinese Daughter* promotes the stereotypical view of the Chinese American community as exotic and "foreign"—through its emphatic descriptions of cultural practices such as cooking or handicraft design—and as a site of emergence for a polite "model minority" eager for mainstream acceptance. One ground for this critical perspective on Wong's work is her own statement that she agreed to let the publisher purge the "personal"—and implicitly the less "polite"—aspects of her autobiography, a purging that allowed her book to be used to affirm the assimilationist demands of the cultural establishment (Chin et al. 1974, xxiv–xxx; Kim 1982, 70–72). Along the same lines, Patricia Lin-Blinde suggests that Wong's work "in no way adds anything in terms of real knowledge where the general public's picture of Chinese people is concerned," for "what Wong does is essentially to 'repeat' the white world's articulations and expectations as to what Chineseness is or is not," a repetition that is "complete as far as her choice of a form is concerned" (1979, 58). David Leiwei Li similarly argues that "cultural hegemony maintains itself not so much by imposing white writing upon the minority but by soliciting white writing from the objectified minority," because "the autobiographical genre designed for their lot demands the omission of subjective valuations" (1991, 214).

Ironically, Maxine Hong Kingston, who produced in *The Woman Warrior* the single most influential autobiographical text written by an Asian American woman in the 1970s, does not seem disturbed by the "purge" of "personal" emotions from Wong's work. On the contrary, she retrospectively referred to Wong as "the mother of Chinese American literature" as well as the only Chinese American author she read before writing her own book. Kingston reflects: "I found Jade Snow Wong's book myself in the library, and was flabbergasted, helped, inspired, affirmed, made possible as a writer—for the first time I saw a person who looked like me as a heroine of a book, as a maker of a book" (quoted in Amy Ling 1990, 120).[2] Kingston's acknowledgment of the unrecognized merits of Wong's book was preceded by Kathleen Loh Swee Yin's and Kristoffer Paulson's 1982 reinterpretation of the autobiography, in which they suggest that the book's significance lies precisely in its ironic portrayal of "the division of Wong's life and how she questions and rejects the Chinese conventions which no longer apply in the context of the duality of experience she faces" (56). It was followed by the feminist rereading of Wong's work by Amy Ling (1990, 119–24) and Shirley Lim (1992, 252–55), both emphasizing the ambiguities and indeterminacies of the autobiography as a result of the book's representation of the female protagonist's complex and gender-specific experience. Reacting to these revisionist efforts on behalf of *Fifth Chinese Daughter* in affirmation of the community's "long-standing critiques of Wong as a 'model minority' subject," Karen Su argues that such a critical turn reflects two conservative political tendencies in American society: the "growing backlash against issues of race" in the 1980s and the mainstream multiculturalist appropriation of the "model minority" myth in the early 1990s. Su accordingly warns that "feminist recuperations" of Wong's work should be made with a caution against liberal multicultural co-optation of the articulation of gender differences and against abandonment of criticism of U.S. racism exemplified in the initial assessment of Wong's work (1994, 4, 28).

My discussion of the ongoing debate over Wong's work will focus on one issue emerging from the positions voiced by these critics—that of cultural hegemony— because, in my view, the assessment of this issue lies at the heart of the debate. I will ask, in particular, (1) whether the dominant culture is indeed capable of fully controlling the meaning of the ethnic texts it "solicits"; (2) to what extent even a censored work like Wong's can be truly cleansed of its "subjective valuations"; (3) how Wong's political position as constructed through the generic form of autobiography relates to her selfhood in a social sense; (4) whether recognition of the difficulty of assigning a singular ideological meaning to a conservatively canonized text necessarily presupposes forsaking the political gains made by the early Asian American movement; and above all, (5) why women's difference is seen as if it were a neutral ideological entity susceptible to conservative appropriation, while racial difference is seen as naturally resistant to it. In asking these questions, I wish to register a disagreement with the connection that Su has established between the political regressions in American society in the 1980s and 1990s, and feminist rereadings of Wong's work, not because such a connection is impossible but because it does not necessarily describe a real convergence of a unified politics. Indeed, positing such a connection can obscure a significant progressive context, to which the recent re-assessment of Wong's work is more closely related—that is, the internal critique during the 1980s of the race- and class-based paradigm that had dominated Ameri-can minority discourse (e.g., Christian 1980; Carby 1986; Gates 1986; Valerie Smith 1987), as well as a simultaneous attempt to construct woman-centered ap-proaches in Asian American creative and critical practices along a similar political trajectory, an effort that led to the publication of two pathbreaking anthologies, *Making Waves* (1989) and *The Forbidden Stitch* (1989), at the end of the decade.

Without a doubt, the peculiar social and cultural circumstances under which Wong's book was written, published, and originally canonized need to be recog-nized in accounting for its success with the cultural establishment. According to Elaine Kim, the popularity of *Fifth Chinese Daughter* initially grew out of three contexts: a new receptivity in the American literary market to representations of "Chinese family lives" from the mid-1930s through the late 1940s owing to the United States' political and military alliance with Nationalist China (although this new interest in Chinese American life remained largely an extension of the "liberal" side of traditional mainstream perceptions of this minority group as "unassimilable" practitioners of exotic or foreign customs); the dominance of the ethnicity paradigm for immigrant acculturation, a paradigm within which Asian Americans were incorporated only as cultural other on unequal terms; and America's need to stress a national tradition of racial tolerance and equality of op-portunity during cold war ideological exchanges with communist countries that charged the United States with racial discrimination and class oppression (1982, 60). The official endorsement of Wong's *Fifth Chinese Daughter* in the 1950s, in this sense, does suggest the popular canonization of this Chinese American woman writer's autobiography as a hegemonic process of selective appropriation and domestication.[3]

Despite the fact that Wong's work was initially used to shore up conventional norms and values in common sense terms, the meaning of her text, in view of the book's mixed reception since the 1970s, obviously did not simply mirror the con-servative political climate of the cold war. This phenomenon suggests that cul-tural hegemony is maintained not through *systematic* solicitation of consent to pre-siding values but through selective establishment of hegemonic relations in areas vital to the immediate interests of the ruling ideology. Even within such areas, as Tony Bennett suggests, hegemonic domination is rarely exercised without simul-taneously producing potential forms of opposition that the reigning power is un-able to recognize because of the limitations of its contingent concerns (1993, 72–73). From this perspective, the censored "personal" elements in Wong's work may be only those identifiable as directly harmful under the political atmosphere of the mid-1940s and early 1950s, while other ideological potentials in Wong's work were allowed to exist in suppressed or embryonic forms at other levels of the autobiography.

Belated recognition of such potential in Wong's book during and after the 1980s shows that the Asian American autobiographical articulation cannot be seen as a transparent, unmediated account of women's subjective experience or as an unproblematic realization of their desired selfhood, and that the dominant culture's successful censorship of some elements in such an articulation does not preclude its failure to detect or to censor other ideological possibilities in it. This surplus dimension of Wong's work suggests that no ideology is a simple, organic entity that informs a text in a unitary, stable, and easily definable fashion, and that any ideological domination, in its asymmetrical coverage of activities, always "potentially contains space for alternative acts and alternative intentions which are not yet articulated as a social institution or even project" (Williams 1979, 252). In this sense, neither the texts' lack of perceived challenge to the dominant culture at the time of its publication nor its recognizable strategy of unnegotiated accommodation to the political establishment can provide a ground for retrospective prescriptions of what narrative strategies the author should or should not have taken. The extent to which this text's ideological implications are self-contradictory and contingent on its shifting contexts of meaning-making indicates the limitations of interpreting a work such as Wong's as if it were only an instantiation or a simple reflection of the dominant ideology of its time. This is not to deny that *Fifth Chinese Daughter* can and did serve politically conservative ends at the time of its canonization. It is to emphasize that hegemonic subjectivity is always precarious, and that fixing Wong's autobiography as a work that always "needs to be criticized" for "what it stands for" (Su 1994, 20) would prevent us from raising important questions about specific processes of cultural production and reproduction.

One such question is obviously how to account for the specific historical conditions under which the alternative potentials of Wong's work are either neglected or recognized. In his discussion of the changing horizon of reading, Hans Robert Jauss makes a distinction between a text's initial "perceptual" and its subsequent "reflective" interpretations. According to Jauss, initial reading often fulfills the significances of the text that meet existing social and cultural norms and resists other significances because of their incompatibility with the "horizontal structure" of such reading experience. A transformative reading process, Jauss suggests, entails a continuous readjustment of expectation and evaluation in a three-act hermeneutic execution—thematic, interpretive, and motivational—which dialogically opens up the given horizon of expectations and reveals textual significations hidden from previous interpretations (1982, 141–43). Although limited by its lack of theorization on sociomaterial influences or constraints on specific acts of interpretation, and by its narrow focus on the aesthetic consumption rather than the cultural production of literature, Jauss's distinction is useful for the purpose of my analysis in its implicit recognition of the existence of ideological layers in a single text. Building on Jauss's observation, I would suggest that the significance of the gendered articulation in *Fifth Chinese Daughter* did not acquire ideological cogency for readers of the early 1950s because its recognition depended on the impingement of feminism on the Asian American community in the 1970s and 1980s, a condition that enabled readers and critics such as Yin, Paulson, Kingston, Lim, and Ling to identify retrospectively with, enlarge, and disseminate previously unrecognized grievances in the book as an ideological project.

The overriding factor in the selection and popular canonization of Wong's work in the 1950s was the political need for celebrating the American social system in the midst of cold war ideological confrontations. The devaluation of Wong's work after the early 1970s by many Asian American critics similarly reflected powerful calls for an awakening of ethnic pride within Asian American communities, a development largely shaped by efforts to overcome race and class barriers and by social struggles to end economic inequality in American society. The oppositional force of such calls was understandably directed against the assimilationist impulses that defined the dominant culture's position and precluded contestations from the subordinated social groups. During this phase of the struggle to initiate a race- and class-based cultural resistance, the issue of gender was not seen as a sufficient base for ethnic solidarity and consequently went largely unrecognized as an important rallying point for Asian Americans' collective interests. In this ideological climate, *Fifth Chinese Daughter* was read as a text in the opponent's camp because of its explicit tendencies toward cultural accommodation. Later discovery of sparks of contestation in *Fifth Chinese Daughter* by Asian American critics reflected the emergent contentions of Asian American feminists who were challenging the objectivity of previously all-encompassing articulations of Asian American cultural integrity by male voices in the community. Under such circumstances, readers with a horizon of expectations strongly informed by feminist perspectives would locate the "ideological seams" in Wong's text, bring into full play the previously unfulfilled significance of the work's gender perspective, and attempt to expand the significance of Wong's work into a collective endeavor in which Asian American women's alternative voice could become part of the values that the community was seeking to create in the larger social realm. Absence of that voice thus became substantiated into an ideological presence for many readers. From this perspective, acknowledgment of the ongoing validity of earlier critiques of *Fifth Chinese Daughter* must be made in full recognition of their unintentional complicity with the cultural establishment in erasing gendered concerns in Wong's work, just as feminist rereadings of the autobiography need to take note, as Su cautions, of the entanglement of gender with race and class.

The opening up of the previously "resisted" significance in *Fifth Chinese Daugh-*

ter in terms of Wong's "divided narrative voice" and her struggle and search for an identity "within the forces of the fragmented world of Chinese American women" (Yin and Paulson 1982, 58–59) does not, however, simply illustrate the existence of layers in the horizon of expectations as new audiences engage texts; it also makes possible a reading of gender in Wong's articulation in ways that reassert the category's structurally related, though textually diluted, dimension of race. Su's symptomatic reading of the significance of Wong's work, even though advanced as a critique of the author's assimilationism, is instructive:

> Jade Snow Wong upholds [her] *claim* to theoretical inclusion while appropriately adhering to the practical exclusion of herself—she stays in her proper place. If Jade Snow, the character, and Wong, the author, are finally participants, they participate in the service of American ideology by *voicing* the very terms of their exclusion while simultaneously professing otherwise. The inherent contradictions in the divided voice of *Fifth Chinese Daughter* effectively force Wong's mimicry to expose the ambivalent rhetoric of American ideology itself. (1994, 38)

This nuanced analysis offers an ironic but insightful critique of race relations in American society by taking seriously the contradictions in the female protagonist's double voice. And it shows, once again, that no text is inherently conservative or reactionary and that its significance depends on historically constituted acts of interpretation and modes of consumption (see also Barrett 1988, 700–701). Textual contradictions or differences are not in themselves a guarantee of ideological subversion; for the reader, who chooses either to unpack such contradictions and differences in the historical conjunctions within which they take shape or to bypass them and their connections, is ultimately responsible for a text's ideological significance and its aesthetic valuation. Su is certainly correct when she points out that some of the contradictory responses to *Fifth Chinese Daughter* reveal a reductive interpretive tendency among Asian American critics who read Wong's work either totally negatively or entirely in positive terms, that is, "bad politics = bad art" or "good politics = good art" (1994, 26–27). I would add that such a reductive view of the relationship between art and politics is not uncommon in current Asian American cultural criticism in general, namely, to see a text's ideological effect as equivalent to its literary effect or vice versa, an equation that characteristically leads critics to "consider aesthetic value only in so far as it can be attributed to supposedly 'progressive' texts" (Barrett 1988, 699). The flip side of this view, predictably, is to judge a literary work always in terms of ideological struggle, a struggle that is seen as always consciously waged and always capable of bearing out the critic's own political intentionalities. In its extreme form, this approach simplifies both politics and aesthetics, and prevents investigation of Asian American literature of the 1957–1980 period as a truly historical process.

The interplay between different ideological significances assigned to *Fifth Chinese Daughter* at different times by readers within the same ethnic community thus highlights the complexities of reader expectations when confounded by race, class, gender, national origins, and other historical considerations. An interrogation of critical assessments of an ethnic work of literature clearly needs to recognize the fact that the ethnic writer can never fully anticipate how initial "perceptual" interpretations of his or her work involve horizons of expectations that may privilege certain significances and resist others, as we have seen in the case of Maxine Hong Kingston's surprise over mainstream reviews of *The Woman Warrior.* This interrogation must also recognize that subsequent "reflective" interpretations of an ethnic text may shift its horizons as new readers, new historical circumstances, and new interpretive strategies or perceptual proclivities make available the resisted significances effaced by first readings. Thus, readers' horizons of expectations possess a social dialogism: they shape judgments of a literary work's "cultural influence"—its potential to challenge the presiding assumptions and systems of values of its time (Gunn 1979, 144–45)—and when changed over time, can ground the excavation of the hidden significances in a text, becoming what Edward Said calls "producers of circumstances" (1983, 33).[4]

The historicity of the horizon of expectations implies that the complex ideological meaning in Asian American literary discourse can be best conceived only through fully situated and fully historical readings and rereadings. The contestatory positions of texts such as *America Is in the Heart, No-No Boy,* and *Eat a Bowl of Tea* when originally published clearly set them apart from other pre-1970s works such as Betty Lee Sung's *Mountain of Gold* or Virginia Lee's *The House that Tai Ming Built.* But the point of my analyses of responses to *Fifth Chinese Daughter* is that literary texts are constitutive of culture in different ways. Although we can sometimes retrospectively interpret Asian American texts such as Bulosan's, Okada's, or Chu's as having the potential to change the reader's horizon of expectations, a work's contestatory features cannot be viewed in absolute terms, nor, in my view, should those features constitute a norm against which to measure other works. Instead, a work's multivalent features should be seen as a point of entry into sustained investigations of the cultural contexts of its emergence and reception —including the condition of the emergence of new interpretive positions—and of the interactive and mutually defining relationship between its layered meanings and the reader's layered horizon of expectations. Alternative readings of even a text as ideologically conservative as *Fifth Chinese Daughter* illustrate both the tensions between the primary context of a text's meaning-making and the historical constraints initial readers had to confront in interpreting it, and between the specificity of its initial significances and the changing social, cultural, aesthetic, and ideological contexts in which the text is subsequently assessed and reassessed.

Ethnic Authenticity: A Necessary but Weak Choice

Ever since the mid-1970s, the issue of ethnic authenticity has been a crucial site for the Asian American community's self-contestation about how it relates to mainstream culture and the majority society. One recurring theme of this ongoing polemic, as we have seen, was reflected in the negative assessments of Maxine Hong Kingston's autobiography *The Woman Warrior* by the editors of *Aiiieeeee!* regarding the use, or the alleged misuse, of Asian cultural traditions in literary representations of Asian American images. During the initial debate over the issue, commentators on various sides of the controversy tended to argue about the editors' position on moral grounds and in terms of such binary views as historical truth versus cultural appropriation, artistic freedom versus censorship, or masculine univocality versus feminist difference. More recent attempts to address the controversy have been strongly influenced by poststructuralist problematization of historicist assumptions about origin, which typically casts the issue of authenticity in a negative light, or simply dismisses it as of little theoretical or political consequence. What seems missing from these approaches is a serious examination of ethnic authentication as a political process through which Asian American writers had to pass in their cultural struggles in order to gain an oppositional— and ironic—consciousness about their being America's racial other. In particular, I would suggest, critical examination of authenticity claims needs to consider the phenomenon as "a form of historical contingency," as well as to investigate the structural tension between its tendencies toward "arbitrary" and "conditional" contingency within the given historical imperative, or, to use two traditional categories, between the symbolic-idealist and the social-materialist dimensions of the construction of Asian American cultural identity.[5]

Strategies of reclaiming cultural heritage or affirming community traditions, as shown in my readings in Chapters 4 and 5, spring partly from Asian American writers' need to invent a metaphor to counter the exclusionary Euro-American cultural typology of migration and assimilation and partly from their need to speak across social and historical ruptures to present-day concerns. The adoption of "non-Western" or nonstandard literary models (Kingston's experiments with talk-story, Chin's use of the image of Guan Goong, Chu's invocation of tea, and Okada's deployment of the Momotaro tale) implies Asian American writers' suspicion of the epistemological reliability of established literary conventions, just as the representation of localized experience with oppression implies these writers' deliberate projection of disturbing reminders of mainstream history and culture that resists acknowledgment of the experience of its submerged members. George Lipsitz calls the valorization of ethnic community heritage in literature "counter-memory," with which the ethnic writer looks "to the past for the hidden histories excluded from dominant narratives" and attempts to reframe such narratives in order to be seen or heard publicly (1990, 213), an analysis that aptly describes Chin's and Kingston's general approach in their writings.

The extensive ethnic archival work involved in the fashioning and deployment of such strategies constituted an important form of cultural struggle for Asian American writers in the 1970s and part of the 1980s. As Glenn Omatsu observes, during the Asian American cultural revival in the 1970s, writers and artists took part in "historical rooting"—reclaiming the past and recovering "buried cultural traditions"—in order to "create new visions of community life" on the basis of the writers' and artists' active participation in emancipatory social movements (1994, 20, 30–31). As both a product of and a contributor to these struggles, projects of "historical rooting" were motivated mainly by political rather than cultural considerations: the purpose was to appeal to inside knowledge and collective solidarity and to construct a spatiality that could provide legitimation for large-scale mobilization and collective action in the historical present. The kinds of resources that a figure such as Frank Chin found in the Guan tradition and in heroic Asian American immigrant achievements directly mirror such political considerations. Underlying deployment of these cultural strategies was not, I would emphasize, a naive impulse to return to some unblemished origin, but rather a moral critique of the historical rupture in the present through a "critical revisiting" of or an "ironic dialogue" with the past—to use Linda Hutcheon's words (1988, 4)—and through a symbolic expression of desire for a source of stability and assurance, within a self-consciously evoked and critically understood frame of reference.

In analyzing such strategies in terms of whether they can lead to effective political solidarity, the critic needs to begin with a recognition of what Ernesto Laclau calls the "double requirement" for an effective counterhegemonic cultural operation: an alternative cultural meaning must articulate itself as simultaneously *subordinated to* and *differentiated from* the given knowledge (1993, 285). Hypothetically, such a double requirement can be met through the subaltern's balanced engagement with the vector of similarity and continuity and the vector of difference and rupture (Hall 1990/1994, 395). Yet owing to the fact that Asian American writers often waged their cultural struggle from the "permanent trace" (Laclau 1993, 285) of their material disenfranchisement within their given social and political space, their use of authenticating strategies often privileges the arbitrarily contingent (or the symbolic-idealist) dimension over the conditionally contingent (or the social-materialist) dimension of their construction of cultural identity. Such a historically determined orientation in Asian American writers' authenticity claims, as is shown in Kingston's approaches to *The Woman Warrior* and *China Men,* often involves a conscious or unconscious simplification of the problematic relationship between historical events and their representation, and an exaggeration of the accountability of the symbolic-idealist for the social-materialist. This skewed operation of ethnic authentication, which is further complicated and destabilized by individual writers' varying investments in the strategy, tends to produce several ambiguous consequences: (1) a radical undecidability in the meaning of the cultural identity it constructs; (2) unintended results, including possible betrayal of the writer's original political intentions, through reliance on non-Western cultural symbols or conventions; and (3) an unintentional preservation of Asian Americans as cultural other, at least in part, according to the terms of Western knowledge production. The inherent contradictions between the moral necessity and the epistemological limitations of making authenticity claims in a largely Euro-centric culture therefore points up the essentially rhetorical nature of the strategy, as well as the political ambiguity of the space imagined by Asian American writers in their cultural struggles.

This situation is partly responsible for the ethnic community's internal debates over the accuracy of its individual members' accounts of its ancestral cultural resources, debates that can be seen as part of the intersubjective negotiations within the community springing from the different assumptions that inform strategies of ethnic authentication in relation to their variously experienced material world. When some Asian American critics accuse Kingston of "faking" Chinese history and cultural tradition in *The Woman Warrior,* for example, they typically measure the text's representations of Chinese and Chinese American women's lives against "reality" based on received—and presumably more authentic—versions of Chinese history or cultural traditions. Yet history-making is never ideologically and culturally innocent; whatever the interpretive perspective and formal coherence with which "authentic" historical fact is related, no historical account can "represent a perfect equivalent of the phenomenal field it purports to describe, in size, scope, or the order of seriality in which the events occurred" (White 1978, 111). A further complication in the critical debate about the "truth" of *The Woman Warrior*'s representation of Chinese American women's experience is its rather free rendering or appropriation of Chinese myths and legends. For some critics, the "truth" of Asian American experience is "public" and common and best conveyed through "realist" representation, whereas for Kingston, clearly influenced by modernist and postmodernist skepticism, "truth" is emergent, perspectival, and based on metaphorically constructed connections with her individual experience. A more balanced analysis might recognize, as Kingston did in reference to the reception of her first book, that "mythic" authentication strategies have limitations and provide little guidance for readers accustomed to understanding Asian American images stereotypically, particularly at a time of this minority literature's historical emergence. On the basis of such a recognition, Shawn Wong contends that there is "a need to know what the real is" (quoted in Solovitch 1991, 11). But I would add emphatically that even if, by a stroke of magic, we ultimately had access to a full and authentic past and succeeded in transparently representing what had actually happened, such an accomplishment would be no

guarantee that the reader would necessarily trust a writer's representation, nor
would a presumably restored authentic self grounded in that past necessarily lead
to its institutional acceptance.[6]

As an instance of such claims, consider Chin's borrowing of the figure of Guan
Goong from Chinese literary history as a model both for the Chinese American
writer's "warrior" resistance to racial oppression and for Chinese American heroism. This act of cultural recovery is neither as faithful nor as innocent as Chin
claims. In reviving Guan Goong as a counterhegemonic cultural emblem, he emphasizes qualities of the figure useful for his purposes—martial prowess, generosity, commitment to justice, and readiness to help the weak and contest the
powerful—while he obscures aspects of Guan not useful in an American context,
such as his devotion to the interests of the ruling class and the feudal emperor of
the East Han Dynasty rather than to the common people, and his well-known
temperamental flaws, conceit and jealousy.[7] Chin's selective use of the story of
Guan Goong involves both disruption of the conventional significance that Chinese literary historians find in this figure and extension of aspects of Guan Goong
that are morally empowering to the burgeoning Asian American movement.
Chin's vision of Guan Goong is clearly ordered by issues in the present-day Asian
American life, and by his strategy of emphasizing the moral importance of Guan's
heroism in formations of an "authentic" tradition for Asian American writing. It
is worth pointing out in this connection that while Chin's use of Guan Goong is
informed by the symbolic-idealist tendency in his oppositional construction of
Asian American identity, his insistence on the effectiveness of this figure remains
bound up, as I have shown in Chapter 4, with his emphasis on racial stereotyping
as merely cultural and completely dominant (a conviction that can be further illustrated by his binary formulation of "racist hate" and "racist love"). As a consequence, Chin sees little possibility of carrying out effective struggles against
racial stereotyping on the terrain where Asian American cultural voices must co-
habit with the dominant racial ideology, and he ignores other forms of social production and maintenance of Asian Americans as racial other. These are key reasons
why Chin indiscriminately attacks any ambivalent expression of desire by Asian
American writers, while increasingly embracing a supposedly pure or genuine
Chinese version of the heroic tradition despite his awareness of the rhetorical nature of his own strategy. In his insistence on idealizing and normalizing a recov-
ered Chinese cultural tradition, Chin overtextualizes the intended political meaning of his authenticating strategy, increases the distance between the rhetoric he
uses and the social issue he critiques, and, in claiming ethnic purity, produces a
closure in his communication with Asian American writers' counterdiscourse
against racial stereotypes.

In contrast to Chin's insistent return to a Chinese origin, Kingston seems to
adopt an opposite, though obviously no less problematic, approach. As Shirley

Lim has recognized, Kingston privileges a narrative strategy in her treatment of the issue of ethnicity in *The Woman Warrior* which positions her not as an advantaged insider of the Asian culture but as similarly disadvantaged as her Anglo readers in "finding that Asian component bizarre, distasteful, and difficult to comprehend." By appropriating and anticipating the mainstream reader's response to Chinese culture, Lim further observes, Kingston's strategy thus replicates "the instability and uncertainty of identification that the non–Asian American reader undergoes in relation to the difficult ethnic world being presented" (1993, 161).[8] Kingston's self-conscious search for common areas with mainstream values through calculated distancing from "bizarre" aspects of Chinese culture sheds light on our understanding of the nature of Chin's claims of a total identification with a "heroic tradition" in that same culture. To some extent, the two writers' contrasting attitudes toward Chinese cultural tradition suggests how gender and generational differences can create psychological distances in narrative perspectives from a shared cultural resource of resistance (Kingston is second-generation Chinese American while Chin is fifth-generation American-born). Yet within the political context of the two writers' specific use of authenticating strategies, their differing attitudes may be seen more appropriately as emblems of their different assessments of the extent to which Chinese culture can be used to carry out counterhegemonic projects and of their different degrees of awareness of the limitations of adopting such a strategy. As I showed earlier in this chapter, Chin identifies with Chinese culture only selectively. He finds most offensive the perpetuation in American popular imagination of Asians as nothing but practitioners of cooking, exotic customs, and alien traditions. For him, these images directly contribute to mainstream society's categorization of Asian Americans in terms that deny them their histories and their social relevance to American society. In this sense the "China" that Chin refuses to identity with is not fundamentally different from what Kingston distances herself from: it is a China constructed by Western cultural discourse and encoded with Western prejudices against and contempt for everything it represents. It is clear that both Chin and Kingston internalize the contradictions of such a Western construct of China as American-borns growing up during the early decades of the cold war years. The difference between their approaches is that Kingston tries to reappropriate such a construct to the ethnic writer's advantage while Chin attempts to replace it by counteridentification with selective alternative cultural images.

The two writers' unwillingness to identify themselves with stereotypically produced images of China in American culture is contrasted with their shared reliance on a largely imagined premodern Chinese culture as a ground for subject formation. Implicit in their ambivalent attitudes is a recognition of the difficult historical relationship between the United States and China both before and after World War II, a relationship that affected Chinese Americans negatively, its ramifications reflected in the portrayals in *Eat a Bowl of Tea, The Woman Warrior,* and *China Men,* as well as in Chin's two plays. I see Chin's and Kingston's use of a premodern China for historical commentary on their American present as both strategically necessary and ideologically confining. Although premodern Chinese culture provides the writers with some degree of flexibility in positioning themselves with regard to their present-day concerns, such reference also requires that they abide minimally by the assumptions and conventions of the culture they appropriate. Totally disregarding such assumptions and conventions, as Kingston often does, may render the appropriation less effective, while claims of total identification, such as Chin frequently makes in his later writings, threaten to render the effort of little relevance to actual Asian American concerns. In particular, I would argue that these writers' reliance on Chinese culture to envision Asian American issues about race, gender, or class (along with their simultaneous distancing from contemporary China as a political entity) reflect some inherent contradictions of being Chinese American in contemporary America. Such contradictions are well articulated by the historian Sucheng Chan when she observes:

> [T]he acculturation process experienced by Asians in America has run along two tracks: even as they acquired the values and behavior of Euro-Americans, they simultaneously had to learn to accept their standing as racial minorities—people who, because of their skin color and physiognomy, were not allowed to enjoy the rights and privileges given acculturated European immigrants and native-born Americans. In short, if they wished to remain and to survive in the United States, they had to learn to "stay in their place." . . . (1991, 187)

A recognition of such contradictions suggests that the strategy of ethnic authentication was a risky choice historically available to Asian American writers of the pre-1980s period and that the interventionary value of the strategy lay not in the actual images associated with it but in the images' ironic evocation of the nature of Asian Americans' social status as well as in their potential for reorienting Asian American writers' cultural struggle toward wider sociocultural terrains.

To reckon with the "truth" obtained through the strategy of ethnic authentication, a critic must recognize the inherent limitations of individual acts of culture collecting, which necessarily involve, as James Clifford suggests, concealment, distortion, or extension of certain cultural meanings that distance, time, and social rupture mark as different (1987, 231–32). The arbitrary and rhetorical nature of such a strategy points toward the danger of treating the ethnic author as "authentic" and equating literary representation with phenomenal reality: it runs the real risk of leading naive readers to a reductionist overemphasis on the documentary aspect of Asian American literary works and reinforces mainstream assumptions that ethnic writing is generally more factual than literary, more political than artful, and hence an embodiment of an unmediated and uninflected art of naive representation. Yet, when ethnic writers experiment with alternative literary modes, they take the risk that mainstream culture will misinterpret their positions, especially through the application of conventional cultural codes to elements of a work that invite misreading simply because the text assumes rather than provides the knowledge needed to contextualize their implications. As members of an emergent culture, Asian American writers must often face mainstream readers with little knowledge of Asian American history and experience, and influenced by assimilationist and other either/or conceptual categories. It is a measure of the confrontational posture of the writers discussed in this book that their authentication strategies tend to place on their readers the obligation to acquire new contextual knowledge and conceptual frameworks.

An awareness of the linguistic entanglement of the emergent with the conventional, as well as of mainstream culture's tendency to mistranslate the meaning of ethnic texts, should alert us to arguments about "authenticity" on the basis of contrasting an actually lived experience with its rhetorical representation or with the unpredictable results of such representation's reception. Instead of measuring an author's strategies of authentication against abstractions of Asian American sensibility, we must situate discussions of "authenticity" fully within the matrix of a text's reading environment, its self-enunciation, and the historical condition of its construction. In addition, investigations of implicit or explicit authenticity claims also need to take into account how a particular writer "matches" the schema of meanings of non-Western history or myth with the actualities of the historical present he or she negotiates. In other words, the aim of an ethnic writer is not "to see the object as in itself it really is," but rather to adjust the schema with which the readers see, or fail to see, that history. Such a representation of the past may unavoidably involve the ethnic writer's violation of the "mental set" of both the existing horizon of expectation and the ancestral historical or cultural materials in order to address present-day issues effectively.[9]

When recognizing both the conjunctural need and the epistemological limitations of strategies of ethnic authentication, we should also remember that such strategies are constructed out of a space of irreconcilable ideological differences. As can be seen in my readings of *No-No Boy, The Woman Warrior,* and *The Year of the Dragon,* the complex operations of these strategies in the work of Asian American writers of the 1957–1980 period largely unfold within this ambivalent but contested space: these texts dynamically engage the cultural and political conditions under which they are produced, challenge the cultural assumptions of readers rooted in traditional values and ethics, and foreground the present concerns that inhere in their authenticity claims, claims that everywhere depend on historicization of rhetoric for their force of persuasion. At the same time, as we have also seen, Asian American writers often make such claims as self-conscious strategic choices: they critically reconnect to lost history without reinscribing old categories of abuse, and they assert ethnic subjectivity without constituting it according to available orientalist designs.

Responsibility: Writers and Critics

The debate over authenticity claims, like the strategy's construction, is fundamentally political, especially because of its implications for the kind of Asian American agency being imagined and promoted. This inevitably raises the question of responsibility that Asian American writers and critics bear in creative and theoretical projections of their individual visions in relation to their communities' struggles for justice at the social level. Such a question has, as we have seen, engaged the attention of various critics since the early 1970s with regard to Kingston's position in *The Woman Warrior,* and it forms a crux of the assessment of more recent works such as David Henry Hwang's *M. Butterfly* (1986), Sara Suleri's *Meatless Days* (1987), Bharati Mukherjee's *Jasmine* (1989), and Amy Tan's *The Joy Luck Club* (1989).[10]

Assumptions about literary creation enter strongly into arguments that lend significant weight to a writer's creative freedom, assumptions that can be traced back to postromantic perspectives that privilege the writer's intellectual autonomy and envision creativity as essentially a private process marked by the artist's individual traits and commitments. (In contemporary American life, these assumptions are often supported by appeal to First Amendment rights.) From such perspectives, the writer's responsibility is mainly to speak his or her "inner" vision rather than to articulate perceptions according to external agendas or non-artistic concerns, a formulation that masks complications raised by a writer's gender, race, ethnicity, class, cultural position, or political allegiance.[11] For example, Kingston's initial claims of such freedom in response to charges that she lacked ethnic responsibility in writing *The Woman Warrior*—"Why must I 'represent' anyone besides myself? Why should I be denied an individual artistic vision?" (1982, 63)—indicate both the abstractness of the formulation itself and the complexity of cultural reproduction when it involves the interpretation of a literary work by a writer of color. Yet, as I have tried to show in my discussion of ethnic authenticity, whether Asian American writers consciously assume the role of spokesperson for their communities or warily guard against the limitations imposed by that role, readers tend to measure their works as either confirming or resisting the ethnic group's culturally assigned status, a fact that may be inescapable for Asian American writers who are inextricably implicated in knowledge production in the United States. In other words, whether an Asian American writer is self-consciously perspectival or programmatically independent, his or her text participates ideologically in public discourse with both the established culture and underrepresented ethnic communities, a participation that necessarily involves the author's writing project in the dynamics generated by what Sau-ling Wong defines as "competing claims" on the writer: the need to project ethnic solidarity on the one hand and the necessity to affirm the specificities of personal vision on the other (1988, 4–5). It is precisely within this context that Edward Said makes the observation that "there is no such thing as a private intellectual" (1994, 12). The fundamental question of responsibility is then not whether an Asian American writer agrees with a single version of Asian American history or identity but rather how constructively he or she deals with the competing claims Wong highlights. Wong not only recognizes the multiple political constraints faced by ethnic writers from emergent cultures but also cautions against the pitfall of assigning such writers a definitive responsibility as public "representatives" of their communities, a responsibility that implies a virtual lack of freedom to negotiate the conflicting demands of artistic creation. Nevertheless, I would add that the difficulty of negotiating such "competing claims" should not be underestimated because of the existence of multiple determinants for the outcomes of the negotiation, and that a constructive reconciliation between the two lies *ultimately* not in the ethnic writer's own intentional efforts but rather in the work's critical reception in discursive reading formations.

Whatever an Asian American writer's sense of authorial responsibility, he or she has no practical control over the way written discourse functions under given circumstances, even when the writer makes "informed" aesthetic choices and dialogic projections designed to leave little room for readers to misappropriate that discourse by applying conventional cultural codes. More specifically, Asian American writers often face at least two kinds of risks in publishing their works in a culture largely conditioned by Eurocentric assumptions: the risk of unpredictable effects of articulating their positions, and, more predictably, the risk of the majority culture's misappropriating their representations of ethnic experience. Given these factors, no writer can know how to avoid undecidable risks or to find a "safe" ground outside the force fields in which Asian American literature has to make its presence felt. Similarly, my attempt to describe and analyze various constraints on Asian American literary voices presupposes no "neutral" or ideologically "advantageous" space external to this historical moment and its cultural politics from which to examine the issue of responsibility. But I feel strongly that attention to such constraints offers possibilities of "prevention of harm" (Smiley 1992, 105) in Asian American writers' efforts to achieve progressive cultural pluralism, and enables critics to deal with the consequences of risk taking constructively. One possible result of such attention, if maintained critically, pervasively, and accumulatively, is that it enlarges the reservoirs of potentially functional alternative cultural codes in society, as well as setting *"limits* to the degree to which

a society-in-dominance can easily, smoothly and functionally reproduce itself"
(Hall 1985b, 113).

Maxine Hong Kingston's negotiation with the publication and reception of *The
Woman Warrior* and *China Men,* seen in this light, illustrates how an author's
recognition of the complexities of "risk taking" in a work can lead to fruitful efforts to reconstruct her readers' horizons of expectations. Obviously, my personal
judgment that Kingston's intertextual negotiations were responsible, as were
Chin's in his dramas of the early 1970s, is a retrospective and inevitably presentist
exercise informed by currently available analytical methods. Just as obviously,
there is no guarantee that such negotiations will necessarily produce progressively
"desirable" results or that the writer involved will maintain their negotiating efforts in a consistently self-reflexive fashion.[12] But, as Cornel West might argue,
there is a sure guarantee that the status quo will remain or regress if no such efforts are made at all (1990, 20). From this perspective, the issue of the writer's responsibility does not have to be seen as motivated by a prescriptive or regulating
impulse (a position that precisely renders the question of responsibility meaningless); rather, it arises primarily from taking a historical perspective on the contradictions faced by Asian American writers who express themselves creatively—and
politically—as historically disenfranchised racial, sexual, or cultural subjects in
America. Such contradictions, as I have shown, frequently manifest themselves as
tensions between these writers' attempts to articulate fully their artistic visions
and various external forces that often prevent such articulations from achieving
their immediate cogency; between the undecidable impact of their art and cultural mistranslations of such impact into their social experiences; and between the
writers' need to adjust their positions of enunciation upon assessing the effects of
their prior interventions and their willingness or ability to do so under the conditions they face.

In the process I have described, Asian American critics have played a unique
role of simultaneously collaborating with and critically transforming evolving
Asian American creative voices through debates over issues examined in this
study. The strategies used by Okada, Chu, Chin, and Kingston in their writings
between 1957 and 1980, for example, reflect the historical specificity of the circumstances that helped promote or limit these writers' deployment of the positions adopted in their works. The grounds for my preferences for transformative
reading of these texts presuppose, first, a recognition of the interventionary value
of their exertion of "minimizable essence" (Spivak 1993, 18) to ensure a contested
exchange,[13] without either collapsing the engagement of communication between the "center" and the peripheries or sacrificing subordinate cultures' interests in challenging that construct, and second, the possibility that a revisionary
redescription of these works in light of such a recognition may lead to discovery of
residual possibilities of meaning that can be developed to meet the emerging

needs of Asian America's present and future. In stating the issue in this way, however, I do not assume that the critic's task is to prescribe retrospectively or prospectively what individual Asian American works should or should not mean. On the contrary, I urge critics to be vigilant against assuming that their articulations are somehow better than those of the writers, creating new forms of closure or exclusion in the process of opening fresh areas of hermeneutic or theoretical investigation, and privileging some modes of literary expression over others or refusing to raise and contemplate certain questions while allowing others to thrive. In short, critics must bear the responsibility for being aware of the limitations of their own positions or discourses and, by projecting them as absolute grounds for critical judgment, of the possibility of inflicting violence on the creative voices they analyze.

Various critics have commented on the role of the intellectual in relation to institutional power, cultural hegemony, and the upward mobility intellectuals have gained from the emphasis on academic theories of difference. The issues raised include recognition of how such intellectuals' own ideological positions and political commitments are implicated in their judgments of any particular writer's work, the extent to which they are responsible for institutionalized knowledge production and dissemination, and the contradiction between their vested interest in structurally transforming the institutions in which they work, and their financial dependence on the same institutions for "innovative" teaching and research (e.g., Rey Chow 1993, 15–17; Dirlik 1994; Godzich 1994, 15–35; Ross 1988; Said 1994; West 1987). Critics' individual assessments of the extent and scope of domination and the effects and nature of particular forms of dissent often imply the degrees of their own awareness of and engagement with the social issues in question. As I have discussed at various points in this book, calls by Asian American theorists for cultural heterogeneity and multiplicity constitute a necessary challenge to essentialist notions of identity politics that dominated the early phase of postwar Asian American literary discourse. Yet in finding many pre-1980s positions inherently problematic and hence always already limited, these theorists raise a presentist rather than a truly critical question. For such judgments are premised on the problematic belief that the past is not only bygone—and therefore temporally and spatially sealed—but also easily detachable from its historical present. What these critics often ignore is that the historical or textual objects of their critiques frequently function outside academically certified spheres of knowledge and are directly associated with pressing social and economic problems that cannot be easily engaged through theoretical diagnoses or prescriptions. It is not my argument that critics who oppose essentialist "identity politics" by emphasizing heterogeneous differences are necessarily unconcerned about the material conditions they theoretically signify. I only point out that their critique of essentialist positions, however well grounded and necessary, is often made too easily on the basis of intellectually constructed visions and to the neglect of the possibility that a theoretically sound idea may be ineffective in application and that a theoretically untenable social practice may indicate not its own falsehood but rather theory's inability to exhaust realities.

The ongoing discrepancy between theoretical articulation and worldly existence marks a particularly challenging area of negotiation faced by the critic, especially when his or her theoretical and political representations tend to generate and then follow different logics or dynamics. A dramatic case in point is noted by Ella Shohat:

> While poststructuralist feminist, gay/lesbian, and postcolonial theories have often rejected essentialist articulations of identity, along with biologistic and transhistorical determinations of gender, race and sexual orientation, they have at the same time supported "affirmative action" politics, implicitly premised on the very categories they themselves reject as essentialist. This leads to a paradoxical situation in which theory deconstructs totalizing myths while activism nourishes them. (1995, 167)

Although it addresses an extreme form of mutual interruption between theory and practice, this example usefully suggests that theory and practice do not automatically inform each other toward transformative praxis unless they are organized to do so by the critic, who, as Shohat suggests, has an unavoidable responsibility to reconcile institutionally based deconstructive critiques of essence with social demands for equality through constructive politics. It is important, of course, to identify intersections between poststructuralism and academic minority discourse. But Shohat's example obviously points to a disjunction that is especially difficult to negotiate, namely, that between an academically practiced minority discourse empowered by poststructuralism and racial minorities' socially experienced disadvantage external to or unbounded by the imagined structure of theory. It is to the Asian American critic's involvement in the creation and maintenance of such a disjunction that the following discussion turns.

To a large extent, the difficulty in negotiating the above-mentioned disjunction lies precisely in what is often taken to be a major theoretical breakthrough in the kind of materialist cultural criticism practiced by academic theorists, including Asian American cultural critics: the linkage between culture and the material world. Securing such a linkage has been a valuable contribution of contemporary cultural studies pioneered by the theoretical practice of British cultural studies from the 1950s through the early 1980s.[14] The need to break down the barrier between the social and the cultural initially grew out of British cultural critics' imperative to address

> the failure of the traditional marxist left to confront, in both theoretical and political terms, the beginnings of late capitalism, the new forms of economic

and political colonialism and imperialism, the existence of racism within the
so-called democratic world, the place of culture and ideology in relations of
power, and the effects of consumer capitalism upon the working classes and
their cultures. (Grossberg 1993, 25)

The central task of this critical project is to deconstruct the orthodox Marxist formulation of the hierarchical relationship between economic base and superstruc-
ture, a relationship seen as harboring two theoretical reductions: economic determinism and cultural elitism. Because such reductions effectively separated culture
from society, denied cultural struggle as a viable form of social action, and contributed to the hegemonic power of late capitalism, Birmingham critics turned,
at different stages of the development in cultural studies, to discourse theory,
semiotics, psychoanalysis, and structuralism, despite the contradictory implications of such positions for the original critical commitment of cultural studies to
humanist Marxisms.[15] While these efforts were remarkably successful in relating
social, cultural, and signifying practices as tightly integrated processes, they also
gave rise to the tendency to use "culture" as the initial site of social analysis or political engagement, because "culture," no longer considered merely superstructural, had now become a general way of talking about all social relations and activities. But such a theoretical breakthrough was made not through a developed
theory of culture but rather essentially through the Saussurean theory of language. In this model, culture becomes a determining, productive field through
which social realities are generated, experienced, and interpreted, a mirroring of
the logic that language organizes and constructs and that ultimately provides us
with our only access to reality (e.g., Falck 1989, 9–12; Turner 1990, 13, 15;
Walsh 1993, 237–39).[16] While such a formulation of culture effectively eradi-
cates the reductionism of orthodox Marxism's base/superstructure formulation, as
well as its attendant argument about "false consciousness," it simultaneously reduces, with the aid of other structuralist and poststructuralist insights, social
practice to culture and culture to linguistic discourse or systems of signification—
a reduction that in turn becomes the ground for explanatory operations. For complex reasons, this side effect of cultural studies' early attempts to complicate its
critique of late capitalist culture has become a main ingredient in today's poststructuralist cultural criticism.[17]

In Asian American cultural criticism, one aspect of cultural studies' early efforts
to link the social to the cultural, Louis Althusser's notion of the "material existence" of ideology, has been especially influential since the early 1990s because of
its effective conceptualization of ideologies as materially inscribed "practices" and
"rituals" capable of both producing social relations and initiating subject formation
(see Lowe 1995b, 60–62).[18] Because, according to Althusser, there is virtually no
practice outside of ideology, and since "the category of the subject is only constitu-

tive of all ideology in so far as ideology has the function . . . of 'constituting' concrete individuals as subjects" (1970/1980, 45), ideological result is then social result. Despite its obvious contributions to a reconceptualization of culture, Althusser's notion of ideology depends, as critics have pointed out, on a partial
appropriation of psychoanalytical insights on the one hand and on an uneven theorization of subject formation on the other.[19] Yet because of its tendency to privilege
a linguistic construction of subjectivity, Althusser's view has a special appeal to
poststructuralist critics who practice a top-down approach to theory: it allows them
to stage subversive operations from an ideological field that is already material by
assigning unlimited power to the interpellated subject—ironically contrary to Althusser's belief in the death of the subject—so that this subject can intervene in the
signifying processes and practices and therefore produce social change (see also
Chaney 1994, 191; Turner 1990, 215). An important strategy for this poststructuralist reworking of Althusser's notion of interpellation emphasizes the incomplete, the asymmetrical, or the residual nature of the interpellative process, and the
semiautonomous status of the subject which is now exposed not to one but to a
number of social forces (see Lowe 1995b, 55–56).[20] This situation then allows the
Althusserian subject to find an exit from the aporias of the ideological structure of
interpellation through a self-inflicted fragmentation.

Despite its creative augmentation of the explanatory power of the Althusserian
model, this effort does not supply what is fundamentally missing from Althusser's
original theoretical formulation of ideology: a conceptualization of the construction of alternative space in which to organize and articulate agency—through
lived historical subjects of the state—into "social and historical structures of resistance" (Grossberg 1992, 126). To some extent, this silence in Althusser's theory of
ideology's function in the reproduction of the social relations of production, as
critics suggest, reflects the doubts among French left intellectuals about the efficacy of political practice in the aftermath of the disintegration of revolutionary
politics in France and elsewhere in the world in the 1950s and 1960s. It also reflects the increasing preoccupation of Western humanistic intellectuals with the
determining nature of systems of representation in the face of such failure.[21] This
historically produced defect in Althusserianism is clearly not easy to repair
through dialectical reworking of the arsenal of Althusser's ideological apparatus[22]—for the reformulated Althusserian subjects, flexible as they have become,
are but "individualized and dispersed" rebels (Grossberg 1992, 126), whose successful interventions depend on a heightened linguistic awareness, as well as on a
desensitized regard for the social and the collective. Within this reformulation,
"lived experience" remains not only a deeply suspect category but also an untheorized—and hence theoretically hegemonized—term.

The discussion here is deliberately minimalist but one that may suffice for the
present need of illustrating Shohat's example of the inconsistent theorist at once

committed to the academic discourse of critiquing essentialism and yet keenly aware of its moments of non-working. Underlying this paradoxical situation, I would suggest, lies two further problematics perhaps more fundamental to the kind of cultural criticism now being practiced generally: it does not have a fully theorized aesthetics nor, as a left criticism, does it seriously engage with the question of aesthetic pleasure; and it inherits from structuralist or poststructuralist Marxism, as we have seen, two problematic legacies—a reified concept of ideology and a partial theorization of the question of agency (see Barrett 1988, 701; Pecora 1989, 196, 271).[23] These problematics in turn are responsible for two notable tendencies in current cultural criticism that reproduce the theory/practice dichotomy alluded to by Shohat. First is an overgeneralized negation of teleological history through a construction of ideological opacity and aesthetic playfulness (typically à la psychoanalysis) as the most rigorous and effective form of political opposition. Second is a shifting, especially under challenge, away from such an aestheticized ideological criticism to overt institutional criticism, an engagement that is, of course, crucial to any materialist cultural studies attuned to the Gramscian vision of the organic intellectual. But, as Shohat's example shows, such shifting does not always proceed as a dialogic engagement with the *institutional dimension* of literary or cultural production; rather, it often serves to defuse the obvious tension between critics' political and theoretical representations, or, in some cases, simply to fend off charges of textualism inherent in poststructuralism as a kind of "left formalism" (Erkkila 1995, 569).[24]

Under such circumstances, a responsible critic is faced with the unavoidable task of negotiating what Stuart Hall calls a "double engagement" with theory and practice. On the one hand, one must recognize that material conditions are not sufficient grounds for social practice and hence cultivate an appreciation for "a necessary level of abstraction" in theory; on the other, one must also acknowledge the need to reintegrate theory self-consciously with other levels and kinds of determination and practice at specific political junctures.[25] The purpose of this double engagement, according to Hall, is to achieve contingent forms of "intelligibility" which would allow a dissemination of theory and its gradual realization through practice without reducing one to the other (1986, 57–59, 53). Such an engagement, I would add, can be maintained only through critics' conscious effort to grasp the nature of their social and theoretical experiences, to attend to their interrelated but different requirements, and to negotiate their common grounds as well as their divergent concerns. In this double engagement, the relationship between theory and practice will necessarily remain conflictual and contradictory because of the difficulty of translating theory seamlessly and permanently into practice. What often stands in the way and needs constant negotiation is what Pierre Bourdieu calls "a remainder" of translation (1983, 327). In current Asian American cultural criticism, this remainder tends to be obscured by urges to collapse the ontological into the epistemological, the nondiscursive into the discursive, the actual into the desirable, and the subject empowered by ideology into the subject as an ideological or a structural effect. In facing the challenges of such a remainder of translation in critical bricolage and in the kind of cultural politics we deploy or refuse to engage ultimately resides the critic's responsibility.

Conclusion

From the perspective of the majority culture, Asian Americans may very well be constructed as different from, and other than, Euro-Americans. But from the perspectives of Asian Americans, we are perhaps even more different, more diverse, among ourselves: being men and women at different distances and generations from our "original" Asian cultures—cultures as different as Chinese, Japanese, Korean, Filipino, Indian, and Vietnamese—Asian Americans are born in the United States and born in Asia; of exclusively Asian parents and of mixed race; urban and rural; refugee and nonrefugee; communist-identified and anticommunist; fluent in English and non–English speaking; educated and working class. As with other diasporas in the United States, the Asian immigrant collectivity is unstable and changeable, with its cohesion complicated by intergenerationality, by various degrees of identification and relation to "homeland," and by different extents of assimilation to and distinction from "majority culture" in the United States.

—Lisa Lowe, "Heterogeneity, Hybridity, Multiplicity"

Throughout this book, I have tried to suggest that the Asian American literary discourse from the 1950s through 1980 was constituted by dynamic, complex negotiations leading to an increasing awareness of and critical self-consciousness about the kind of complexity described by Lowe in the epigraph. This process, as I have also tried to show, is marked not by linear developments or sharp dividing lines, but by contradictions and incongruities open to multiple developments and outcomes. The various texts examined in this study have similarly demonstrated that their articulations do not simply reproduce monochromatic cultural positions or types; rather, their discourses are richly at odds with both the established cultural practices against which they emerged, and with the predictability—and the univocality—of certain contemporary theoretical projections of the nature of "traditional" Asian American literary voices. In particular, I have argued that there is nothing inherently "domestic" about these texts. On the contrary, the representations of wartime internment of Japanese Americans described in *No-No Boy,* of the decay of Chinatown bachelor society portrayed in *Eat a Bowl of Tea,* of the strained encounter between Fred and his Chinese mother in *The Year of the Dragon,* and of the Chinese male immigrant laborers recruited to build America's Transcontinental Railroad in *China Men* are all deeply and unavoidably inflected with the authors' diasporic concerns and with their implicit commentary on America's imperial role in international power politics, a role that seriously affects the daily life of their characters. It is the critic, I have argued, who, for contingent political reasons, tends to read rigidity into the "domestic" aspect of these works as a fixed paradigm or to misperceive the relative lack of textual maneuverability in them as a sign of their inherent failure to articulate differences—hence of their tacit alignment with totalization—rather than as an indication of their ironic commentary on America's inability to deliver its democratic promise to Asian immigrants and their American-born descendants in the period in question. Indeed, a self-conscious foregrounding of the international or diasporic dimensions of these texts is crucial to understanding the cultural and political dynamics in an age of unprecedented global movement of capital, population, economic force, and cultural practice. But such a foregrounding should not be made either out of an underestimation of the difficulty of working through the social contradictions in Asian Americans' daily experiences, or out of the mistaken belief that a diasporic perspective is a necessarily advantageous critical position and therefore must be unconditionally emulated or reproduced.

The basic point I have tried to make is that, ultimately, history can develop only contrapuntally. Edward Said describes such a process as follows: "We must be able to think through and interpret together experiences that are discrepant, each with its particular agenda and space of development, its own internal formations, its internal coherence and system of external relationships, all of them coexisting and interacting with others" (1993, 32). In this process, there are always prefigurative traces in the past and unresolved contradictions in the present, and there often exist cultural elements whose political inclinations remain undefined to us unless we critically engage with and interrogate them under specific historical conditions. This means that critics who practice transformative reading need to be open to unacknowledged heterogeneous connections between "traditional" and "contemporary" Asian American projects, and refuse to make absolute either the "dominant" or the "residual" or the "emergent" in their readings. Such an approach also requires that forward-looking attempts to reformulate earlier Asian American studies projects be carried out with a serious recognition of the internal complexities of the tradition from which they launched themselves and of the specific intersubjective connections between "contemporary" and "traditional" positions. Giving attention to these entangled relationships, I suggest, is vital to the creation of fresh openings for critical engagement with the challenges posed for Asian American writers and critics by their past, their present, and their future.

One such challenge, the construction of new forms of political solidarity in this age of global capitalism, cannot be avoided. Various Asian Americanists have advanced provocative scenarios for meeting the challenge: Sau-ling Wong's reaffirmation of the four founding principles for ethnic studies formulated by Ling-chi Wang (1995a, 20), Paul Takagi's and Margot Gibney's reemphasis on "participatory action research" (1995, 123), and Lane Hirabayashi's and Marilyn Alquizola's call for reengagement with the "original critical, counterhegemonic stance" of Asian American studies (1994, 351). These passionate calls testify to the continued operation of America's racial state and to these critics' keen awareness that the notion of cultural hybridity will have little political relevance unless it is viewed as "an excruciating act of self-production" through coalitional mobilizations of the "multiple traces" of "unequal histories and identities" in contemporary Asian American life (Radhakrishnan 1996, 159, 160). They also indicate a broad-minded strategic concern with the need to mobilize counterhegemonic forms of political coalition despite the internal differences and contradictions between and among various Asian American communities.

I have suggested that existing definitions and categories informing Asian American studies may not constitute adequate rallying points for viable and extensive coalition building as we cross into the next century, nor can the exact content and form of early cultural nationalist struggles be adequately reproduced in a period of "scattered hegemonies" (Grewal and Kaplan 1994) and globalized, multileveled cultural and economic operations. In view of these developments, Asian American coalition workers need to develop strategies that are not only able to register the politics of a given praxis but also willing to engage with the discursive consequences of global corporate power's active interventions in contemporary Asian American life, with a recognition that political alliances cannot be stable or explicit under ordinary circumstances but may acquire contingent shapes in certain crisis situations.[1] To facilitate political solidarity under such conditions, Asian American critics and theorists need to reconceptualize both the meaning and procedure of coalition building, while rearticulating their commitment to collective struggle premised on effective human agency. Under ordinary circumstances, for example, we can advocate maximum expression of and attention to multiple discourses of difference, especially when there are power imbalances, taking seemingly heterogeneous articulations in dialogic terms, while recognizing seemingly united voices as inherently different, contested, and negotiated utterances. In crisis situations, we attempt to identify and articulate the nature of the tension, risk defining battlefronts, and negotiate provisional consensus and coalitions along tactical lines that at once recognize the importance of and go beyond class, race, and gender as the sole determinants of shared social interests. Such efforts, if maintained consistently and self-reflexively, promise over time to preserve transformative results and build further space for Asian American writers and critics to struggle and to negotiate our cultural vision for a better future.

Notes

CHAPTER 1

1. Such a critique can be found, for example, in Elaine Kim's essay "Beyond Railroads and Internment: Comments on the Past, Present, and Future of Asian American Studies." Kim uses "railroads" and "internment" as synonyms for the "developmental narratives" of the "essentializing" Asian American cultural nationalism embodied in the "sacred Asian American texts" by such "dead yellow men" as Carlos Bulosan, John Okada, and Louis Chu (1995, 12, 18). It also figures prominently in Lisa Lowe's and Shirley Lim's various comments on such Asian American writers as Louis Chu, Maxine Hong Kingston, Monica Sone (Lowe 1991, 34–35; 1995, 64n 1), Frank Chin, John Okada, and Carlos Bulosan (Lim 1993, 153, 155–56; 1997, 287). Shelley Wong similarly argues that works by Bulosan, Jadw Snow Wong, Kingston, Okada, Shawn Wong, David Mura, and Gish Jen, "shared a certain formal resemblance in their respective relationships to the developmental narrative. The *bildung* that is traced in these narratives usually involves the evolution of an individual character in his or her search for identity and of identification with the larger society. This identity can also be either retrospective or projective, in the sense that some protagonists are committed to recovering or retrieving a lost or submerged identity, while others anticipate the forging of a new identity" (1995, 128–29).

2. The full quotation reads: "One thing that has struck me particularly in the current theorization of Asian-American studies à la the postmodern is what I would call the fetishization of the present, which takes place doubly. First, the notion that our sense of time has become flattened out: we dwell entirely in the present, dismissive of both the past and the future as being contaminated by master narratives of the historical and the teleological. Second, in practice the object of scrutiny tends almost always to be the contemporary, or close to it."

3. With regard to such a view of history, the historian Gordon Chang observes that "the

radical skepticism that occupies the heart of much of postmodern theory, i.e., that the representation of, or even just the search for, historical truths and realities is an impossibility and even a deception because of the constitutive role of language, in which meaning is itself elusive; that no meaningful distinction exists between fiction and historical writing because of the subjectivity of all authors; that the absence of a unified subject makes efforts to advance historical explanation about community or individuals in history, including Asian American history, [is] fundamentally problematic" (1995, 91). See also Mohanty (1995) and Niethammer (1992, 7–23).

4. In phrasing the second half of my question, I draw on Satya Mohanty's observation in a different context that "plurality is thus a political ideal as much as it is a methodological slogan. But the issue of competing rationalities raises a nagging question: how do we negotiate between my history and yours? How would it be possible for us to recover our commonality, not the ambiguous imperial-humanist myth of the shared human attributes that are supposed to distinguish us all from animals, but, more significantly, the imbrication of our various pasts and presents, the ineluctable relationships of shared and contested meanings, values, material resources? It is necessary to assert our dense peculiarities, our lived and imagined differences; but could we afford to leave untheorized the question of how our differences are entwined and, indeed, hierarchically organized? Could we, in other words, afford to have *entirely* different histories, to see ourselves as living—and having lived—in entirely heterogeneous and discrete spaces?" (1992, 128)

5. The quoted remarks are taken from E. Ann Kaplan's discussion of the problematics of what she calls "utopian" and "commercial" postmodernisms in current Western theoretical discourse. The full passage reads: "The common term makes sense if we see the diverse theories as responding to a similar cultural situation: namely, the aftermath of the 1960s. Both concepts of postmodernism arise in the wake of theories and debates about race, class, sex and gender during the past twenty years. Significantly, however, in both cases the thinking has abandoned dialectics, as it had to if it was to embody the end of binarisms. But it is precisely here that the important question remains: if abandoning binarisms necessitates abandoning dialectics, how can we envision an intellectual, psychic, social or cultural life that moves forward, that renews itself, that is self-critical and purposive?" (1988, 5).

6. In his critique of European utopian thinking from the Victorian period to the emergence of poststructuralism, Vincent Pecora offers an analysis of a little examined but crucial context of contemporary theory's privileging of the conceptual over the social: that is, Western intellectuals' anthropological reduction of human behavior to semiotics through adaptation of Ferdinand de Saussure's synchronic linguistics (see also my brief discussion of this problematic in contemporary cultural studies in Chapter 6). Among the thinkers Pecora examines are Georges Bataille, Franz Boas, Emile Durkheim, Jacques Derrida, Martin Heidegger, Marcel Mauss, and Claude Lévi-Strauss (1997, 220–66).

7. Reflecting the strength of Lowe's theoretical formulation is Elaine Kim's and Norma Alarcón's coedited *Writing Self, Writing Nation* (1995), a collection of theoretically challenging essays on *Dictée*. This collection demonstrates the "hybrid and multilingual" subject in Cha's work as a possible new model for the "conversion of the individual into a subject of discourse" (see Lowe 1995b, 64).

8. Lowe's conceptualization of Asian American literary history is specifically reflected in her positive analysis of the migratory agency in Peter Wong's 1986 film *A Great Wall* as an example of diasporic nomadism and in her negative interpretation of Louis Chu's 1961 realist novel *Eat a Bowl of Tea* as an emblem of a masculinist Asian American cultural nationalism. Lowe therefore implicitly proposes, as Sau-ling Wong points out, an "overdrawn" opposition between an "essentialist" Asian American past and an "enlightened" Asian American present, ironically, precisely according to the developmental logic Lowe sets out to problematize (see Wong 1995a, 14–15).

9. This is Lowe's restatement of Gramsci's remark that the tendency toward unity in the subaltern classes' formation of historic bloc "can only be demonstrated when a historical cycle is completed and this cycle culminates in a success" (Gramsci 1971, 54–55), on the basis of his recognizing the subaltern groups' "fragmented and episodic" nature as well as their multiple affiliations with the dominant political formations. These observations by Gramsci, however, seem to be made within different frames of reference in the *Notebooks*. For example, his observation about the subaltern groups' "fragmented and episodic" status is in fact the foundation for his suggestion that these groups had to go through several phases of negotiation, mobilization, and adjustment before they ultimately "developed from subaltern groups to hegemonic and dominant groups" (1971, 52–53). Of the various phases of such attempts at self-organization, Gramsci designates two as essential to establishing a new historical bloc: the subaltern classes' achieving an "autonomy vis-à-vis the enemy they had to defeat"; and their winning "support from the groups which actively or passively assisted them" (1971, 53). What Gramsci emphasizes here is both the complexity of and the practical need for the subaltern groups to fashion provisional unifying politics or to negotiate provisional hegemonies among themselves in order to make common claims on society and, ultimately, to achieve a "unified" status in "the form of the state" (1971, 52, 53). This emphasis constitutes the fundamental premise of the Gramscian notion of hegemony in relation to the historic bloc. Yet Gramsci's remark that the tendency toward unity in the subaltern classes' formation of historic bloc "can only be demonstrated when a historical cycle is completed and . . . culminates in a success" is made, I would suggest, in reference to a very different kind of political scenario, which Peter Gibbon has identified in his reconstruction of Gramsci's central concepts in the *Notebooks* (1983). In rematerializing Gramsci's prison writings against poststructuralist abstractions, Gibbon particularly mentions Gramsci's contemplation of the need for Western Europe to reconceive the struggle undertaken by the Soviet Union in the revolutionary era (i.e., to recognize that a full hegemony cannot be attained before the capture of state power)—a contemplation that, Gibbon suggests, reflects Gramsci's "favorable description" of the socialist political order newly established in the USSR as the epitome of the final realization of proletarian hegemony, as well as his optimistic evocation of a traditional superstructural determinism (1983, 339). Gramsci's assumption is that the achievement in postrevolutionary hegemonic institution building in the Soviet Union offers a possible model for constructing practical forms of working-class "popular morality" in Italy in the 1920s. This assumption then leads him to speculate that "the subaltern classes, by definition, are not unified and cannot unite until they are able to become a 'state'" (1971, 52). Despite its suggestiveness, Gramsci's statement remains politically vague—because he never elaborates on it in the *Notebooks*—in

comparison with his relatively more consistent discussions of the political conditions he considers necessary for the attainment of hegemony, as well as with his emphatic reminder that preparation for hegemony is a matter of monopolistic penetration of the masses (see Gibbon 1983, 338–40). From this perspective, Gramsci's tentative statement can hardly be used as a general paradigm for analyzing contemporary American minority cultural politics.

In critiquing Asian American identity politics, Lowe appropriates Gramsci's speculations in ways that give prominence only to the seemingly discursive moment of Gramsci's discussion of the subaltern struggle. In so appropriating Gramsci's idea, Lowe deftly rejects the teleology of Gramsci's less mechanical notion of determinism implicit in the successive social formations he describes (Gramsci is, after all, a Leninist strategist). But she also reverses Gramsci's historical materialist procedure by using his contingent statement as both the essence of his theory on the subaltern struggle and the starting point of her own argument for the fundamental condition of Asian American heterogeneous differences.

10. For a discussion of Nietzschean perspectivism in relation to postmodern theory, see McGowan (1991, 70–88).

11. In making this observation, I draw on Lawrence Grossberg's discussion of the relationship between articulation, agent, and agency. Relevant aspects of Grossberg's argument can be briefly summarized as follows: such a relationship holds the key to understanding how history is made and how articulations are put into place; agency resides not necessarily in the immediate results of a speaking or acting agent but rather in the tendential forces produced by progressive but undecidable social and cultural struggles within limited spaces; and continuous articulations into the social vector can bend their environment toward their needs or interests (1992, 113–30). The analysis that follows is partially influenced by Grossberg's observations.

12. Lisa Lowe also points out that "some of the most powerful practices may not always be the explicitly oppositional ones, may not be understood by contemporaries, and may be less covert and recognizable than others" (1991, 29).

13. The notion of "negotiation" began to circulate, without consistent development or definitional unity, in some context-oriented cultural and pragmatic theories in the early 1980s. Among critics associated with this concept are Stephen Greenblatt, Dominick LaCapra, Clifford Geertz, Mikhail Bakhtin, and various Birmingham cultural critics. My discussion of "negotiation" draws mainly on the perspectives of Antonio Gramsci, Raymond Williams, Stuart Hall, and Cornel West, among others.

14. Gramsci observes: "The war of position demands enormous sacrifices by infinite masses of people. So an unprecedented concentration of hegemony is necessary, and hence a more 'interventionist' government, which will take the offensive move openly against the oppositionists and organize permanently the 'impossibility' of internal disintegration—with controls of every kind, political, administrative, etc. . . . In politics, in other words, the war of maneuver subsists so long as it is a question of winning positions which are not decisive, so that all the resources of the State's hegemony cannot be mobilized" (1971, 238–39). There are many different readings of Gramsci's war metaphor. My appropriation of it relies on Stuart Hall's interpretation (1985a, 14). For two alternative perspectives, see Perry Anderson (1976) and Harris (1992, 24–29).

15. Poststructuralist readings of Gramsci's politico-military strategy tend to privilege "war of position," with an emphasis, by dint of selective references, on Gramsci's discounting of the relevance of any "war of maneuver," hence describing a politics of fluid plurality that refuses any essentialist fixations (see Gibbon 1983, 331–32). But Gramsci himself seems more cautious about the relationship between his theoretical view and his political practice, when he observes that "the general criterion should be kept in mind that comparisons between military art and politics, if made, should always be taken *cum grano salis*—in other words, as stimuli to thought, or as terms in a *reductio ad absurdum*" (1971, 231).

16. My use of the phrase "the productivity of confrontation" derives from the following observation made by Ernesto Laclau and Chantal Mouffe regarding Gramsci's war metaphor: "This transition to a nonmilitary conception of politics reaches a limit precisely at the point where it is argued that the *class* core of the new hegemony—and, of course, also of the old—remains constant throughout the entire process. In this sense, *there is* an element of continuity in the confrontation, and the metaphor of the two armies in struggle can retain part of its productivity" (1985, 70).

17. Alan Wald points out in this connection that while oppression among some European immigrants may have existed in a *degree* equivalent to that which was experienced by some people of color, it was not equivalent in *kind* (1987, 25).

18. For an elaboration by Spivak on the "strategic use of essentialism," see, for example, her collection of essays, *Outside in the Teaching Machine* (1993, 1–23).

19. A fuller quote from Wong reads: "For Asian American writers in the 1970s and 1980s, the choice of realist forms such as the autobiography and the *Bildungsroman* was determined in part by the demand for such narratives as evidenced by the enthusiastic reception granted earlier such works but also by the need to provide a corrective to what many viewed as disabling misrepresentations of Asian Americans in mainstream literature and culture. The countering of such disabling fictions required the production of positive fictions grounded in the development of an authentic Asian American identity. These realist forms allowed writers to depict the particularities of the Asian American experience and to directly thematize pressing political and social issues confronting Asian Americans. . . . Recognizing the literary work as the site for both the construction and contestation of cultural meanings, and recognizing the broad-based appeal and accessibility of realist forms, Asian American writers continued throughout this period to work within these forms in order to consolidate the Asian American identity needed to galvanize an oppositional social movement" (1995, 129–30).

20. Lisa Lowe particularly identifies the nineteenth-century European novelistic tradition as emblematizing the "developmentalism" of the ethnicity-immigration paradigm. She observes, with regard to the danger of reading Carlos Bulosan's *America Is in the Heart* from such a perspective: "If the novel is read as either a narrative of immigrant assimilation or even as a successful self-definition (the hero leaves the poverty and the lack of opportunity of the Philippines to become a laborer in the United States; he achieves a state of self-consciousness that allows him to become a journalist and to author his autobiography), both characterizations privilege a telos of development that closes off the most interesting conflicts and indeterminacies in the text. In addition, reading the novel as an analog of the

European novel subordinates Asian American culture in several significant ways: not only does the form itself structurally imply an integration and submission of individual particularity to a universalized social norm (which, in the case of the Asian American novel, is racial and ethnic difference coded as anterior to, less than, Western civilization), but in privileging a nineteenth-century European genre as the model to be approximated, Asian American literature is cast as imitation, mimicry, the underdeveloped Other" (1995a, 55).

But in view of the studies of nineteenth-century realist narratives made by Gunter Gebauer and Christoph Wulf (1992, 221–54), Wallace Martin (1986, 57–80), Brook Thomas (1996, 1–52, 270–97), Eric Sundquist (1988b, 501–3), and Samuel Weber (1979), Lowe's observation seems based more on ideological than on theoretical considerations. For as these critics persuasively argue in their respective studies, investigation of nineteenth-century European realist novels can be meaningfully conducted only within the context of their developing responses to Enlightenment assumptions about the nature of imitation, their idealistic expansion of mimetic aesthetics into a constitutive character of social reality (hence raising the question of how reality was defined at that time), and the ironic waning of their representational power in the face of growing commercialism, the epistemological consequences of expanding nationalist ideologies, and the difficulty posed for representation by vast socioeconomic dislocations. With regard to the nineteenth-century French realist novels, Gebauer and Wulf particularly point out: "It is a defining characteristic of nineteenth-century French novels that they occasion a confrontation between the fictional and real social world, a collision organized with the fiction that leads to the destruction of essential elements of the fictional world—a mimesis of *illusions perdues*" (225). From this perspective, they further observe that even "in the Balzacian novel, images are no longer regarded as symptoms or indications but are themselves among the elements out of which society is constructed. . . . Their truth is preconceptual, a doxa; it lies in the concentration and intensity of literary representation. Social reality thus becomes an epicosmos of the realistic novel. The novel does not simply illustrate reality; rather, it is the means by which the truth associated with the sensuousness and substance of reality is rendered accessible to experience" (222–23). For discussions of twentieth-century developments of realist narratives, see, for example, McGowan (1991, 6–12), Gebauer and Wulf (1992, 281–93, 276–80), Bakhtin (1981, 259–422), and White (1978, 185–213).

21. The kind of realism being problematized by these critics can be found in the most rigid claims of naturalism in some classical reflection theories or in the vulgar "socialist realism" proposed by Andrei Zhdanov in the Soviet Union in the early 1930s. But even with these extreme versions of "realism," claims should not be totally equated with results. For discussions of the complexity of realism in relation to some of its problematic tendencies, see Jay (1973, 173–74) and Robins (1993, 226–31).

22. For an effort to address the complexity of the so-called mimetic representation in Asian American literary works, see Cheung (1993, 12–13). Regarding the antirealist tendency in poststructuralism in general, Fredric Jameson observes: "The assimilation of realism as a value to the old philosophical concept of mimesis by such writers as Foucault, Derrida, Lyotard, and Deleuze has reformulated realism/modernism debate in terms of a Platonic attack on the ideological effects of representation" (1977/1988, 135–36). Some critics disagree with Jameson's lumping together of Derrida with poststructuralism or

postmodernism in terms of attack on representation and argue that this generalization results from a misreading of the early Derrida, who attacks correspondence theories not because they enthrall the signifier to the signified but because they liberate the signifier from
its constitutive relation to other signifiers within the totality of the differential system of
signs (e.g., Carroll 1987, 98–104; Owens 1983, 59). For a further critique of the antirealist tendency in postmodernism, see Arac (1989, 294–305).

23. Stephen Sumida was among the first Asian American critics to problematize the reductionism of Ted Gong's sociological reading of *Eat a Bowl of Tea* (1986, 64–66).

24. For discussions of realism as a form of social engagement, see, for example, Brecht
(1964, 107–15), Adorno (in Gebauer and Wulf 1992, 281–93), and Levine (1993, 16–17).

25. Reed's discussion is specifically concerned with James Agee's and Walker Evans's
1941 photographic documentary work *Let Us Now Praise Famous Men*.

26. I have quoted Lentricchia's phrase from H. Aram Veeser's "Introduction" in *New
Historicism Reader* (1994, 4). For a discussion of Asian American identity politics from a
critical postcolonial perspective, see Jenny Sharpe's "Is the United States Postcolonial?"
(1995). Arif Dirlik particularly argues, with regard to poststructuralist critiques of the
Asian American nationalist projects of the 1960s and 1970s, that these projects have in
fact rarely moved from their earlier historicist presentations of Asian America to culturalist
positions (1996, 23–24n 44).

27. See During (1992, 95–98), Pecora (1997, 272–75), Said (1983, 185–88), and
White (1987, 105–20). Regarding the nature of his knowledge/power nexus, Foucault observes: "There is no power relation without the correlative constitution of a field of knowledge, nor any knowledge that does not presuppose and constitute at the same time power
relations" (1979, 27).

28. The passing of the Immigration Act of 1965, which was fully implemented in
1968, reopened the door for Asian immigration to the United States. But these immigration reforms favored professionals or people fleeing totalitarian regimes in Asia. Many of
these new Asian immigrants were politically oriented toward mainstream America. Such
developments in post-1965 Asian immigration has been noted by Sucheng Chan (1990,
140–41) and Glenn Omatsu (1994, 42–50). In making this observation, however, I only
aim to reconstruct the contingent context of the editors' position in relation to the cold
war dimension of post-1965 Asian immigration to America; I do not presume that these
positions were taken by all Asian immigrants in the period or that the new immigrants'
desire for integration was immune to change during their subsequent stay in the United
States.

29. Here and elsewhere in this book, I selectively utilize Bhabha's theoretical perspectives on nationalism and subject formation, perspectives that to some extent depart from
his typically psychologized approaches to these issues. In reading Bhabha against the grain,
I emphasize the complexity of his positions, which I see as open to materialist appropriations.

30. Awareness of this fact is reflected in the writings of a key member of the editorial
collective of *Aiiieeeee!*, Frank Chin, who was personally involved in the redress movements
in the 1970s (1979, 2–14).

31. By "postnational," I refer to positions that can go beyond various American excep-

tionalisms and critically engage with such social and political issues as race, gender, class, or nation in their diverse forms, and contribute to a better understanding of the nature of Asian American literary and cultural practices within a critically national and diasporic perspective. For a recent critical effort toward this direction, see, for example, Kaplan and Pease (1993).

32. Existing postcolonial theories' inadequate attention to the complexity of nationalism can be recognized, for example, in Edward Said's reflections on the subversive role of the Third World cosmopolitan exile: "Nationalism is an assertion of belonging in and to a place, a people, a heritage. It affirms the home created by a community of language, culture and customs; and by so doing, it fends off exile, fights to prevent its ravages. Indeed, the interplay between nationalism and exile is like Hegel's dialectic of servant and master, opposites informing and constituting each other. All nationalisms in their early stages develop from a condition of estrangement. . . . Triumphant, achieved nationalism then justifies, retrospectively as well as prospectively, a history selectively strung together in a narrative form: thus all nationalisms have their founding fathers, their basic, quasi-religious texts, their rhetoric of belonging, their historical and geographical landmarks, their official enemies and heroes" (1990, 359). This characterization of the relations between exile and nationalism, nuanced as it is, problematically constructs the latter as uniform and teleological in nature, while it ignores conditions under which types of nationalisms cannot be programmatically triumphant or successful according to given linguistic or tropological paradigms (see also the distinctions Said makes between "filiation" and "affiliation," 1983, 16–24). In a way, the kind of elision of power differential in Said's conceptualization also informs much idealized celebration of a Fanonian "third space" and of diasporic subjectivity in recent Asian American cultural criticism. From this perspective, what Sau-ling Wong refers to as a phenomenon of "denationalization" in Asian American critical discourse should perhaps be rethought as that of the poststructuralist theoretical simplification or abstraction of nationalism as a political question.

33. I have quoted Benjamin's remark from Patrick Williams and Laura Chrisman's "Introduction" in their coedited *Colonial Discourse and Post-Colonial Theory*. By this remark, Benjamin originally refers to an important feature of commodity production, "where the need for the commodity to present itself as always new, different, desirable, masked the underlying, unchanging nature of capitalist relations of production" (Williams and Chrisman 1994, 12). Within the context of my appropriation of Benjamin's idea, I emphasize the historical dialectic of his thinking rather than the mechanism of commodity production that he describes. See also the following remark by Benjamin: "History is like Janus, it has two faces: whether it looks at the past or the present, it sees the same thing" (quoted in Ferris 1996, 1).

CHAPTER 2

1. For in-depth discussions of the internment of Japanese Americans and the draft process, see Weglyn (1976) and Daniels (1993). Subsequent references to Okada's novel cite the 1979 edition.

2. Of the 21,000 nisei males eligible to register for the draft, some 4,600 answered the

two questions with an explicit "no" or with no response (Takaki 1989, 397). Upon answering no to the two questions, nisei were immediately separated from other internees and put into a designated segregation center along with other "troublemakers." Not until a year after their segregation were no-no boys charged, tried, and convicted.

3. For earlier attempts to address the "unreliable" narrative perspective as well as the rhetorical complexity of *No-No Boy*, see, for example, Sumida (1986, 64–66; 1989, 227–28).

4. During this era, for example, one historian asserted "the seamlessness" of United States culture, under the assumption that the values of various classes were "fundamentally similar" (Boorstin 1953, 157, 170), while another scholar held that material abundance had shaped a common American character and that social inequality, if existent, must violate "our national ideals" and "impair public morale" (Potter 1954, 91, 127). For analyses of other aspects of cold war American culture, see Temperly and Bradbury (1981/1989, 289–322) and May (1988).

5. For a discussion of the political and cultural implications of the stereotypical images of Chinese and Japanese in the period, see Amy Ling (1990, 56–58). Along with the massive evacuation of Japanese Americans during the first half of the 1940s, numerous community-based Japanese American publications disappeared; many issei writers destroyed works written in Japanese in order to avoid suspicion of disloyalty, while nisei writers who persisted in writing had to go "underground"—by confining their creative work to internment camp audiences. Toshio Mori's collection of short stories, *Yokohama, California,* for example, was scheduled for publication in 1941, but did not come out until after the war. For a further discussion of wartime suppression of Japanese American creative activities, see Cheung (1988, xii–xiii).

6. For a further discussion of assessments of Wong's autobiography, see Chapter 6.

7. The role of parental prohibition in the no-no boy controversy is an issue of considerable historical complexity. Part of the complexity lies in the fact that some mainland nisei were from families connected to the Japanese American population in Hawaii, a population partly constituted by immigrants from Okinawa. As a result, many of these Japanese American families had friends or relatives in this Japanese island. During the American invasion of Okinawa in the final phase of the war, some Japanese American soldiers who participated in the battles in the Pacific witnessed their Japanese relatives resisting or being killed by the invading American army. For a fictional account of such an encounter, see Sylvia Watanabe's short story "The Caves of Okinawa" (1992).

8. Prior to this act, U.S. citizenship had been reserved for white persons through a 1790 federal law and many subsequent anti-Asian immigration restrictions at both the federal and state levels after the Civil War. As a result, the prewar population of the Japanese American community was characterized, as Donna Nagata observes, by "unique age distributions" and "distinct age peaks." By 1940, for example, the average age of issei males was between fifty and sixty-four, whereas issei women were generally ten years younger. Most of their American children were born between the 1910s and the 1920s (1993, 4–5). For a discussion of the complex legal issues and procedures surrounding the internment, see Sundquist (1988).

9. My analysis of the power dynamics in this context draws on John Gaventa's discus-

sion of the relationship between power and resistance in a relatively closed hegemonic situation, a situation that I find similar to the overall circumstances faced by Japanese American internees during World War II, despite their ability to make occasional protests within the camps (1980, 5–12).

10. In view of the continued Asian immigration to the United States today, as well as of America's ongoing difficulty in resolving the race issue in terms defined by the nation's democratic ideals, "generational conflict"—which signifies the passing of the immigration generation's social dilemma on to their American-born children—will continue to serve as a useful site for commenting on the nonlinear nature of Asian immigration and on various Asian ethnic groups' social status in American society.

11. Although Okada's portrayal of Mrs. Yamada's expression of allegiance to the Japanese emperor (13–14) can be seen as a rhetorical construction in *No-No Boy,* her preoccupation with rumors from the Japanese community in Brazil that ships are being sent by the Japanese government to take the loyal Japanese home does have a factual basis. In her novel *Brazil Maru,* Karen Tei Yamashita describes the wartime division of a Japanese community in São Paulo between "makegumi," those who believed in Japanese victory, and "kachigumi," those who believed in Japan's defeat. The former group, controlled by pro-Japanese forces, not only spread news about Japanese victories but also exerted considerable pressure over the latter (1992, 102–9). But the wartime conditions experienced by Japanese Americans, as Michi Weglyn (1976) and Ronald Takaki (1989) have pointed out, were quite different.

12. Despite the apparent satiric force of Kenji's characterization, his death early in the novel prevents him from playing a symptomatically more central role than Emi in elucidating both the novel's rhetorical range and its ideological import.

13. My discussion of Okada's negotiating stance in relation to the reader, the publisher, and the authorial intent draws on Cathy Davidson's analysis of the disjunctions in the sentimental structure of the production of nineteenth-century American romantic novels, that is, the gaps between the officially espoused public morality, the private behavior of the characters who supposedly validate that morality, the writer's demands for artistic license, and the culturally conditioned readerly expectations (1986, 135, 136–40).

14. My observation about the aftermath of the cultural establishment's rejection of *No-No Boy* relies in part on the annotated bibliography of Asian American literature coedited by Cheung and Yogi (1988). For analyses of Miyamoto's and Murayama's novels, see Sumida (1991, 216–22, 110–37). Momoko Iko's play *The Gold Watch,* which engages the issue of the internment with poignancy and insight, was premiered at the Inner City Cultural Center, Los Angeles, in 1971 and published in *Aiiieeeee!* in 1974.

15. The reason is that the Hawaiian economy depended on Japanese American workers, who constituted some 70 percent of its total labor force during the war. Relocation of Japanese Americans to the mainland would therefore have been too disruptive to Hawaii's economy while tying up too many ships that might otherwise be more gainfully utilized.

CHAPTER 3

1. I make use of Sigmund Freud's concept of the return of the repressed in this chapter's title to refer to the novel's critical revelation of the mechanism of racial gendering of Chi-

nese male immigrants in American culture in the pre–1965 period. This revelation promises but does not guarantee a recovery of Chinese American women's agency because of deep-rooted patriarchal assumptions and practices in American society in general and in Chinatown communities in particular. My selective appropriation of Freud's idea does not aim to illustrate the psychoanalytical process he theorizes (1963, 111–12). Subsequent references to Chu's novel cite the 1989 edition.

2. Critics tend to see a "diasporic" experience as not only overlapping but also exceeding an "immigration" experience, with the former term connoting an open-ended scenario of continued displacement and emergence, and the latter a linear process of migration and settlement (e.g., Campomanes 1992; Lim 1997). Relevant as it may be as a way of critiquing ethnic essentialism, this distinction has a tendency to obscure the actual hegemonic operation of America as a racial state, in which the outcomes of Asian immigration are not only fundamentally different from those of European immigration but also deeply entwined with the conditions and ideologies associated with "diaspora." In my analysis, I emphasize the inseparability of Asian immigration and Asian diaspora, as well as the critical potential that derives from such a comparative perspective.

3. My observation about the audience of *Eat a Bowl of Tea* therefore differs from Elaine Kim's suggestion that Chu's novel, because of its creative translation of idioms and images from Cantonese dialects, was "deliberately not addressing Anglo American readers" (1990a, 156).

4. Another predecessor to Chu's novel is H. T. Tsiang's *And China Has Hands* (1937), the first novelistic account of Chinatown bachelor society in English. This novel, though roughly composed, is unique for its realistic details about Chinese laundrymen's life in New York (see Kim 1982, 109).

5. These laws remained in effect in some states until 1967, when the Supreme Court ruled them unconstitutional.

6. This is also reflected in Chu's portrayal of how Mei Oi's father, Lee Gong, ponders the international situation that surrounds his New York Chinatown experience: the consequence of the Sino-Japanese War on his home country, Mao Tse-tung's seizing power of China from Chiang Kai-shek in 1949, and the Korean War in the Far East (18).

7. This term was coined by Howard Temperly and Malcolm Bradbury in reference to the revival of literary realism in the United States in the 1950s (1981, 316).

8. My positing realism against modernism here is a contingent gesture, with a recognition of the latter as a complex and variously defined phenomenon. In particular, I recognize the inherently political nature of modernism's withdrawal from the social to the aesthetic as a radical resistance to the ever-growing dominance of commercial culture and a society increasingly succumbing to its power (Adorno, discussed in Jay 1973, 189–90; 1984, 111–60), as well as modernism's contradictory affiliations with and responses to commercial capitalism and realism (McGowan 1991, 11–12). Regarding modernism's relationship with realism, Hayden White observes that it is less a question of rejecting the realist project or denying history than anticipating a new form of historical reading (1992, 52). Craig Owens further points out, in a provocative analysis of Lukácsian realist claims, that "'realism' is defined—rigorously, philosophically—in opposition to idealism. In Lukács's characterization, the idealist is concerned primarily, if not exclusively, with subjective percep-

tions of reality rather than the tangible existence of the object of perception—and thus, following Kant, with the forms rather than the contents of consciousness. The realist avoids such formalism by focusing on the objective social and historical forces that shape both external reality and our perceptions of it. Depicting contemporary reality in all its complexity, the realist exposes the contradictions that traverse late capitalist society—contradictions which also traverse and structure any representation of it. . . . Viewed in this way, realism itself cannot transform the world (as so many modernist utopian programs for art propose to do); rather, depicting reality as it appears from a modernist perspective, realism prepares the way for its transformation" (1992, 255–56).

9. My use of the term "carnivalesque realism" derives from what Bakhtin calls "grotesque realism," a term by which he refers to "the material bodily principle" in the work of Rabelais (and of other writers of the Renaissance) for ironic representation of the world. Bakhtin observes: "In grotesque realism . . . the bodily element is deeply positive. It is presented not in a private, egotistic form, severed from other spheres of life, but as something universal, representing all the people. As such it is opposed to severance from the material and bodily roots of the world; it makes no pretense to renunciation of the earthy, or independence of the earth and the body. . . . The essential principle of grotesque realism is degradation, that is, the lowering of all that is high, spiritual, ideal, abstract; it is a transfer to the material level, to the sphere of earth and body in their indissoluble unity" (1984, 19–20). In my appropriation of Bakhtin's concept, I selectively foreground his dialogic combination of the essential elements of carnival and realism rather than his emphasis on bodily functions.

10. For example, Elaine Kim argues that the story of *Eat a Bowl of Tea* is entirely about men and about "their struggles for a self-determined political identity," with women defined only in relation to them "as voiceless obstacles to or objects of their search for America" (1990b, 72–73). Ruth Hsiao contends that, in Chu's depiction of his male protagonist's ultimate regaining of his manhood, he "not only restore[s] the ruffled, old-order social hierarchy" but also "suggests the birth of a new age patriarchy" (1992, 152). For Lisa Lowe's more extensive criticism of the novel, see her 1991 essay (34–35).

11. In using the phrase "formal embodiment of the material truncation," I draw on Abdul JanMohamed's and David Lloyd's analysis of minority discourse as a cultural product of damage (1990, 4–5).

12. I am grateful to Micheline Soong for her contribution to my analysis of Mei Oi's social status in China and in New York Chinatown bachelor society.

13. *Gim Peng Moy (Jin Ping Mei)*, also known as *The Golden Lotus,* is a novel written by Xiao Xiao Sheng during the Ming Dynasty (1368–1644). Because the novel is known for its explicit descriptions of the female protagonist's sexuality, Ah Sing metonymically uses its title to refer to Mei Oi's adultery with Ah Song.

14. Elaine Kim attributes the Chinatown leaders' harsh treatment of Ah Song to his lack of major clan connections in the Wang Association (1982, 115–16). While agreeing with such an observation, I would suggest that Ah Song's outsider status may also be a result of his apparent disrespect for family, which is indicated by his lack of commitment to the rich widow he has married, his flirtation with Lao Woo's wife, and his seduction of the newly married Mei Oi.

CHAPTER 4

1. Before Chin's plays were published, he had already won the Joseph Henry Jackson prize in 1965 for his as-yet-unpublished story "A Chinese Lady Dies" (see Robert Murray Davis 1988, 75). Subsequent references to Chin's plays cite the 1981 edition.

2. Critics have made a thoughtful distinction between Chin as a critic and Chin as an artist (e.g., TuSmith 1993, 45). Here I suggest that these two aspects of Chin can productively converge under given conditions.

3. Chin is clearly using the phrase "Chinese whoremother" sarcastically to refer to the cultural deprivation suffered by Chinese Americans through incorporation of a dominant language of the late 1960s counterculture. But this usage also reflects Chin's insensitivity to the sexism in such language.

4. For an analysis of the relationship between early Chinese immigration history, the role of theatrical performance in the immigrant community, and appropriations of Kwan Kung as a historical figure, see Robert Lee (1992).

5. See Abe (1991) and Nee and Nee (1973, 377–89).

6. For Fredric Jameson, postmodernism is a dominant cultural condition marked by a total loss of the social space for political opposition. Such a perception of America's late capitalist culture leads him to see the "Third World," which he imagines allegorically in a somewhat monolithic fashion, as the only possible site for effective counterhegemonic struggle (1986). In my analysis of Chin's plays, I appropriate Jameson's idea of "the cultural dominant" invertedly, that is, not as a substantiation of his original formulation of postmodernism but rather as ironic commentary on the social and cultural dilemmas faced by Asian Americans. In addition, examining Chin's work through the ironic lens of the Jamesonian idea of the postmodern can lead to a historically more concrete understanding of the role of the "Third World," a phenomenon that, as Chin's plays show, is disruptively present in the capitalist order of the United States and difficult to appropriate as simply oppositional in an idealized fashion. For two alternative positions about postmodernism and its conditions, see, for example, Mike Davis (1988) and Reed (1992, 151–58).

7. See, for example, Palumbo-Liu (1994, 78–79) and Reinhard (1995, 57–67). My limited reference to Freud's perspective via Lacan is meant not to illustrate the complex psychoanalytical procedures involved, but to elucidate the historicity of the interventionary possibilities yielded by Chin's critical engagement with racial, sexual, and cultural doubles in his plays.

8. Both Chin and Shawn Wong pointed out in 1974 that African Americans have been "quicker to understand and appreciate the value of Asian American writing than whites. . . . The blacks were the first to take us seriously and sustained the spirit of many Asian American writers. [I]t was not surprising to us that Howard University Press understood us and set out publishing our book *Aiiieeeee!* with their first list. They liked the English we spoke and did not accuse us of wholesale literary devices" (viii, vi).

9. Chin's shift of creative attention also reflects the course of development of ethnic movements in American society in the early 1970s in general. According to one study, this period saw the radical fervor of ethnic protest subside along with the decline of the massive student activism of the late 1960s. Such decline resulted mainly from the ascendancy to

political power of neoconservatives and the simultaneous economic recession in the United States as American troops began to withdraw from Vietnam. One of the consequences was the splintering of social movements. For example, the New Left perspective did not succeed in creating constituencies among most students of color because it failed to embrace their experiences and needs. Its call for personal liberation was not well received by those who saw themselves as a community seeking to break free from societal racism. And the optimism of the New Left's belief in "Revolution Now!" did not sit well with intellectuals of color, either, who were all too aware of the slow process of realizing concrete demands. As a result, many radicals turned their attention to their respective communities and focused on bread-and-butter issues (Barlow 1991, 9). My analysis of Chin's second play is, from this perspective, specifically concerned with the representational problems faced both by the playwtight himself and by his artist figure. For a brief mention of Chin's dramatization in this play of "the burden and dilemma" Chinatown poses "as an existential space" for Chinese Americans in the 1970s, see Li (1991, 217).

10. The president of the local chapter of the Chinese Benevolent Association in San Francisco and New York is traditionally called the Mayor of Chinatown by the press and the president of the United States. The implication of the honorary title is a recognition of an understanding between the press and the Chinese Benevolent Association that they are the exclusive source of Chinatown news—hence "good news only" (see Chin 1972a, 61).

11. In reference to the ironic implications of orientalist desire, Ali Behdad further points out that there is always "a split between the Western vision of its Other, the cleavage of the masked and the exposed, the cut between maximum visibility and total inscrutability," because of the discursive paradox of gazing (1990, 37).

12. In making this argument, I appropriate David Chaney's observation about tourism in relation to late modern drama: "To the extent that post-modern tourists have abandoned a search for cultural meaning, they have also accepted the limitations of artificiality to any form of social action when there has been a radical dramatization of everyday life" (1993, 166).

13. For a discussion of Virginia Lee's work in terms of memory and literary ancestral home, see Amy Ling (1990, 97–103).

14. Vincent Crapanzano elaborates on this paradox in his discussion of the ethnographer's critical interpretation of cultural other (1986, 52).

15. My discussion of Chin's male artist as a Faust figure draws on David Harvey's comment on Faust as symptomatic of the limitations of modernity (1989, 16). For a thoughtful discussion of Chin as a Joycean artist figure, see Robert Murray Davis (1992).

16. Many critical attempts have been made to distinguish modernity from postmodernity: Ihab Hassan's stylistic differentiation (1982/1987), Jameson's argument about the emergence of "the cultural dominant" in the early 1960s (1983, 124–25), Harvey's observation about postmodernity as emerging "full blown" between 1968 and 1972 (1989, 38), and Spivak's designation of the worldwide electronification of the stock market in 1974 as the beginning of postmodernity (quoted in Bill Martin 1992, 208 n. 8).

17. Despite my reservation about Fischer's use of the term "postmodernist art" to describe Chin's literary creation in general, I find his assessment of the significance of Chin's art quite accurate and incisive: "No greater indictments of racism in America exist than

Charlie Mingus's *Beneath the Underdog,* Raul Salinas's 'A Trip Through the Mind Jail,' the angry writings of Frank Chin, the portraits of trauma by James Welch or Gerald Viznor. None of these, however, merely indicts, and certainly none blames only oppressors outside the self and ethnic group; all fictively demonstrate the creation of new identities and worlds. Rather than naive efforts at direct representation, they suggest or evoke cultural emergence" (1986, 202).

18. These writers include, among others, Charles Altieri, David Antin, John Barth, William Burroughs, John Cage, Arthur Miller, and Charles Olson.

19. This is my condensed reworking—through refocusing on issues of race, gender, and class—of Dick Hebdige's lengthy discussion of the multi-positionalities of postmodernism as a contested yet underdefined term (1993, 70–71).

20. Colin Falck points out in this regard that crisis of meaning and intensified linguistic self-consciousness—including "a general weakening of confidence in language and in linguistically based meaning as a whole"—is an important aspect of postromantic philosophical linguistic sensibility (1989, 159–60). See also Hutcheon (1988, 168).

21. My observation here is indebted to Craig Owens's 1983 essay "The Discourse of Others: Feminists and Postmodernism" (1987, 60), which introduced me to Lacan's remark.

CHAPTER 5

1. In so raising the issue, however, I do not invoke the Barthesian dictum of "death of the author" but rather call attention to the complexity of intentionalities. Subsequent references to *China Men* cite the 1980 edition.

2. For a further discussion of the "expansive" ideological apparatus in the post-1960s United States, see Hogue (1986, 158–60).

3. In a sociological study of Asian American women's lack of participation in feminist movements in the era, Esther Chow points out that the feminist movement in the United States has been from its inception predominantly white and middle class. Apart from some of the obvious external causes of Asian American women's lack of impact on the movement, Chow mentions several internal factors that particularly discouraged Asian American women's involvement in social activism. One of them is their psychological constraint as a result of their prolonged dual status as both racial minority and women, a status that requires a double—but simultaneous—liberation in the realms of ethnicity and gender. Because of the unevenness of the civil rights movement in the era, Chow suggests that women were often reluctant to join in the feminist movement because it necessarily pitted their ethnic identity against their gender identity (1989, 362, 367).

4. My use of the phrase "revolution within a revolution" echoes Todd Gitlin's similar remark—"revolution in the revolution"—about the American feminist movement in relation to American New Left (1987, 362).

5. In addition, this self-reference has a male version in Chinese (奴才), which can be similarly translated into the English word "slave." Critics should therefore be careful not to equate Kingston's rhetorical strategy constructed out of the American context with social realities in China, because such an equation would inadvertently affirm the West's assumptions about its cultural other in monolithic terms, and consequently undermine the speci-

ficities of Kingston's Chinese American feminist argument. For an informative analysis of Chinese women's oppression and their struggle for self-determination in different historical periods, see Amy Ling (1990, 1–20).

6. According to Sara Evans, American feminist protests were historically most vocal among southern white women—in the nineteenth century, in the early twentieth century, and in the early years of the civil rights movement. As a result, there was a tradition among American feminists of linking the sin of slavery to that of sexual oppression (1979, 25–28).

7. Henderson suggests that the emergent black feminist discourse needs a two-step intervention into the existing discourse(s): as a first step, self-inscription through disruption—the initial response to hegemonic and ambiguously (non)hegemonic discourse—and then, as a second step, revision through rewriting and rereading, an attempt to enter into dialogue with discourses of the other (1989, 24–30).

8. I hope that my reading of China men's selective—and complicitous—silence about history would in a way complement King-Kok Cheung's analysis of the "provocative silence" in Kingston's same work, an analysis made in the context of her argument against the privileging of speech over silence in Euro-American feminist criticism (1993, 100–125). My discussion is concerned more with the nuances of historicity.

9. My discussion of the productive tension between the historical and mythic plots in Kingston's work benefits from the theoretical model that emerges from Sally Keenan's insightful analysis of the interplay among history, myth, mythology, gender, and postcoloniality in Toni Morrison's *Beloved* (1993).

10. In making this observation, I draw on Donald Pease's discussion of the limitations of the national narrative. He writes: "The national narrative produced national identities by way of a social symbolic order that systematically separated an abstract, disembodied subject from resistant materials, such as race, class, and gender. This universal body authorizes the discrimination of figures who can be integrated within the national symbolic order and matters (of race, gender, class) external to it. Because the coherence of the national narrative depends upon the integrity of its universal subject, that figure is transformed into a tacit assumption and descends into the social unconscious" (1994, 3).

11. Hayden White observes: "The Epic plot structure would appear to be the implicit form of chronicle itself" (1973, 8).

12. Although Taiwan was the only "China" recognized by the United States during the first three decades after 1949, the Chinese in the United States were keenly aware of the hostility between the two parts of China (see also my analysis of the political context of the publication of Louis Chu's *Eat a Bowl of Tea* in Chapter 3), as well as of the fact that the immediate post-1965 Chinese immigration to the United States almost exclusively consisted of Chinese from Taiwan and Hong Kong—places rarely confused with "China" as a geopolitical entity by Chinese Americans when *China Men* was written and published. In addition, the widely publicized normalization of U.S.-China relations throughout the 1970s—the "Ping Pong diplomacy" of 1971, Nixon's visit to China in 1972, the establishment of an American liaison office in Beijing (headed by George Bush) in 1976, and the establishment of diplomatic relations between and United Sates and China in 1979—also highlighted the difference between "China" and "Taiwan" for Chinese Americans in the 1970s.

13. Despite Kingston's critiques of the reductive historicism that partially informs the efforts to recover an "Asian American heroic tradition," she also emphasizes, as I have shown in the foregoing analysis in this chapter, the deep tension between some Asian American writers' idealized conceptualization of Asian American cultural integrity and institutional denials of early Chinese immigrants' equal participation in the masculine heroic discourse authorized by the given social and racial hierarchies in the United States. From a somewhat different perspective, David Li suggests that China men are full (though unconscious) accomplices in America's imperialist project of manifest destiny: "Unknowingly, they paved the way for the realization of a manifest destiny and secured the harbors on the West Coast, not only completing the continental expansion of America but also opening the new highway of trade for America to enjoy, in the words of President Polk, 'an extensive and profitable commerce with China, the other countries of the East.' That is, the Chinese ironically became accomplices in the exploitation of their ancient empire. Probably it is their unconscious participation in the grand scheme that disqualifies them for membership in canonical American history, a history which Kingston now sets out to remember" (1990, 490). Such an assessment of the historical role of Chinese immigrant laborers in the building of the American nation, while illustrating the operation of cultural hegemony to a certain extent, does not offer a fully historical perspective on the global processes into which these laborers were inserted as displaced racial and class subjects, nor on the nature of the social antagonism they experienced under the given conditions.

14. I have borrowed the term "paraliterary space" from Linda Hutcheon's *A Poetics of Postmodernism* (1988, 11), a term that she uses to discuss a range of contemporary literary texts, including Kingston's *China Men,* as examples of "historiographic metafiction." However, my critical assumptions about Kingston's work differ from Hutcheon's.

CHAPTER 6

1. The first such conference was held at the Oakland Museum in 1975, followed by the Pacific Northwest Asian American Writers' Conference in Seattle in 1976 and by the Talk Story Conference in Honolulu in 1978. Subsequently, other Asian American literary conferences took place on both coasts of the continent as well as in Hawaii. Since 1985, there have been national meetings of the Association for Asian American Studies (see Sumida 1989a, 151).

2. In 1976, the year *The Woman Warrior* became a major commercial success (it would earn the National Critics Circle Award for nonfiction the following year), Wong was chosen as "the person best representing Asian Americans for a PBS documentary about American racial minorities" (Kim 1982, 60), a choice that interestingly reflects back on the commercial and political success of *Fifth Chinese Daughter* in the cold war years of the 1950s.

3. Elaine Kim observes that in the early 1950s, the U.S. State Department negotiated for the rights to publish *Fifth Chinese Daughter* in other languages and arranged for Jade Snow Wong to take a speaking tour in 1952 to forty-five Asian locations from Tokyo to Karachi, where she spoke about the benefits of American democracy from the perspective of a Chinese American woman (1982, 60).

4. Giles Gunn makes a distinction between what he calls a literary work's "historical

impact" and its "cultural influence" in relation to the "horizon of expectations" with which it interacts. By the former, Gunn refers to a work's tendency to confirm and support conventional modes of thinking or reflect popular cultural perceptions of its time by merely supplying new content to the collective experience (1979, 144–48).

5. I have entwined R. Radhakrishnan's perspective on ethnic authenticity as a form of historical contingency (1996, 162) with H. Veeser's discussion of the principles of New Historicism as registering two interrelated contingent concerns—its "arbitrary contingency" and its "conditional contingency" (1994, 4). My purpose is to show that ethnic authentication is an internally complex political-rhetorical strategy. In borrowing such traditional materialist categories as "idealist-symbolic" and "social-materialist," I aim only to illustrate the two categories that I appropriate from Veeser, rather than to invoke the questionable mechanical theory of reflection or of "false consciousness" implicit in those traditional materialist terms.

6. Kenneth Burke similarly observes that a writer's consciously providing the context of his or her literary portrayal gives no assurance that the reader will go along with his or her use of facts in fiction, however accurate the details, because "sheer fantasies can somehow 'ring true,' though the story never actually happened, and never will happen" (1982, 38).

7. Some of Guan Goong's less flattering features can be detected through a symptomatic reading of *Romance of the Three Kingdoms* from a critically historical perspective (see especially Chapters 1 and 5 of the novel; Lou [1310–1385/1987]).

8. This observation is part of Lim's larger argument that Kingston's 1976 work has already acquired non–Asian American characteristics and hence should not be measured against the presumed "ethnic" assumptions. As a critique of authoritarian imposition of a single artistic standard on Asian American literary creation and interpretation, I am very much in agreement with Lim's analysis. But in view of the ideological ambiguity of Kingston's cultural politics, especially the inadequately debated charge that Kingston's publication of *The Woman Warrior* was motivated only by the urge for assimilation, Lim's characterization of Kingston's strategy for her 1976 autobiography strikes me as a little surprising.

9. My discussion here is informed by E. H. Gombrich's observations about the relationship between artistic representations and viewers' reception (1960, 60, 88). For an elaboration on Gombrich's theoretical perspectives, see Gunn (1979, 149–51).

10. For an overview of the debate over the reception of *The Woman Warrior,* see Solovitch (1991). For analyses of the issues surrounding the reception of works by Hwang, Suleri, Mukherjee, and Tan, see, for example, *The Big Aiiieeeee!* (Chan et al. 1991, 2–3), Grewal (1993; 1994), and Sau-ling Wong (1995b).

11. For an informative analysis of the issue of moral imagination in American culture, see Gunn (1987, 19–40).

12. In fact, Kingston seems to have abandoned this particular negotiating strategy after she wrote *China Men* and engaged in what appears to be a thinly veiled personal assault on Chin in her 1989 novel *Tripmaster Monkey: His Fake Book,* despite arguments to the contrary. A fully historicized analysis of the factors at issue in this exchange remains to be made.

13. For adaptations of Charles Taylor's related concept of "minimal rationality," see Mohanty (1992, 137–40) and Bhabha (1992, 57).

14. British cultural studies, contrary to what it is often made to seem, has been internally divergent and intellectually and ideologically conflictual, with unstable boundaries and complex political tendencies. One indication of its complexity is its internal "warfare" both before and after the founding of the Center for Contemporary Cultural Studies (CCCS) in 1964: that between E. P. Thompson and Raymond Williams over the latter's reformulation of culture as "material" in the 1950s and early 1960s, that between Raymond Williams and Stuart Hall over the choice between "culturalist" and "structuralist" approaches from the 1970s onward (during which Hall became the director of the CCCS), that between Ernesto Laclau and Stuart Hall over the formulation of specific cultural strategies during the Thatcherite 1980s, and, more generally, that between an urge toward Gramscianism and that toward Althusserianism (Harris 1992, 36–47; McGuigan 1992, 13–42).

15. For the early positions of British cultural studies, see, for example, E. P. Thompson's *Poverty of Theory and Other Essays* (1978), Richard Hoggart's *Uses of Literacy* (1958), and Raymond Williams's *Culture and Society, 1980–1950* (1966).

16. Early cultural critics particularly relied on the distinction made by Saussure between his theorization of *langue* (the determining repertoire of possibilities within a language system) and that of *parole* (specific utterance constrained by such a system) for a model for understanding cultural operations, with an emphasis on the role of the former over that of the latter (see Turner 1992, 13). Such an account of culture through the linguistic model, an account often made in conjunction with Saussure's related distinctions between synchrony and diachrony and between syntagmatic and paradigmatic, "opens possibilities for cultural—and political—praxis precisely at points where it betrays its own rhetoricity" (Attridge 1987, 204).

17. Stuart Hall comments extensively on the negative consequences of "a fatal dislocation" in one of cultural studies' key efforts to link the social to the material, that is, Louis Althusser's theorization of ideology in his 1970 essay "Ideology and Ideological State Apparatus." Hall argues that, since Althusserianism, an enormous amount of sophisticated theorizing had been devoted to the role of unconscious processes in the creation of subjects constituted through discourses, but there had been very little development of theories about ideology's relationship to the reproduction of the social relations of production. This uneven development of cultural theory, according to Hall, results from Althusser's failure to theorize adequately the second aspect of his concern with ideology: "The question of reproduction has been assigned to the marxist, (male) pole, and the question of subjectivity has been assigned to the psychoanalytic, (feminist) pole. Since then, never have the twain met. The latter is constituted as a question about the 'insides' of people, about psychoanalysis, subjectivity and sexuality, and is understood to be 'about' that. It is in this way and on this site that the link to feminism has been increasingly theorized. The former is 'about' social relations, production and 'hard edges' of productive systems, and that is what marxism and the reductive discourses of class are 'about.' This bifurcation of the theoretical project has had the most disastrous consequences for the unevenness of the subsequent development of ideology, not to speak of its damaging political effects" (1985b, 102–3).

18. For the quoted words, see Louis Althusser's "Ideology and Ideological State Apparatus" (1970/1980, 39, 43).

19. For critical comments on these limitations of Althusser's theory on ideology, see, for

example, Hall (1985b, 102–3, 106–7), Higgins (1986, 115–19), Močnik (1993), and Paul Smith (1988, 16–23).

20. For critical comments on such a reformulation of Althusser's notion of "interpellation," see Grossberg (1992, 117–27), Probyn (14–16), Radhakrishnan (1996, 10), and Žižek (1994, 321–25).

21. For discussions of the political contexts of the rise of poststructuralist Marxisms, see Perry Anderson (1988, 328–29), Elliott (1993, 33), Kellner (1995, 23), and Pecora (1992, 59, 61).

22. Despite some critics' passionate defense of Althusserianism, Althusser himself recognized the limitations of his functionalist overemphasis on the role of ideology in "Ideology and Ideological State Apparatuses." See his 1977 essay "Notes on the ISAs" (1977/1983, 4).

23. Vincent Pecora particularly points out that one consequence of such a dilemma is that critics often waver between the basic left-Hegelian procedure and an unconscious reconstitution of the aesthetic as the dominant category of social interaction (1989, 271). My analysis of the problems in Asian American cultural criticism benefits from Pecora's insight.

24. It is during this shifting, I would suggest, that a mistranslation often takes place: that is, from a disavowal of aestheticized ideological criticism emerges a generalized substitution of reading and interpreting literary texts with metacommentaries based solely on ideological presumptions. This development in recent cultural criticism typically draws support from three theoretical sources: the poststructuralist repudiation of interpretation as a manifestation of cultural essentialism (see Mohanty 1997, 95–105), British cultural studies' tendency to dismiss high culture (see Aronowitz 1993, 127), and Pierre Bourdieu's wholesale denunciation of aesthetic as nothing but an indicator of class privilege and of conspicuous consumption, despite the obvious virtues of his theorization of cultural capital (e.g., 1983, 1985). Consequently, the task of decoding culture becomes simplified in practice while little attempt is made to theorize specific reading strategies for specific Asian American literary texts.

25. Hall further observes in this connection: "Every social practice is constituted within the interplay of meaning and representation and can itself be represented. In other words, there is no social practice outside of ideology. However, this does not mean that, because all social practices are within the discursive, there is nothing to social practice *but* discourse. I know what is vested in describing processes that we usually talk about in terms of idea as practices; 'practices' feel concrete. They occur in particular sites and apparatuses—like classrooms, churches, lecture theaters, factories, schools and families. And that concreteness allows us to claim that they are 'material.' Yet differences must be remarked between different kinds of practices" (1985b, 103).

CONCLUSION

1. My comments on the ideological and circumstantial contingencies of contemporary Asian American political alliance draw upon two critical perspectives on coalition building: Caren Kaplan's synthesis of Bernice Johnson Reagon's textual strategy for constructing black women's solidarity through the autobiography form (1992, 116, 133, 135) and Yen Le Espiritu's discussion of the implications of anti-Asian violence for contemporary coalition building among Asian Americans of diverse backgrounds and persuasions (1992, 134–76).

Bibliography

Abe, Frank. 1991. "Frank Chin: His Own Voice." *Bloomsbury Review*, September, 3–4.

Althusser, Louis. 1970/1980. "Ideology and Ideological State Apparatus." In *Essays on Ideology*, 1–60. London: Verso.

———. 1977/1983. "Notes on the ISAs" (extracts). *Economy and Society* 12.4: 455–65.

Anderson, Benedict. 1983/1991. *Imagined Communities: Reflections on the Origin and Spread of Nationalism*. London: Verso.

Anderson, Perry. 1976. "The Antinomies of Antonio Gramsci." *New Left Review* 100: 5–81.

———. 1988. "Modernity and Revolution." In *Marxism and the Interpretation of Culture*, ed. Cary Nelson and Lawrence Grossberg, 317–33. Urbana: University of Illinois Press.

Arac, Jonathan. 1989. *Critical Genealogies: Historical Situations for Postmodern Literary Studies*. New York: Columbia University Press.

Aronowitz, Stanley. 1993. *Roll Over Beethoven*. Hanover, N.H.: University Press of New England.

Asian Women United of California, ed. 1989. *Making Waves: An Anthology of Writings by and about Asian American Women*. Boston: Beacon Press.

Attridge, Derek. 1987. "Language as History/History as Language: Saussure and the Romance of Etymology." In *Post-Structuralism and the Question of History*, ed. Derek Attridge et al., 183–211. New York: Cambridge University Press.

Bakhtin, Mikhail M. 1981. *The Dialogic Imagination*. Trans. Caryl Emerson and Michael Holquist. Austin: University of Texas Press.

———. 1984. *Rabelais and His World*. Trans. Hélène Iswolsky. Bloomington: Indiana University Press.

Barlow, Andrew. 1991. "The Student Movement of the 1960s and the Politics of Race." *Journal of Ethnic Studies* 19.3: 1–22.

Barrett, Michèlle. 1988. "The Place of Aesthetics in Marxist Criticism." In *Marxism and the

Interpretation of Culture, ed. Cary Nelson and Lawrence Grossberg, 697–713. Urbana: University of Illinois Press.

Barth, John. 1958. *The End of the Road.* Garden City, N.Y.: Doubleday.

———. 1960. *The Sot-Weed Factor.* New York: Grosset & Dunlap.

———. 1980/1984. "The Literature of Replenishment: Postmodernist Fiction." In *The Friday Book: Essays and Other Non-Fiction,* 193–206. New York: G. P. Putnam's Sons.

Baudrillard, Jean. 1983. *Simulations.* Trans. Paul Foss et al. New York: Semiotext(e).

Behdad, Ali. 1990. "Orientalist Desire, Desire of the Orient." *French Forum* 15.1: 37–51.

Bellow, Saul. 1959. *Henderson the Rain King.* New York: Popular Library.

Bennett, Tony. 1987. "Texts in History: The Determinations of Readings and Their Texts." In *Post-Structuralism and the Question of History,* ed. Derek Attridge et al., 63–81. New York: Cambridge University Press.

———. 1993. "Useful Culture." In *Relocating Cultural Studies: Developments in Theory and Research,* ed. Valda Blundell et al., 67–85. New York: Routledge.

Bhabha, Homi K. 1990a. "DissemiNation: Time, Narrative, and the Margins of the Modern Nation." In *Nation and Narration,* ed. Homi K. Bhabha, 291–322. New York: Routledge.

———. 1990b. "Location, Intervention, Incommensurability: A Conversation with Homi Bhabha." *Emergencies* 1: 65–88.

———. 1992. "Postcolonial Authority and Postmodern Guilt." In *Cultural Studies,* ed. Lawrence Grossberg et al., 55–66. New York: Routledge.

———. 1994. *The Location of Culture.* New York: Routledge.

Boorstin, Daniel J. 1953. *The Genius of American Politics.* Chicago: University of Chicago Press.

Bourdieu, Pierre. 1983. "The Field of Cultural Production, or: The Economic World Reversed." *Poetics* 12.4–5: 311–56.

———. 1985. "The Market of Symbolic Goods." *Poetics* 14.1–2: 13–44.

Bové, Paul A. 1995. "Preface: Literary Postmodernism." In *Early Postmodernism: Foundational Essays,* ed. Paul A. Bové, 1–16. Durham N.C.: Duke University Press.

Brecht, Bertolt. 1964. *Brecht on Theater.* Trans. John Willet. New York: Hill & Wang.

Bulosan, Carlos. 1943/1973. *America Is in the Heart.* Seattle: University of Washington Press.

Burke, Kenneth. 1982. "Realism, Occidental Style." In *Asian and Western Writers in Dialogue: New Cultural Identities,* ed. Guy Amirthanayagam, 26–47. London: Macmillan.

Cabral, Amilcar. 1973/1994. "National Liberation and Culture." In *Colonial Discourse and Post-Colonial Theory,* ed. Patrick Williams and Laura Chrisman, 53–65. New York: Columbia University Press.

Campomanes, Oscar V. 1992. "Filipinos in the United States and Their Literature of Exile." In *Reading the Literatures of Asian America,* ed. Shirley Geok-lin Lim and Amy Ling, 49–78. Philadelphia: Temple University Press.

Carby, Hazel. 1986. *Reconstructing Womanhood: The Emergence of the Afro-American Novel.* New York: Oxford University Press.

Carroll, David. 1987. *Paraesthetics: Foucault, Lyotard, Derrida.* New York: Methuen.

Cha, Theresa Hak Kyung. 1982/1995. *Dictée.* Berkeley, Calif.: Third Woman Press.

Chakrabarty, Dipesh. 1994. "Postcoloniality and the Artifice of History: Who Speaks for

'Indian' Pasts?" In *The New Historicism Reader,* ed. H. Aram Veeser, 342–69. New York: Routledge.

Chan, Jeffery Paul. 1979. "Introduction." In *Eat a Bowl of Tea,* 1–5. Seattle: University of Washington Press.

Chan, Jeffery Paul, et al., eds. 1991. *The Big Aiiieeeee! An Anthology of Chinese American and Japanese American Literature.* New York: Meridian.

Chan, Sucheng. 1991. *Asian Americans: An Interpretive History.* Boston: Twayne.

Chaney, David. 1993. *Fictions of Collective Life: Public Drama in Late Modern Culture.* London: Routledge.

———. 1994. *The Cultural Turn: Scene-Setting Essays on Contemporary Cultural History.* London: Routledge.

Chang, Diana. 1956/1994. *Frontiers of Love.* Seattle: University of Washington Press.

Chang, Gordon. 1995. "History and Postmodernism." *Amerasia Journal* 21.1&2: 89–93.

Chatterjee, Partha. 1993. *The Nation and Its Fragments: Colonial and Postcolonial Histories.* Princeton, N.J.: Princeton University Press.

Chen, Jack. 1980. *The Chinese of America.* San Francisco: Harper & Row.

Cheung, King-Kok. 1988. "Introduction." In Hisaye Yamamoto, *Seventeen Syllables and Other Stories,* xii–xiii. Latham, N.Y.: Kitchen Table/Women of Color Press.

———. 1990. "The Woman Warrior versus The Chinaman Pacific: Must a Chinese American Critic Choose Between Feminism and Heroism?" In *Conflicts in Feminism,* ed. Marianne Hirsch and Evelyn Fox Keller, 234–251. New York: Routledge.

———. 1993. *Articulate Silences: Hisaye Yamamoto, Maxine Hong Kingston, Joy Kogawa.* Ithaca, N.Y.: Cornell University Press.

Cheung, King-Kok, and Stan Yogi, eds. 1988. *Asian American Literature: An Annotated Bibliography.* New York: Modern Language Association of America.

Chin, Frank. 1972a. "Confessions of the Chinatown Cowboy." *Bulletin of Concerned Asian Scholars* 4.3: 52–70.

———. 1972b. "'Don't Pen Us Up in Chinatown." *New York Times,* 8 October, 1, 5.

———. 1973. "Confessions of a Number One Son," *Ramparts* 11.9: 41–48.

———. 1977. "Letter to Y'Bird." *Y'Bird Magazine* 1.1: 42–45.

———. 1979a. "Afterword." In *No-No Boy,* 253–60. Seattle: University of Washington Press.

———. 1979b. "Redress for Japanese Americans? What For?" *Rikka* 6.3: 2–14.

———. 1981. *The Chickencoop Chinaman* and *The Year of the Dragon.* Seattle: University of Washington Press.

———. 1982. "Chinaman's Chance," *WCH Way* 4: 162–81.

———. 1985. "This Is Not an Autobiography," *Genre* 18.2: 109–30.

———. 1988. "Railroad Standard Time." In *The Chinaman Pacific & Frisco R.R. Co.,* 1–7. Minneapolis, Minn.: Coffee House Press.

Chin, Frank, and Jeffery Paul Chan. 1972. "Racist Love." In *Seeing through Shuck,* ed. Richard Kostelanetz, 65–79. New York: Ballantine.

Chin, Frank, and Shawn Wong, eds. 1974. *Yardbird Reader #3.* Berkeley: California Yardbird Publishing.

Chin, Frank, et al., eds. 1974. *Aiiieeeee! An Anthology of Asian American Writers.* Washington, D.C.: Howard University Press.

Chow, Esther Ngan-Ling. 1989. "The Feminist Movement: Where Are All the Asian American Women?" In *Making Waves: An Anthology of Writings by and about Asian American Women,* ed. Asian Women United of California, 362–77. Boston: Beacon Press.

Chow, Rey. 1993. *Writing Diaspora: Tactics of Intervention in Contemporary Cultural Studies.* Bloomington: Indiana University Press.

Christian, Barbara. 1980. *Black Women Novelists: The Development of a Tradition, 1892–1976.* Westport, Conn.: Greenwood Press.

Chu, Louis. 1961/1989. *Eat a Bowl of Tea.* Seattle: University of Washington Press.

Chua, Cheng Lok. 1982. "Golden Mountain: Chinese Versions of the American Dream in Lin Yutang, Louis Chu, and Maxine Hong Kingston." *Ethnic Groups* 4.1–2: 33–59.

Clifford, James. 1987. *The Predicament of Culture: Twentieth-Century Ethnography, Literature, and Art.* Cambridge, Mass.: Harvard University Press.

Crapanzano, Vincent. 1986. "Hermes' Dilemma: The Masking of Subversion in Ethnographic Description." In *Writing Culture: The Poetics and Politics of Ethnography,* ed. James Clifford and George E. Marcus, 51–77. Berkeley: University of California Press.

Daniels, Roger. 1993. *Prisoners Without Trial: Japanese Americans in World War II.* New York: Hill and Wang.

Davidson, Cathy N. 1986. *Revolution and the Word: The Rise of the Novel in America.* New York: Oxford University Press.

Davis, Mike. 1988. "Urban Resistance and the Spirit of Postmodernism." In *Postmodernism and Its Discontents: Theories, Practices,* ed. E. Ann Kaplan, 79–87. New York: Verso.

Davis, Robert Murray. 1992. "Frank Chin: Iconoclastic Icon." *Redneck Review of Literature* 23: 75–78.

De Man, Paul. 1979. *Allegories of Reading: Figural Language in Rousseau, Nietzsche, Rilke, and Proust.* New Haven, Conn.: Yale University Press.

Denning, Michael. 1987. *Mechanic Accents: Dime Novels and Working-Class Culture in Nineteenth-Century America.* London: Verso.

Dirlik, Arif. 1994. "The Postcolonial Aura: Third World Criticism in the Age of Global Capitalism." *Critical Inquiry* 20: 328–56.

———. 1996. "Asians on the Rim: Transnational Capital and Local Community in the Making of Contemporary Asian America." *Amerasia Journal* 22.3: 1–24.

During, Simon. 1992. *Foucault and Literature: Towards a Genealogy of Writing.* New York: Routledge.

Eco, Umberto. 1976. *A Theory of Semiotics.* Bloomington: Indiana University Press.

Elliott, Gregory. 1993. "Althusser's Solitude." In *The Althusserian Legacy,* ed. E. Ann Kaplan and Michael Sprinker, 17–37. London: Verso.

Ellison, Ralph. 1952. *Invisible Man.* New York: Vintage.

Erkkila, Betsy. 1995. "Ethnicity, Literary Theory, and the Grounds of Resistance." *American Quarterly* 47.4: 563–94.

Espiritu, Yen Le. 1992. *Asian American Panethnicity: Bridging Institutions and Identities.* Philadelphia: Temple University Press.

Evans, Sara M. 1979. *Personal Politics: The Roots of Women's Liberation in the Civil Rights Movement and the New Left.* New York: Knopf.

Falck, Colin. 1989. *Myth, Truth, and Literature: Towards a True Postmodernism.* New York: Cambridge University Press.

Federman, Raymond. 1988. "Self-Reflexive Fiction." In *Columbia Literary History of the United States,* ed. Emory Elliott et al., 1142–57. New York: Columbia University Press.

Ferris, David S. 1996. "Introduction: Aura, Resistance, and the Event of History." In *Walter Benjamin: Theoretical Questions,* ed. Davis S. Ferris, 1–26. Stanford, Calif.: Stanford University Press.

Fischer, Michael. 1986. "Ethnicity and Post-Modern Arts of Memory." In *Writing Culture: The Poetics and Politics of Ethnography,* ed. James Clifford and George E. Marcus, 195–233. Berkeley: University of California Press.

Foucault, Michel. 1972. *The Archaeology of Knowledge and the Discourse on Language.* Trans. A. M. Sheridan Smith. New York: Pantheon.

———. 1976/1980. *The History of Sexuality.* Trans. Robert Hurley. New York: Vintage.

———. 1979. *Discipline and Punish: The Birth of the Prison.* Trans. Alan Sheridan. New York: Vintage.

Fowler, Roger. 1981. *Literature as Social Discourse: The Practice of Linguistic Criticism.* London: Billing and Son.

Freud, Sigmund. 1919/1957. "The 'Uncanny.'" In *The Standard Edition of the Complete Psychological Works of Sigmund Freud.* Vol. 17. Trans. James Strachey, 219–52. London: Hogarth Press and Institute of Psycho-Analysis.

———. 1963. *General Psychological Theory,* ed. Philip Rieff. New York: Collier.

Fuss, Diana. 1989. *Essentially Speaking: Feminism, Nature, and Difference.* London: Routledge.

Gates, Jr., Henry Louis, ed. 1986. *"Race," Writing, and Difference.* Chicago: University of Chicago Press.

Gaventa, John. 1980. *Power and Powerlessness: Quiescence and Rebellion in an Appalachian Valley.* Urbana: University of Illinois Press.

Gebauer, Gunter, and Christoph Wulf. 1992. *Mimesis: Culture, Art, Society.* Trans. Don Reneau. Berkeley: University of California Press.

Genette, Gérard. 1972/1980. *Narrative Discourse: An Essay in Method.* Trans. Jane E. Lewin. Ithaca, N.Y.: Cornell University Press.

Gibbon, Peter. 1983. "Gramsci, Eurocommunism, and the Comintern." *Economy and Society* 12.3: 328–66.

Gitlin, Todd. 1987. *Sixties: Years of Hope, Days of Rage.* New York: Bantam.

Godzich, Wlad. 1994. *The Culture of Literacy.* Cambridge, Mass.: Harvard University Press.

Goellnicht, Donald C. 1992. "Tang Ao in America: Male Subject Positions in *China Men.*" In *Reading the Literatures of Asian America,* ed. Shirley Geok-lin Lim and Amy Ling, 191–214. Philadelphia: Temple University Press.

Gombrich, E. H. 1960. *Art and Illusion: A Study in the Psychology of Pictorial Representation.* New York: Pantheon.

Gong, Ted. 1980. "Approaching Cultural Change Through Literature: From Chinese to Chinese American." *Amerasia Journal* 7.1: 73–83.

Gramsci, Antonio. 1971. *Selections from the Prison Notebooks.* Trans. Quintin Hoare and Geoffrey Nowell Smith. New York: International Publishers.

Grewal, Inderpal, 1993. "Reading and Writing the South Asian Diaspora: Feminism and Nationalism in North America." In *Our Feet Walk the Sky: Women of the South Asian Diaspora,* ed. Women of South Asian Descent Collective, 226–36. Berkeley, Calif.: Aunt Lute.

———. 1994. "Autobiographic Subjects and Diasporic Locations: *Meatless Days* and *Borderlands.*" In *Scattered Hegemonies: Postmodernity and Transnational Feminist Practices,* ed. Inderpal Grewal and Caren Kaplan, 231–54. Minneapolis: University of Minnesota Press.

Grewal, Inderpal, and Caren Kaplan, eds. 1994. *Scattered Hegemonies: Postmodernity and Transnational Feminist Practices.* Minneapolis: University of Minnesota Press.

Grossberg, Lawrence. 1992. *We Gotta Get Out of This Place: Popular Conservatism and Postmodern Culture.* New York: Routledge.

———. 1993. "The Formations of Cultural Studies: An American in Birmingham." In *Relocating Cultural Studies: Developments in Theory and Research,* ed. Valda Blundell et al., 21–66. New York: Routledge.

Gunn, Giles. 1979. *The Interpretation of Otherness: Literature, Religion, and American Imagination.* New York: Oxford University Press.

———. 1987. *The Culture of Criticism and the Criticism of Culture.* New York: Oxford University Press.

Hagedorn, Jessica. 1990. *Dogeaters.* New York: Pandora.

Hall, Stuart. 1980. "Cultural Studies: Two Paradigms." *Media, Culture, and Society* 2: 52–72.

———. 1980/1993. "Decoding and Encoding." In *Culture, Media, Language,* ed. Simon During, 90–103. London: Routledge.

———. 1985a. "Gramsci's Relevance for the Study of Race and Ethnicity." *Journal of Communication Inquiry* 10.2: 5–27.

———. 1985b. "Signification, Representation, Ideology: Althusser and the Post-Structuralist Debates." *Critical Studies in Mass Communication* 2.2: 91–114.

———. 1986. "On Postmodernism and Articulation: An Interview." *Journal of Communication Inquiry* 10.2: 45–60.

———. 1988. "The Toad in the Garden: Thatcherism among the Theorists." In *Marxism and the Interpretation of Culture,* ed. Cary Nelson and Lawrence Grossberg, 35–73. Urbana: University of Illinois Press.

———. 1990/1994. "Cultural Identity and Diaspora." In *Colonial Discourse and Post-Colonial Theory: A Reader,* ed. Patrick Williams and Laura Chrisman, 392–403. New York: Columbia University Press.

Harper, Phillip Brian. 1994. *Framing the Margins: The Social Logic of Postmodern Culture.* New York: Oxford University Press.

Harrington, Michael. 1959. "Our Fifty Million Poor: Forgotten Men of the Affluent Society." *Commentary* 28: 19–27.

———. 1960. "Slum, Old and New." *Commentary* 30: 118–24.

Harris, David. 1992. *From Class Struggle to the Politics of Pleasure: The Effects of Gramscianism on Cultural Studies.* New York: Routledge.

Harvey, David. 1989. *The Condition of Postmodernity.* Cambridge, Mass.: Blackwell.

Hassan, Ihab. 1982/1987. "Toward a Concept of Postmodernism." In *The Postmodern Turn: Essays in Postmodern Theory and Culture,* 84–96. Columbus: Ohio State University Press.

Hebdige, Dick. 1993. "A Report on the Western Front: Postmodernism and the 'Politics' of Style." In *Cultural Reproduction,* ed. Chris Jenks, 69–103. New York: Routledge.

Heller, Joseph. 1961. *Catch-22.* New York: Simon and Schuster.

Henderson, Mae Gwendolyn. 1989. "Speaking in Tongues: Dialogics, Dialectics, and the Traditions of the Black Woman Writer." In *Changing Our Own Words: Essays on Criticism, Theory, and Writing by Black Women,* ed. Cheryl A. Wall, 16–37. New Brunswick, N.J.: Rutgers University Press.

Higgins, John. 1986. "Raymond Williams and the Problem of Ideology." In *Postmodernism and Politics,* ed. Jonathan Arac, 112–22. Minneapolis: University of Minnesota Press.

Hirabayashi, Lane R., and Marilyn C. Alquizola. 1994. "Asian American Studies: Reevaluating for the 1990s." In *The State of Asian America: Activism and Resistance in the 1990s,* ed. Karin Aguilar–San Juan, 351–64. Boston: South End Press.

Hogue, W. Lawrence. 1986. *Discourse and the Other: The Production of the Afro-American Text.* Durham, N.C.: Duke University Press.

Hom, Marlon. H. 1982. "Chinatown Literature During the Last Ten Years (1939–1949) by Wenquan." *Amerasia Journal* 9.1: 75–100.

hooks, bell. 1990. *Yearning: Race, Gender, and Cultural Politics.* Boston: South End Press.

Hsiao, Ruth Y. 1992. "Facing the Incurable: Patriarchy in *Eat a Bowl of Tea.*" In *Reading the Literatures of Asian America,* ed. Shirley Geok-lin Lim and Amy Ling, 151–62. Philadelphia: Temple University Press.

Hsiao-Hsiao Sheng. 1617/1939. *The Golden Lotus.* Trans. Clement Egerton. London: Routledge & Kegan Paul.

Hsu, Kai-yu. 1972. "Frank Chin." In *Asian-American Authors,* ed. Kai-yu Hsu and Helen Palubiaska, 47–48. Boston: Houghton Mifflin.

Hutcheon, Linda. 1988. *A Poetics of Postmodernism: History, Theory, Fiction.* New York: Routledge.

Hwang, David Henry. 1986. *M. Butterfly.* New York: Plume.

Ichioka, Yuji. 1988. *The Issei: The World of the First Generation Japanese Immigrants, 1885–1924.* New York: Free Press.

————. 1998. "The Meaning of Loyalty: The Case of Kazumaro Buddy Uno." *Amerasia Journal* 23.3: 45–71.

Iko, Momoko. 1971/1974. "The Gold Watch." In *Aiiieeeee! An Anthology of Asian American Writers,* ed. Frank Chin et al., 89–114. Washington, D.C.: Howard University Press.

Inada, Fusao Lawson. 1976. "Introduction." In *No-No Boy,* i–vi. Seattle: University of Washington Press.

Iser, Wolfgang. 1987. "Representation: A Performative Act." In *The Aims of Representation: Subject/Text/History,* ed. Murry Krieger, 217–32. Stanford, Calif.: Stanford University Press.

Jameson, Fredric. 1977/1988. "Reflections on the Brecht-Lukács Debate." In *The Ideologies of Theory: Essays, 1971–1986.* Vol. 2, 133–47. Minneapolis: University of Minnesota Press.

———. 1983. "Postmodernism and the Consumer Society." In *The Anti-Aesthetic: Essays on Postmodern Culture,* ed. Hal Foster, 111–25. Port Townsend, Wash.: Bay Press.

———. 1986. "Third-World Literature in the Era of Multinational Capitalism." *Social Text* 15: 65–88.

———. 1991. *Postmodernism, or, The Cultural Logic of Late Capitalism.* Durham, N.C.: Duke University Press.

JanMohamed, Abdul R., and David Lloyd. 1990. "Introduction: Toward a Theory of Minority Discourse: What Is to Be Done?" In *The Nature and Context of Minority Discourse,* ed. Abdul R. JanMohamed and David Lloyd, 1–16. New York: Oxford University Press.

Jauss, Hans Robert. 1982. *Toward an Aesthetic of Reception.* Trans. Timothy Bahti. Minneapolis: University of Minnesota Press.

Jay, Martin. 1973. *The Dialectical Imagination: A History of the Frankfurt School and the Institute of Social Research, 1923–1950.* Boston: Little, Brown.

———. 1984. *Adorno.* Cambridge, Mass.: Harvard University Press.

Kaplan, Amy. 1993. "'Left Alone with America': The Absence of Empire in the Study of American Culture." In *Cultures of United States Imperialism,* ed. Amy Kaplan and Donald Pease, 3–21. Durham, N.C.: Duke University Press.

Kaplan, Amy, and Donald E. Pease, eds. 1993. *Cultures of United States Imperialism.* Durham, N.C.: Duke University Press.

Kaplan, Caren. 1992. "Resisting Autobiography: Out-Law Genres and Transnational Subjects." In *De/Colonizing the Subject,* ed. Sidonie Smith and Julia Watson, 115–38. Minneapolis: University of Minnesota Press.

Kaplan, E. Ann. 1988. "Introduction." In *Postmodernism and Its Discontents: Theories, Practices,* ed. E. Ann Kaplan, 1–9. New York: Verso.

Keenan, Sally. 1993. "'Four Hundred Years of Silence': Myth, History, and Motherhood in Toni Morrison's *Beloved.*" In *Recasting the World: Writing after Colonialism,* Jonathan White, 45–81. Baltimore, Md.: Johns Hopkins University Press.

Kellner, Douglous. 1995. *Media Culture: Cultural Studies, Identity, and Politics between the Modern and the Postmodern.* New York: Routledge.

Kim, Elaine H. 1982. *Asian American Literature: An Introduction to Their Writings and Their Social Contexts.* Philadelphia: Temple University Press.

———. 1990a. "Defining Asian American Realities Through Literature." In *The Nature and Context of Minority Discourse,* ed. Abdul R. JanMohamed and David Lloyd, 146–70. New York: Oxford University Press.

———. 1990b. "'Such Opposite Creatures': Men and Women in Asian American Literature." *Michigan Quarterly* 9.1: 68–93.

———. 1995. "Beyond Railroads and Internment: Comments on the Past, Present, and Future of Asian American Studies." In *Privileging Positions: The Sites of Asian American Studies,* ed. Gary Y. Okihiro et al., 11–19. Pullman: Washington State University Press.

Kim, Elaine, and Norma Alarcón, eds. 1995. *Writing Self, Writing Nation.* Berkeley, Calif.: Third Woman Press.

Kingston, Maxine Hong. 1976. *The Woman Warrior: Memoirs of a Girlhood among Ghosts.* New York: Alfred A. Knopf.

———. 1980. *China Men.* New York: Alfred A. Knopf.

———. 1982. "Cultural Mis-readings by American Reviewers." In *Asian and Western Writers in Dialogue: New Cultural Identities,* ed. Guy Amirthanayagam, 55–65. London: Macmillan.

———. 1989. *Tripmaster Monkey: His Fake Book.* New York: Alfred A. Knopf.

Kramer, Jane. 1976. Review of *The Woman Warrior: Memoirs of a Girlhood among Ghosts. New York Times Book Review,* 7 November, 1, 18.

Lacan, Jacques. 1977. "The Agency of the Letter in the Unconscious or Reason since Freud." In *Écrits: A Selection,* trans. Alan Sheridan, 146–78. New York: Norton.

———. 1982. "Guiding Remarks for a Congress on Feminine Sexuality." In *Feminine Sexuality,* ed. Juliet Mitchell and Jacqueline Rose, 86–98. New York: Norton and Pantheon.

Laclau, Ernesto. 1993. "Power and Representation." In *Politics, Theory, and Contemporary Culture,* ed. Mark Poster, 277–96. New York: Columbia University Press.

Laclau, Ernesto, and Chantal Mouffe. 1985. *Hegemony and Socialist Strategy: Toward a Radical Democratic Practice.* London: Verso.

Lang, Berel. 1992. "The Representation of Limits." In *Probing the Limits of Representation: Nazism and the "Final Solution,"* ed. Saul Friedlander, 300–317. Cambridge, Mass.: Harvard University Press.

Lee, Chin-Yang. 1957. *Flower Drum Song.* New York: Farrar, Straus & Cudhay.

Lee, Robert G. 1992. "In Search of the Historical Guan Gong." *Asian America* 1: 26–43.

Lee, Virginia. 1963. *The House That Tai Ming Built.* New York: Macmillan.

Leer, David Van. 1991. "Society and Identity." In *The Columbia History of the American Novel,* ed. Emory Elliott et al., 485–509. New York: Columbia University Press.

Levine, George. 1993. "Looking for the Real: Epistemology in Science and Culture." In *Realism and Representation,* ed. George Levine, 3–26. Madison: University of Wisconsin Press.

Li, David Leiwei. 1990. "*China Men:* Maxine Hong Kingston and the American Canon." *American Literary History* 2.3: 482–502.

———. 1991. "The Formation of Frank Chin and Formations of Chinese American Literature." In *Asian Americans: Comparative and Global Perspectives,* ed. Shirley Hune et al., 211–24. Pullman: Washington State University Press.

———. 1992. "The Production of Chinese American Tradition: Displacing American Orientalist Discourse." In *Reading the Literatures of Asian America,* ed. Shirley Geoklin Lim and Amy Ling, 319–32. Philadelphia: Temple University Press.

Li, Ruzhen. 1828/1965. *Flowers in the Mirror.* Trans. Lin Tai-yi. Berkeley: University of California Press.

Lim, Shirley Geok-lin. 1986. "Twelve Asian American Writers: In Search of Self-Definition." *MELUS* 13.1–2: 57–77.

———. 1992. "The Tradition of Chinese American Women's Life Stories: Thematics of

Race and Gender in Jade Snow Wong's *Fifth Chinese Daughter* and Maxine Hong Kingston's *The Woman Warrior.*" In *American Women's Autobiography, Fea(s)ts of Memory,* ed. Margo Cully, 252–67. Madison: University of Wisconsin Press.

———. 1993. "Assaying the Gold: Or, Contesting the Ground of Asian American Literature." *New Literary History* 24.1: 147–69.

———. 1997. "Immigration and Diaspora." In *An Interethnic Companion to Asian American Literature,* ed. King-Kok Cheung, 289–311. New York: Cambridge University Press.

Lim, Shirley Geok-lin, and Mayuni Tsutakawa, eds. 1989. *The Forbidden Stitch: An Asian American Women's Anthology.* Corvallis, Ore.: Calyx.

Lin, Yutang. 1948. *Chinatown Family.* New York: John Day.

Lin-Blinde, Patricia. 1979. "The Icicle in the Desert: Perspective and Form in the Works of Two Chinese-American Writers." *MELUS* 6.3: 51–71.

Ling, Amy. 1981. "A Perspective on Chinamerican Literature." *MELUS* 8.2: 76–81.

———. 1990. *Between Worlds: Women Writers of Chinese Ancestry.* New York: Pergamon.

Ling, Jinqi. 1995a. "Race, Power, and Cultural Politics in John Okada's *No-No Boy.*" *American Literature* 67.2: 359–81.

———. 1995b. "Reading for Historical Specificities: Gender Negotiations in Louis Chu's *Eat a Bowl of Tea.*" *MELUS* 20.1: 35–51.

———. 1997. "Identity Crisis and Gender Politics: Reappropriating Asian American Masculinity." In *An Interethnic Companion to Asian American Literature,* ed. King-Kok Cheung, 312–37. New York: Cambridge University Press.

Lipsitz, George. 1990. *Time Passages: Collective Memory and American Popular Culture.* Minneapolis: University of Minnesota Press.

Lou, Guanzhong. 1310–1385/1987. *Romance of the Three Kingdoms.* Changsha, Hunan: Yue Lu Press.

Lowe, Lisa. 1991. "Heterogeneity, Hybridity, Multiplicity: Marking Asian American Differences." *Diaspora* 1.1: 22–44.

———. 1993. "Literary Nomadics in Francophone Allegories of Postcolonialism: Pham Van Ky and Tahar Ben Jelloun." *Yale French Studies* 82.1: 43–61.

———. 1995a. "Canon, Institutionalization, Identity: Contradictions for Asian American Studies." In *The Ethnic Canon: Histories, Institutions, and Interventions,* ed. David Palumbo-Liu, 48–68. Minneapolis: University of Minnesota Press.

———. 1995b. "Unfaithful to the Original: The Subject of *Dictée.*" In *Writing Self, Writing Nation,* ed. Elaine H. Kim and Norma Alarcón, 35–72. Berkeley, Calif.: Third Woman Press.

Lyotard, Jean-François. 1984. *The Postmodern Condition: A Report on Knowledge.* Trans. Geoff Bennington and Brian Massumi. Minneapolis: University of Minnesota Press.

Marshall, Brenda K. 1992. *Teaching the Postmodern: Fiction and Theory.* New York: Routledge.

Martin, Bill. 1992. *Matrix Line: Derrida and the Possibilities of Postmodern Social Theory.* Albany: State University of New York Press.

Martin, Wallace. 1986. *Recent Theories of Narrative.* Ithaca: Cornell University Press.

May, Elaine Tyler. 1988. *Homeward Bound: Families in the Cold War Era.* New York: Basic Books.

McDonald, Dorothy Ritsuko. 1979. "After the Imprisonment: Ichiro's Search for Redemption in *No-No Boy.*" *MELUS* 1.6: 19–26.

———. 1981. "Introduction." In *The Chickencoop Chinaman and The Year of the Dragon,* ix–xxix. Seattle: University of Washington Press.

McGowan, John. 1991. *Postmodernism and Its Critics.* Ithaca, N.Y.: Cornell University Press.

McGuigan, Jim. 1992. *Cultural Populism.* London: Routledge.

Medvedev, Pavel N. 1928/1978. *The Formal Method in Literary Scholarship.* Trans. Albert Wehrle. Baltimore, Md.: Johns Hopkins University Press.

Miyamoto, Kazuo. 1964. *Hawaii: The End of the Rainbow.* Rutherford, Vt.: Charles E. Tuttle.

Močnik, Rastko. 1993. "Ideology and Fantasy." In *The Althusserian Legacy,* ed. E. Ann Kaplan and Michael Sprinker, 139–56. New York: Routledge.

Mohanty, Satya P. 1992. "Us and Them: On the Philosophical Bases of Political Criticism." In *Critical Conditions: Regarding the Historical Moment,* ed. Michael Hays, 115–45. Minneapolis: University of Minnesota Press.

———. 1995. "Epilogue: Colonial Legacies, Multicultural Futures: Relativism, Objectivity, and the Challenge of Otherness." *PMLA* 100.1: 108–18.

———. 1997. *Literary Theory and the Claims of History: Postmodernism, Objectivity, Multicultural Politics.* Ithaca, N.Y.: Cornell University Press.

Molesworth, Charles. 1988. "Culture, Power, and Society." In *Columbia Literary History of the United States,* ed. Emory Elliott et al., 1024–44. New York: Columbia University Press.

Mori, Toshio. 1949. *Yokohama, California.* Caldwell, Ida.: Caxton Printers.

Mukherjee, Bharati. 1989. *Jasmine.* New York: Fawcett Crest.

Murayama, Milton. 1975. *All I Asking for Is My Body.* San Francisco: Supa.

Nagata, Donna K. 1993. *Legacy of Injustice: Exploring the Cross-Generational Impact of the Japanese American Internment.* Ann Arbor: University of Michigan Press.

Nee, Victor G., and Brett de Bary Nee. 1972. *Longtime Californ': A Documentary Study of an American Chinatown.* New York: Pantheon.

Niethammer, Lutz. 1992. *Posthistoire: Has History Come to an End?* Trans. Patrick Camiller. New York: Verso.

North, Michael. 1994. *The Dialect of Modernism: Race, Language, and Twentieth-Century Literature.* New York: Oxford University Press.

O'Hara, Daniel T. 1992. "Critical Change and Collective Archive." In *Critical Conditions: Regarding the Historical Moment,* ed. Michael Hays, 39–55. Minneapolis: University of Minnesota Press.

Okada, John. 1957/1976. *No-No Boy.* Seattle: University of Washington Press.

Omatsu, Glenn. 1994. "The 'Four Prisons' and the Movements of Liberation: Asian American Activism from the 1960s to the 1990s." In *The State of Asian America: Activism and Resistance in the 1990s,* ed. Karin Aguilar–San Juan, 19–70. Boston: South End Press.

Omi, Michael, and Howard Winant. 1986. *Racial Formation in the United States: From the 1960s to the 1980s.* New York: Routledge.

Owens, Craig. 1983. "The Discourse of Others: Feminists and Postmodernism." In *The Anti-Aesthetic: Essays on Postmodern Culture,* ed. Hal Foster, 57–82. Port Townsend, Wash.: Bay Press.

198   Bibliography

————. 1992. *Beyond Recognition: Representation, Power, and Culture,* ed. Scott Bryson et al. Berkeley: University of California Press.

Palumbo-Liu, David. 1994. "The Minority Self as Other: Problematics of Representation in Asian American Literature." *Cultural Critique* 28: 75–102.

————. 1995. "Theory and Subject of Asian American Studies." *Amerasia Journal* 21.1&2: 55–66.

Pease, Donald E. 1993. "New Perspectives on U.S. Culture and Imperialism." In *Cultures of United States Imperialism,* ed. Amy Kaplan and Donald Pease, 22–37. Durham, N.C.: Duke University Press.

————. 1994. "National Identities, Postmodern Artifacts, and Postnational Narratives." In *National Identities and Post-Americanist Narratives,* ed. Donald E. Pease, 1–9. Durham, N.C.: Duke University Press.

Pecora, Vincent P. 1989. "The Limits of Local Knowledge." In *The New Historicism,* ed. H. Aram Veeser, 243–76. New York: Routledge.

————. 1992. "What Was Deconstruction?" *Contention* 1.3: 59–79.

————. 1997. *Households of the Soul.* Baltimore, Md.: Johns Hopkins University Press.

Pfaff, Timothy. 1980. "Talking to Mrs. Kingston." *New York Times Book Review,* 18 June, 1, 25–27.

Potter, David M. 1954. *People of Plenty: Economic Abundance and the American Character.* Chicago: University of Chicago Press.

Probyn, Elspeth. 1990. "Travels in the Postmodern: Making Sense of the Local." In *Feminism/Postmodernism,* ed. Linda J. Nicholson, 176–89. New York: Routledge.

————. 1993. *Sexing the Self: Gendered Positions in Cultural Studies.* New York: Routledge.

Rabine, Leslie E. 1987. "No Lost Paradise: Social Gender and Symbolic Gender in the Writings of Maxine Hong Kingston." *Signs* 12.3: 471–492.

Radhakrishnan, R. 1996. *Diasporic Mediations: Between Home and Locations.* Minneapolis: University of Minnesota Press.

Radway, Janice. 1986. "Identifying Ideological Seams: Mass Culture, Analytic Method, and Political Practice." *Communication* 9: 93–123.

Reed, T. V. 1988. "Unimagined Existence and the Fiction of the Real: Postmodernist Realism in *Let Us Now Praise Famous Men.*" *Representations* 24: 174.

————. 1992. *Fifteen Jugglers, Five Believers: Literary Politics and the Poetics of American Social Movements.* Berkeley: University of California Press.

Reinhard, Kenneth. 1995. "The Freudian Things: Construction and the Archaeological Metaphor." In *Excavations and Their Objects,* ed. Stephen Barker, 57–79. Albany: State University of New York Press.

Riesman, David. 1950/1961. *The Lonely Crowd: A Study of the Changing American Character.* New Haven, Conn.: Yale University Press.

Robins, Bruce. 1993. "Modernism and Literary Realism." In *Realism and Representation,* ed. George Levine, 225–31. Madison: University of Wisconsin Press.

Ross, Andrew. 1988. "Introduction." In *Universal Abandon? The Politics of Postmodernism,* ed. Andrew Ross, vii–xviii. Minneapolis: University of Minnesota Press.

Said, Edward W. 1983. *World, Text, and Context.* Cambridge, Mass.: Harvard University Press.

————. 1990. "Reflections on Exile." In *Out There: Marginalization and Contemporary Culture,* ed. Russell Ferguson et al., 357–66. Cambridge, Mass.: MIT Press.

————. 1993. *Culture and Imperialism.* New York: Alfred A. Knopf.

————. 1994. *Representations of the Intellectual.* New York: Pantheon.

Saldívar, José David. 1990. "The Limits of Cultural Studies." *American Literary History* 2: 231–66.

San Juan, E., Jr., 1992. *Racial Formations/Critical Transformations: Articulations of Power in Ethnic and Racial Studies in the United States.* Atlantic Highlands, N.J.: Humanities Press International.

————. 1995. *Hegemony and Strategies of Transgression: Essays in Cultural Studies and Comparative Literature.* Albany: State University of New York Press.

Sangari, Kumkum. 1987/1990. "The Politics of the Possible." In *The Nature and Context of Minority Discourse,* ed. Abdul R. JanMohamed and David Lloyd, 216–45. New York: Oxford University Press.

Santos, Bienvenido. 1948/1979. "Scent of Apples." In *Scent of Apples: A Collection of Short Stories,* 21–29. Seattle: University of Washington Press.

Sato, Gayle K. Fujita. 1992. "Momotaro's Exile: John Okada's *No-No Boy.*" In *Reading the Literatures of Asian America,* ed. Shirley Geok-lin Lim and Amy Ling, 239–58. Philadelphia: Temple University Press.

Schaub, Thomas Hill. 1991. *American Fiction in the Cold War.* Madison: University of Wisconsin Press.

Sharpe, Jenny. 1995. "Is the United States Postcolonial? Transnationalism, Immigration, and Race." *Diaspora* 4.2: 181–99.

Shohat, Ella. 1995. "The Struggle over Representation: Casting, Coalitions, and the Politics of Identification." In *Late Imperial Culture,* ed. Roman de la Campa et al., 166–78. London: Verso.

Sledge, Linda Ching. 1980. "Maxine Hong Kingston's *China Men:* The Family Historian as Epic Poet." *MELUS* 7.4: 3–22.

Smiley, Marion. 1992. *Moral Responsibility and the Boundaries of Community: Power and Accountability from a Pragmatic Point of View.* Chicago: University of Chicago Press.

Smith, Barbara Herrnstein. 1988. *Contingencies of Value: Alternative Perspectives for Critical Theory.* Cambridge, Mass.: Harvard University Press.

Smith, Paul. 1988. *Discerning the Subject.* Minneapolis: University of Minnesota Press.

Smith, Valerie. 1987. *Self-Discovery and Authority in Afro-American Narrative.* Cambridge, Mass.: Harvard University Press.

Soja, Edward W. 1989. *Postmodern Geographies: The Reassertion of Space in Critical Social Theory.* London: Verso.

Solovitch, Sara. 1991. "When East Meets West." *Philadelphia Inquirer Magazine,* 4 August, 11–16.

Sone, Monica. 1953. *Nisei Daughter.* Boston: Little, Brown.

Spivak, Gayatri Chakravorty. 1988. "Can the Subaltern Speak?" In *Marxism and the Interpretation of Culture,* ed. Cary Nelson and Lawrence Grossberg, 271–313. Urbana: University of Illinois Press.

————. 1993. *Outside in the Teaching Machine.* New York: Routledge.

Stam, Robert. 1988. "Mikhail Bakhtin and Left Cultural Critique." In *Postmodernism and Its Discontents: Theories, Practices,* ed. E. Ann Kaplan, 116–35. London: Verso.

Su, Karen. 1994. "Jade Snow Wong's Badge of Distinction in the 1990s." *Critical Mass* 2.1: 3–52.

Suleri, Sara. 1987. *Meatless Days.* Chicago: University of Chicago Press.

Sumida, Stephen. 1986. "First Generations in Asian American Literature: As Viewed in Some Second Generation Works." In *Asian American and Pacific American Education,* ed. Nobuya Tsuchida, 64–70. Minneapolis: Asian/Pacific American Learning Center.

———. 1989a. "Asian American Literature in the 1980s." In *Frontiers of Asian American Studies: Writing, Research, and Commentary,* ed. Gail Nomura et al., 151–58. Pullman: Washington State University Press.

———. 1989b. "Japanese American Moral Dilemmas in John Okada's *No-No Boy* and Murayama's *All I Asking for Is My Body.*" In *Frontiers of Asian American Studies: Writing, Research, and Commentary,* ed. Gail Nomura et al., 222–33. Pullman: Washington State University Press.

———. 1991. *And the View from the Shore: Literary Traditions of Hawai'i.* Seattle: University of Washington Press.

———. 1992. "Protest and Accommodation, Self-Satire and Self-Effacement, and Monica Sone's *Nisei Daughter.*" In *Multicultural Autobiography: American Lives,* ed. by James Robert Payne, 207–43. Knoxville: University of Tennessee Press.

Sundquist, Eric J. 1988a. "The Japanese American Internment: A Reappraisal." *American Scholar* 58: 529–47.

———. 1988b. "Realism and Regionalism." In *Columbia Literary History of the United States,* ed. Emory Elliott et al., 501–24. New York: Columbia University Press.

Sung, Betty Lee. 1967. *Mountain of Gold.* New York: Macmillan.

Sze, Mai-mai. 1945. *Echo of a Cry: A Story Which Began in China.* New York: Harcourt, Brace.

Takagi, Paul, and Margot Gibney. 1995. "Theory and Praxis: Resistance and Hope." *Amerasia Journal* 21.1&2: 119–26.

Takaki, Ronald. 1989. *Strangers from a Different Shore: A History of Asian Americans.* New York: Penguin.

Tan, Amy. 1989. *The Joy Luck Club.* New York: Putnam.

Taylor, Lois. 1976. Review of *The Woman Warrior: Memoirs of a Girlhood among Ghosts. Honolulu Star-Bulletin,* 1 September, B1.

Temperly, Howard, and Malcolm Bradbury. 1981. "War and Cold War." In *Introduction to American Studies,* ed. Malcolm Bradbury and Howard Temperly, 289–322. London: Longman.

Thomas, Brook. 1996. *American Literary Realism and the Failed Promise of Contract.* Berkeley: University of California Press.

Tsiang, Hsi Tseng. 1937. *And China Has Hands.* New York: Robert Speller.

Turner, Graeme. 1990. *British Cultural Studies: An Introduction.* New York: Routledge.

TuSmith, Bonnie. 1993. *All My Relatives: Community in Contemporary Ethnic American Literatures.* Ann Arbor: University of Michigan Press.

Updike, John. 1960. *Rabbit, Run.* New York: Knopf.

Veeser, H. Aram. 1994. "The New Historicism." In *The New Historicism Reader,* ed. H. Aram Veeser, 1–31. New York: Routledge.

Wald, Alan. 1981. "The Culture of 'Internal Colonialism': A Marxist Perspective." *MELUS* 8: 18–27.

———. 1987. "Theorizing Cultural Difference: A Critique of the 'Ethnicity School.'" *MELUS* 14.2: 21–33.

Walsh, David. 1993. "The Role of Ideology in Cultural Production." In *Cultural Reproduction,* ed. Chris Jenks, 228–49. New York: Routledge.

Wang, Alfred S. 1988. "Maxine Hong Kingston's Reclaiming of America: The Birthright of the Chinese American Male." *South Dakota Review* 26: 18–29.

Watanabe, Sylvia. 1992. "The Caves of Okinawa." In *Talking to the Dead,* 24–46. New York: Doubleday.

Waugh, Patricia. 1992. *Practicing Postmodernism: Reading Modernism.* New York: Edward Arnold.

Weber, Samuel. 1979. *Unwrapping Balzac: A Reading of "La Peau de Chagrin."* Toronto: University of Toronto Press.

Weglyn, Michi. 1976. *Years of Infamy: The Untold Story of America's Concentration Camps.* New York: William Morrow.

West, Cornel. 1989. *The American Evasion of Philosophy: A Genealogy of Pragmatism.* Madison: University of Wisconsin Press.

———. 1990. "The New Cultural Politics of Difference." In *Out There: Marginalization and Contemporary Culture,* ed. Russell Ferguson et al., 19–38. Cambridge, Mass.: MIT Press.

White, Hayden. 1973. *Metahistory: The Historical Imagination in Nineteenth-Century Europe.* Baltimore, Md.: Johns Hopkins University Press.

———. 1978. *Tropics of Discourse: Essays in Cultural Criticism.* Baltimore, Md.: Johns Hopkins University Press.

———. 1987. *The Content of the Form: Narrative Discourse and Historical Representation.* Baltimore, Md.: Johns Hopkins University Press.

———. 1992. "Historical Emplotment and the Problem of Truth." In *Probing the Limits of Representation: Nazism and the "Final Solution,"* ed. Saul Friedlander, 37–53. Cambridge, Mass.: Harvard University Press.

Williams, Patrick, and Laura Chrisman, eds. 1994. "Colonial Discourse and Post-Colonial Theory: An Introduction." In *Colonial Discourse and Post-Colonial Theory: A Reader,* ed. Patrick Williams and Laura Chrisman, 1–20. New York: Columbia University Press.

Williams, Raymond. 1977. *Marxism and Literature.* New York: Oxford University Press.

———. 1979. *Politics and Letters: Interviews with "New Left Review."* London: New Left Books.

———. 1989. *Resources of Hope,* ed. Robin Gable. London: Verso.

Wong, Jade Snow. 1945/1950. *Fifth Chinese Daughter.* New York: Harper & Row.

Wong, Sau-ling Cynthia. 1988. "Necessity and Extravagance in Maxine Hong Kingston's *The Woman Warrior:* Art and the Ethnic Experience." *MELUS* 15.1: 3–26.

———. 1993. *Reading Asian American Literature: From Necessity to Extravagance.* Princeton, N.J.: Princeton University Press.

————. 1995a. "Denationalization Reconsidered: Asian American Cultural Criticism at a Theoretical Crossroads." *Amerasia Journal* 21.1&2: 1–27.

————. 1995b. "'Sugar Sisterhood': Situating the Amy Tan Phenomenon." In *The Ethnic Canon: Histories, Institutions, and Interventions,* ed. David Palumbo-Liu, 174–209. Minneapolis: University of Minnesota Press.

Wong, Shelley S. 1995. "Unnaming the Same: Theresa Hak Kyung Cha's *Dictée.*" In *Writing Self, Writing Nation,* ed. Elaine H. Kim and Norma Alarcón, 103–40. Berkeley: Calif.: Third Woman Press.

Wright, Richard. 1953. *The Outsider.* New York: Harper & Row.

Yamamoto, Hisaye. 1950/1988. "The Legend of Miss Sasagawara." In *Seventeen Syllables and Other Stories,* 20–33. Latham, N.Y.: Kitchen Table/Women of Color Press.

Yamashita, Karen Tei. 1992. *Brazil-Maru.* Minneapolis, Minn.: Coffee House.

Yin, Kathleen Loh Swee, and Kristoffer F. Paulson. 1982. "The Divided Voice of Chinese American Narration: Jade Snow Wong's *Fifth Chinese Daughter.*" *MELUS* 9.1: 53–59.

Žižek, Slavoj. 1994. "How Did Marx Invent the Symptom?" In *Mapping Ideology,* ed. Slavoj Žižek, 296–331. London: Verso.

Index

Hutcheon, Linda
    on historicity, 148
    on "historiographic metafiction," 138, 183 n.14
    on language, 181 n.20
Hwang, David Henry, *M. Butterfly,* 154

Ichioka, Yuji
    on dual citizenship, 41
    on postwar stereotype of Japanese Americans, 36, 51
identity, 4, 6, 13–14, 19, 29, 34, 37–38, 41, 44, 51, 88–91, 93, 97–98, 102, 115, 124, 128, 132–36, 148–50
    Asian American cultural, 6, 92, 114
    politics, 24, 118, 128, 135, 137
ideology, vi, 41, 59, 143
    layers of, 146, 159–60
    See also Althusser, Louis; interpellation
Iko, Momoko, *The Gold Watch,* 176 n.14
imperialism
    cultural, 14–15
    editors of *Aiiieeeee!* on, 15
    in *China Men,* 134–36
    See also Kaplan, Amy
Inada, Lawson Fusao, 6, 131
    on John Okada, 48
intellectual, the, 35, 55, 154–62. *See also* responsibility
intentionality, 16, 75–76, 82, 154–56
    of Frank Chin, 81–82
    of Louis Chu, 57, 76–77
    of Maxine Hong Kingston, 111, 119–24, 130
    of John Okada, 37
interracial relations, 82–85, 88–89, 94–96
internment, 31, 38–39, 41, 43, 45, 47, 49–51
    consequence of, 41, 175 n.5
    and draft process, 32, 39, 41, 43, 174–75 n.2
    execution and events of, 31–32, 174 n.1
    and redress movement, 32, 51, 81–82, 173 n.30
interpellation, 21, 27, 161. *See also* Althusser, Louis; ideology
intertextuality
    of Frank Chin's plays, 81–82, 109
    of *China Men,* 112–18, 130–31, 133–35, 137–38
    of *Eat a Bowl of Tea,* 56–58, 74–75, 78
    of *Fifth Chinese Daughter,* 141–42, 144
    of *No–No Boy,* 34–35, 52

issei. *See* generational conflict; Japanese Americans
Iser, Wolfgang, on realism, 77

Jameson, Fredric
    on debate over realism, 172–73 n.12
    on postmodernism, 93, 105, 179 n.6, 180 n.16
    on "schizophrenic disjuncture," 97
JanMohamed, Abdul R., and David Lloyd, on literature of damage, 22, 178 n.11
Japan
    and Pearl Harbor incident, 31
    as postwar U.S. ally, 36
Japanese Americans
    postwar stereotype of (*see also* Ichioka, Yuji)
    wartime displacement of (*see also* internment)
Jauss, Hans Robert. *See also* horizon of expectations
Jay, Martin
    on "negative liberty," 104
    on realism, 172 n.21, 177 n.8

Kaplan, Amy, on U.S. imperialism, 28, 173–74 n.31
Kaplan, Caren, on coalition building, 186 n.1
Kaplan, E. Ann, on postmodernism, 5, 168 n.5
Keenan, Sally, on *Beloved* (Morrison), 182 n.9
Kellner, Douglas, on poststructuralism, 186 n.21
Kim, Elaine H.
    Asian American Literature (1982), 139–40, 142
    on Frank Chin, 112, 114, 119
    on *China Men,* 110, 119, 134, 135
    on "developmental narrative," 167 n.1
    on *Eat a Bowl of Tea,* 60, 63, 70, 177 n.3, 178 n.14
    on female articulation, 116
    on *Fifth Chinese Daughter,* 140, 142
    on *Nisei Daughter,* 37
    on *No–No Boy,* 33
Kingston, Maxine Hong, 9, 11, 22, 28, 150
    China Men, vii–viii, 22, 28, 110–38, 152, 156, 164
    on *China Men,* 111
    on "claiming America," 111, 118, 128, 132, 135–36.
    and critique of masculine ideals, 111–12, 123–25, 127, 137–38
    and pacifism, 117, 134

and *Tripmaster Monkey,* 184 n.12
The Woman Warrior, 109–10, 112–16, 128,
130–32, 135, 140, 146–49, 151–54, 156
on Jade Snow Wong, 140–41, 144 (*see also*
Ling, Amy)
and writer's responsibility, 147, 149, 150–52,
156
Lacan, Jacques, 84, 86, 91, 108, 179 n.7
Laclau, Ernesto
on counterhegemonic articulation, 148
on representation, 20
on subject formation, 78
Lauclau, Ernesto, and Chantal Mouffe, on cultural hegemony, 13, 148, 171 n.16
Lang, Berel, on radical intervention, 14
language, 14–15, 26, 54, 86–87, 89–90, 97–98
misappropriation of, 116, 181 n.5
Lee, Chin–Yang, *Flower Drum Song,* 56
Lee, Robert G., on Guan Goong (Kwan Kung),
179 n.4
Lee, Virginia, *The House That Tai Ming Built,*
100, 146
Leer, David Van, on Existentialism, 35
Levine, George, on realism, 173 n.24
Li, David Leiwei
on *The Chickencoop Chinaman* and *The Year of
the Dragon,* 86, 180 n.9
on *China Men,* 110, 125, 134, 183 n.13
on Chinese American literary canon, 9
on Jade Snow Wong, 140
Lim, Shirley
on diaspora, 177 n.2
on ethnocentrism, 167 n.1 (*see also* developmentalism, American *Bildungsroman*)
on *No–No Boy,* 33
on *The Woman Warrior,* 112, 150–51
on Jade Snow Wong, 141, 144
Lim, Shirley, and Mayumi Tsutakawa, *The Forbidden Stitch,* 142
Lin, Hazel, *The Physicians,* 56
Lin–Blinde, Patricia, on Jade Snow Wong, 140–41
Ling, Amy
on *China Men,* 134
on Chinese women, 182 n.5
on wartime racial stereotype, 175 n.5
on *The Woman Warrior*
on Jade Snow Wong, 141, 144
Lipsitz, George, on "counter–memory," 147–48
Lowe, Lisa

on Althusser, 159, 160
on cultural difference, 5–8, 139
on "developmental narrative," 167 n.1, 169
n.8
on *Dictée,* 19, 168 n.7
on *Eat a Bowl of Tea,* 20, 178 n.10
on Gramsci and cultural politics, 8, 169–70
n.9, 170 n.12
on heterogeneity, 5, 6, 8
on *No–No Boy,* 33, 38
on "nomadism," 7
on realism, 19, 171–72 n.20
Lukács, Georg, on realism, 177–78 n.8. *See also*
Owens, Craig
Lyotard, Jean–François, 24, 105

Making Waves, 142
Marshall, Brenda K., on postmodernism, 105
Martin, Wallace, on realism, 77, 172 n.20
Marxism
and base/superstructure model, 158–59
and "false consciousness," 159, 184 n.5
See also materialism
Marxist literary criticism
aesthetic legacy of, 161, 186 n.21
and debate over realism, 21–22, 172–73
n.22, 177–78 n.8
master narratives, 4, 72, 105, 138
materialism, 8, 106, 161, 170 n.9, 184 n.5. *See
also* Marxism
May, Elaine Tyler, 175 n.4
McCarran Internal Security Act (1950), 55
McCarran–Walter Act (1952), 41
McCarthyism, 55–56, 132. *See also* anticommu-
nism
McDonald, Dorothy Ritsuko
on *No–No Boy,* 33, 45, 47, 48
on Frank Chin, 26, 80, 102
McGowan, John
on modernism, 107
on postmodernism, 105, 170 n.10
on realism, 172 n.20, 177 n.8
McGuigan, Jim, on British cultural studies, 185
n.14
Miyamoto, Kazuo, *Hawaii: The End of the Rainbow,* 50
Močnik, Rastko, on Althusserianism, 185–86
n.19
model minority, 55, 87, 89, 100, 140, 141